Cloud Strategy

CW00815837

A Decision-Based Approach to Successful Cloud Migration

Gregor Hohpe

Cloud Strategy

A Decision-Based Approach to Successful Cloud Migration

Gregor Hohpe

ISBN 9798665253046

Cloud computing changes the role technology plays in enterprises from "keeping the lights on" to boosting innovation through agility, frequent releases, and automation. It only seems appropriate to embrace the same principles when writing a book about this transformation.

This book started out as a Leanpub book. Lean Publishing is the act of publishing an in-progress ebook using lightweight tools and iterations to get reader feedback. You're reading the result of this iterative process, which elevates readers to become active participants.

Contents

Part III: Moving to the Cloud   89

Part IV: Architecting the Cloud   151

Part V: Building (for) the Cloud   225

About This Book

Strategy is the difference between
making a wish and making it come true.

Cloud computing is an amazing resource that can provide fully managed platforms, instant scaling, auto-optimizing and even auto-healing operations, per-second billing, pre-trained machine learning models, and globally distributed transactional data stores. The cloud is also a critical enabler for organizations to compete in economies of speed. So, it's no wonder that most enterprises want to take advantage of such capabilities.

Migrating an entire enterprise to the cloud isn't as easy as pushing a button, though. Simply lifting and shifting legacy applications is unlikely to bring the anticipated benefits, whereas re-architecting applications to run optimally in the cloud can be cost prohibitive. In addition, organizations looking to reap the full rewards from cloud technology also need to consider changes to their business model and their organization. Enterprises thus need a more nuanced strategy than simply proclaiming "cloud first!"

A sound cloud strategy isn't something you can copy from a recipe book or from another organization. Diverse starting points, objectives, and constraints imply different choices and trade-offs. Instead, you need a set of proven decision models that help you analyze your specific situation, evaluate options, understand trade-offs, and articulate your choice to a broad audience.

Unfortunately, most books on cloud computing either stay at a very high level or focus on specific vendors and products. This book closes this gap by questioning existing assumptions, establishing technology-neutral decision models, and presenting a new way to think about your cloud journey.

Life Teaches the Best Lessons

My book *37 Things One Architect Knows About IT Transformation*[1] describes
how architects can drive change in large organizations by riding the "Architect
Elevator" from the penthouse to the engine room. *Cloud Strategy* applies this
mental model to cloud architecture and cloud migrations. Just like *37 Things*,
Cloud Strategy includes many anecdotes and the occasional punch line based
on my real-world experience.

I have been in charge of major cloud transformations in three distinct roles:

- As chief architect of a major financial services provider, I devised and built
  a private cloud platform to speed up application delivery.
- As technical director at a major cloud provider, I advised strategic clients
  in Asia and Europe, including some of the largest retailers and telecom-
  munications companies, on aligning their cloud strategy with their organizational transformation.
- As a Singapore smart nation fellow, I laid out an overarching cloud
  strategy at the national level.

Each environment presented its unique set of challenges but also shared noteworthy commonalities. In this book, I distill them into concrete advice so that
everyone can benefit from my experience and occasional mistakes.

Each technology migration involves specific vendors and products. This book
stays away from individual products as much as possible, using them only as
occasional examples where considered helpful. Documents describing products
are widely available, and whereas products come and go, architectural considerations tend to stay. Instead, as with *37 Things*, I prefer to take a fresh look at some
well-trodden topics and buzzwords to give readers a novel way of approaching
some of their problems.

Cloud Stories

Corporate IT can be a somewhat uninspiring and outright arduous topic. But
IT doesn't have to be boring. That's why I share many of the anecdotes that

---

[1]https://leanpub.com/37things

I collected from the daily rut of cloud migration alongside the architectural reflections.

Readers appreciated several attributes of *37 Things'* writing style and content, which I aimed to repeat for this book:

- *Real Experience* – Rather than painting rosy pictures of what could be done, I try to describe what worked (or perhaps didn't) and why, based on actual experience.
- *Unfiltered Opinion* – I prefer to call things the way they are. Also, I am not shy to highlight downsides or limitations. There are plenty of marketing brochures already, so I'm not keen to add another one.
- *Engaging Stories* – Stories stick, so I try to package complex topics into approachable stories and engaging anecdotes.
- *Less Jargon, More Thought* – IT people are well known for spewing out the latest buzzwords. But few can tell you when to use which products and what assumptions are built into them. I aim for the opposite.
- *Valuable Take-Aways* – Stories are nice, but architects also need concrete advice to make their cloud migration successful. I share what I know.
- *Useful References* – A lot has been written on cloud computing, architecture, and IT strategy. I am not here to regurgitate what already has been written but want to synthesize new insights. I am happy to point you to related material.

So, just as with *37 Things*, I hope that this book equips you with a few catchy slogans that you're able to back up with solid architecture insight.

Better Decisions with Models

Although cloud computing is founded in advanced technology, this book isn't deeply technical. You won't find instructions on how to have your CI pipeline auto-generate YAML Helm Charts for fully automated multicluster container orchestration management in a provider-neutral fashion. You might, however, find guidelines on how you would go about deciding whether such a setup is a good match for your organization.

This book focuses on meaningful decisions, those that involve conscious and sometimes difficult trade-offs. Individual product features step aside in favor of a balanced comparison of architectural approaches. Considering both strengths and weaknesses leads to vendor-neutral decision models, often accompanied by questions that you should ask the vendor or yourself.

Employing the "Architect Elevator" notion to better connect the IT engine room to the business penthouse means that elevating the level of discussion isn't dumbing things down. Rather, it's like a good map that guides you well because it omits unnecessary detail. This book therefore removes noise and highlights critical aspects and connections that are too often overlooked. It will make you see the forest and not just the trees, sharpening your thinking and decision making at the relevant level.

What Will I Learn?

This book is structured into six major sections that roughly follow the cloud journey that a complex organization is likely to undertake:

Part I: Understanding the Cloud

The cloud is very different from procuring a traditional IT product. So, rather than follow a traditional selection and procurement process, you'll have to rethink the way your IT works.

Part II: Organizing for the Cloud

Cloud computing impacts more than technology. Getting the most out of cloud necessitates organizational changes, affecting both structure and processes.

Part III: Moving to the Cloud

There are many ways to the cloud. The worst you can do is transport your existing processes to the cloud, which will earn you a new data center, but not a cloud—surely not what you set out to achieve! Therefore, it's time to question existing assumptions about your infrastructure and operational model.

Part IV: Architecting the Cloud

There's a lot more to cloud architecture than picking the right vendor or product. It's best to dodge all the buzzwords and use architectural decision models, instead. This includes multi- and hybrid-cloud, but perhaps not in the way the marketing brochures laid it out.

Part V: Building (for) the Cloud

The cloud is a formidable platform. However, applications running on top of this platform need to do their part, as well. This section looks at what makes an application cloud-ready, what serverless is all about, and what the big deal is about containers.

Part VI: Embracing the Cloud

Congratulations! You have applications in the cloud, but you're not quite done yet! The cloud may still have one or the other pleasant (or unpleasant) surprise for you.

Although you're most welcome to read all chapters in sequence, the book is designed to be read in any order that best suits your needs. So, you can easily dive into a topic that's most relevant to you and follow the many cross-references to related chapters. A cloud journey isn't linear.

Will It Answer My Questions?

I often warn my workshop participants that they should expect to leave with more questions than they came with. Similarly, this book presents a new way of thinking rather than simply being an instruction sheet. It may therefore also raise new questions. I consider this a good thing for two reasons. First, you'll have better questions in your mind, the ones that lead you to making meaningful decisions. And second, you'll have better tools to answer those questions within their specific context, as opposed to relying on some generic paint-by-numbers framework.

There is no copy-paste for transformation. So, this book likely won't tell you exactly what to do. But it will allow you to make better decisions for yourself. Think about it as learning how to fish (see the cover).

Do's and Don'ts

Much of this book is dedicated to looking beneath the surface of the cloud technology buzzwords, aiming to give enterprises a deeper and more nuanced view on what's really involved in a cloud migration. However, as an architect or IT leader, you're also expected to devise an execution plan and lead your organization on a well-defined path. For that you need concrete, actionable advice.

Several chapters therefore include a *Do's and Don'ts* section at the end that summarizes recommendations and provides words of caution. You can use them as a checklist to avoid falling into the same traps as others before you. Think about yourself as India Jones—you're the one who dodges all the traps filled with skeletons. It's challenging and might be a close call sometimes, but you come out as the hero.

What's with the Fish, Again?

The cover shows a swarm of fish that resembles a large fish. I took it in the Enoshima Aquarium in Japan, just a short train ride south of Tokyo, not far from Kamakura. Keeping with the theme of using personal photos of fish from *37 Things*, I selected this swarm because it illustrates how the sum of the parts has its own shape and dynamic—a swarm is more than just a bunch of fish. The same is true for complex architectures and the cloud in particular.

Getting Involved

My brain doesn't stop generating new ideas just because the book is published, so I invite you to have a look at my blog to see what's new:

> https://architectelevator.com/blog

Also, follow me on Twitter or LinkedIn to see what I am up to or to comment on my posts:

http://twitter.com/ghohpe
http://www.linkedin.com/in/ghohpe

Of course, I am happy if you would like to help spread the word and tell your friends about this book. The best way to do so is by sharing this handy URL:

http://CloudStrategyBook.com

To provide feedback and help make this a better book, please join our private discussion group:
https://groups.google.com/d/forum/cloud-strategy-book

Acknowledgments

Books aren't written by a sole author locked up in a hotel room for a season (if you watched *The Shining*, you know where that leads...). Many people have knowingly or unknowingly contributed to this book through hallway conversations, meeting discussions, manuscript reviews, Twitter dialogs, or casual chats. My heartfelt thanks to all of them for their friendship and inspiration.

Chef kept me company throughout and fed me tasty pizza, pasta, and homemade cheesecake.

Part I: Understanding the Cloud

Dedicating several chapters of a book to understanding the cloud might seem like carrying owls to Athens. After all, cloud computing has become as ubiquitous as IT itself and the (online) shelves are full of related books, articles, blog posts, and product briefs. However, much of the available material is either product centric or promises amazing benefits without giving much detail about how to actually achieve them. In my mind, that's putting the technology cart before the enterprise horse.

Putting Cloud in Context

When embarking on a cloud journey, it's good to take a step back and realize that the cloud is a much bigger deal than it might seem from the onset. This way organizations can avoid treating a cloud transformation like yet another IT project. Instead, they need to prepare for a full-on lifestyle change.

To really appreciate the impact that cloud computing makes, it's good to first realize that IT's role in the enterprise is changing. And to put that in context, it's good to look at how the business evolves. Lastly, to understand why the business needs to change, it's helpful to look at how the competitive landscape has evolved.

Modern organizations that have grown up with the cloud think and work differently from traditional enterprises that are embarking on a cloud migration. It's therefore good to understand why the cloud is such a good fit for them and how (or whether) their structure and their behaviors translate to your organization's situation. Each starting point is different, and so is the journey.

It's *Your* Cloud Journey

Adopting the cloud because everyone else does it might be better than doing nothing, but it's unlikely to be a suitable basis for a sound strategy. Instead, you need to have a clear view of why you're moving to the cloud in the first place and what success looks like to your organization. Then, you can weave a path from where you are to that success. Along the way you'll know that there isn't a simple endpoint or even a stable target picture: cloud platforms evolve and so does your competitive playing field, making it a perpetual journey. It's therefore well worth putting some thought into starting out right and understanding what conscious decisions and trade-offs you are making.

Rethinking Cloud Computing

This part helps you take a fresh look in the context of business transformation. Along the way, you'll realize a few things that the shiny brochures likely didn't tell you:

- That success in the cloud requires an *IT lifestyle change* (Chapter 1)
- That *cloud-ready organizations think in the first derivative* (Chapter 2)
- That *wishful thinking isn't a strategy* (Chapter 3)
- That *principles link strategy and decisions* (Chapter 4)
- That *if you don't know how to drive, buying a faster car is a bad idea* (Chapter 5)

1. Cloud Isn't IT Procurement; It's a Lifestyle Change

You don't buy a cloud, you embrace it.

Corporate IT is fundamentally structured around a *buy over build* approach. This makes good sense because it isn't particularly useful for the average enterprise to build its own accounting, human resources, payroll, or inventory system. The same is true of much of the IT infrastructure: enterprises procure servers, network switches, storage devices, application servers, and so on.

Naturally, enterprises tend to follow the same approach when they look at cloud platforms and cloud vendors. Sadly, this can lead to trouble before the first application is ever migrated to the cloud.

Procuring a Cloud?

Most traditional IT processes are designed around the procurement of individual components, which are then integrated in house or, more frequently, by a system integrator. Much of IT even defines itself by the bill of materials that they procured over time, from being "heavy on SAP" to being an "Oracle Shop" or a "Microsoft House". So, when the time comes to move to the cloud, enterprises tend to follow the same, proven process to procure a new component for their ever-growing IT arsenal. After all, they have learned that following the same process leads to the same desirable results, right? Not necessarily.

The cloud isn't just some additional element that you add to your IT portfolio. It becomes the fundamental backbone of your IT: the cloud is where your data resides, your software runs, your security mechanisms protect your assets, and your analytics crunch numbers. Embracing the cloud resembles a full-on *IT outsourcing* (Chapter 6) more than a traditional IT procurement.

A cloud platform isn't an additional element that you add to your IT portfolio. It resembles full-on IT outsourcing more than IT procurement.

The closest example to embracing the cloud that IT has likely seen in the past decades is the introduction of a major ERP (Enterprise Resource Planning) system—many IT staff will still get goose bumps from those memories. Installing the ERP software was likely the easiest part, whereas integration and customization typically incurred significant effort and cost, often into the hundreds of millions of dollars.

We're moving to the cloud not because it's so easy, but because of the undeniable benefits it brings, much like ERP did. In both cases, the benefits don't derive from simply installing a piece of software. Rather, they depend on your organization adjusting to a new way of working that's embedded in the platform. That change was likely the most difficult part of the ERP implementation but also the one that brought the most significant benefits. Luckily, clouds are built as flexible platforms and hence leave more room for creativity than the "my way or the highway" attitude of some ERP systems.

How the Cloud Is Different

Applying traditional procurement processes to cloud computing is likely to lead to disappointment. That's because most of these processes are based on assumptions that were true in the past but that don't hold for the cloud. Attempting to implement new technology using an old model is like printing out emails and filing the paper. You think no one does it? I still get occasional emails with a "save the environment; don't print this mail" at the bottom. Adopting new technology is fairly easy. Adjusting your way of thinking and working takes much more time.

Two classic examples of existing processes that won't mesh with the cloud model are procurement and operations. Let's have a look at each area and how the cloud changes the way we think about it.

Procurement

Procurement is the process of evaluating and purchasing software and hardware components. Because a good portion of IT's budget flows through it, procurement tends to follow strict processes to assure that money is spent wisely, fairly, and sparsely.

Predictability versus Elasticity

Many IT processes are driven through budget control: If you want to start a project, you need budget approval; likewise if you want to buy any piece of software or hardware. In the traditional view of IT as a cost center[1], such a setup makes good sense: if it's about the money, let's minimize the amount that we spend.

Traditional IT budgets are set up at least a year in advance, making predictability a key consideration. No CFO or shareholder likes to find out nine months into the fiscal year that IT is going to overrun its budget by 20%. Therefore, IT procurement tends to negotiate multiyear license terms for the software they buy. They "lock in discounts" by signing up for a larger package to accommodate any increase in usage over time, despite not being able to fully utilize it right from the start. If this reminds you of the free cell phone minutes that are actually free only after you pay for them in bulk, you might be onto something. And what's being locked in here isn't so much the discount but the customer.

The cloud's critical innovation, and the reason it's turned IT upside down, is its elastic pricing model: You don't pay for resources up front but only for what you actually consume. Such a pricing model enables a *major cost savings potential* (Chapter 29); for example, because you don't pay for capacity that you aren't yet utilizing. However, elasticity also takes away the predictability that IT so much cherishes. I have seen a CIO trying to prevent anyone from ordering a new (virtual) server, inhibiting the very benefit of rapid provisioning in the cloud. Such things can happen when a new way of working clashes with existing incentives.

Feature Checklist versus Vision

To spend money wisely, IT procurement routinely compares multiple vendor offerings. Some organizations, especially in the public sector, even have a

---

[1]https://www.linkedin.com/pulse/reverse-engineering-organization-gregor-hohpe/

regulatory requirement to solicit multiple vendor offers to assure disciplined and transparent spending. To decide between vendors, procurement makes a list of required features and non-functional requirements, scoring each product along those dimensions. They add up the scores and go into negotiation with the vendor with the highest number.

This approach works reasonably well if your organization has a thorough understanding of the product scope and the needs you have, and you are able to translate those into desired product features. Although this process has never been a great one (is the product with a score of 82.3 really better than the one with 81.7?), it was alright for well-known components like relational databases.

Unfortunately, this approach doesn't work for cloud platforms. Cloud platforms are vast in scope, and our definition of what a cloud should do is largely shaped by the cloud provider's existing and upcoming offerings. So, we're caught in a loop of cloud providers telling us what the cloud is so we can score their offering based on that definition. As I jested in *37 Things*, if you have never seen a car and visit a well-known automotive manufacturer from the Stuttgart area, you'll walk out with a star emblem on the hood as the first item in your feature list (see "The IT World is Flat" in *37 Things*). Trust me, speaking to IT staff after a vendor meeting makes even that cheeky analogy seem mild.

Because traditional scoring doesn't work well for clouds, a better approach is to compare your company's vision with the provider's product strategy and philosophy. For that, you need to know *why you're going to the cloud* (Chapter 11) and that *buying a faster car doesn't make you a better driver* (Chapter 5).

Snapshot versus Evolution

Massive checklists also assume that you can make a conscious decision based on a snapshot in time. However, clouds evolve rapidly. A checklist from today becomes rather meaningless by the time the cloud providers hold their annual re:Invent/Ignite/Next event.

Related to the previous consideration, IT should therefore look to understand the provider's product strategy and expected evolution. Not many providers will tell you these straight out, but you can reverse engineer a good bit from their product roadmaps. After all, the cloud platform's constant evolution is one of the main motivators for wanting to deploy on top of it. To speak mathematically, you're more interested in the vector than the current position.

Product versus Platform

Most items procured by IT are products: they serve a specific purpose, perhaps in coordination with other components. This makes it easy to look at them in isolation.

The cloud is a giant platform that forms the basis for software delivery and operations. While some large software systems can also be heavily customized and may be positioned as a platform, the cloud is different in that it's an extremely broad and flexible playing field. Attempting a metaphor, you could say that traditionally IT has purchased artwork, but with cloud it's buying a blank canvas and some magic pens. Therefore, when embarking on a cloud journey many more considerations come into play.

Local Optimization versus Global Optimization

When selecting products, IT commonly looks at each product individually, following a best-of-breed approach that picks the best solution for each specific task.

Cloud platforms contain hundreds of individual products, making a comparison between individual products rather meaningless unless you're limiting your move to the cloud to one very specific use case like pre-trained machine learning models. When looking at the cloud as a platform, though, you need to look at the whole and not just the pieces (remember the book cover?). That means optimizing across the platform as opposed to locally for each component, an exercise that is more complex and will require coordination across different parts of the organization.

Matching the Business to the Software

Procuring a product is traditionally done by matching the product's capabilities against the organization's needs. The underlying assumption is that the product that most closely matches your organization's way of working will provide the most value to your business. If you have a family of five, you'll want a minivan, not a two-seater sports car.

In the case of cloud, though, you're not looking to replace an existing component that serves a specific organizational need. Rather the opposite, you're looking for a product that enables your organization to work in a fundamentally different way (that's what we call "transformation"). As a result, you should be adjusting your organization's operating model to the platform you're buying. Hence, you should see which model underlying the cloud platform you find most appropriate for your organization and work backward from there. Although the platforms might look roughly similar from the outside, upon closer inspection you'll realize that they are built under different assumptions that reflect the provider's culture.

Operations

The cloud doesn't just challenge traditional procurement processes, but operational processes, as well. Those processes exist to "keep the lights on", making sure that applications are up and running, hardware is available, and we have some idea of what's going on in our data center. It's not a big surprise that cloud computing changes the way we operate our infrastructure significantly.

Segregation of Infrastructure from Applications

Most IT departments distinguish infrastructure operations from application delivery, typically reflected in the organizational structure where "change" departments build applications to be handed (or tossed) over to "run" departments to be operated. Critical mechanisms such as security, hardware provisioning, and cost control are the operations teams' responsibility, whereas features delivery and usability are in the application teams' court.

A central theme of cloud computing is infrastructure automation, which gives development teams direct access to infrastructure configuration and thus blurs the lines. Especially aspects like security, cost control, scaling, or resilience *span both application and infrastructure* (Chapter 7).

Control versus Transparency

Traditional IT generally suffers from poor transparency into its system inventory. Therefore, many processes are based on control, such as not giving developers access to configure infrastructure elements, restricting deployments, or requiring manual inspections and approvals. These mechanisms are often at odds with modern software delivery approaches such as DevOps or Continuous Delivery.

The cloud dramatically increases transparency, allowing you to monitor usage and policy violations rather than restricting processes up front. Using the transparency to perform actual monitoring can significantly increase compliance while reducing the process burden—process controls were usually just proxies for desirable outcomes with a weak link to reality. However, it requires you to change your IT lifestyle and dive deeper into the platform's technical capabilities. For example, in an environment with high degrees of automation, you can scan deployment scripts for policy violations.

Resilience Through Redundancy vs. Automation

IT traditionally increases system uptime through redundancy. If the server running an important application fails, there's a fully configured standby server ready to take over, minimizing any disruption. As can easily be seen, such an approach leads to rather unfavorable economics: half the production servers are essentially doing nothing. Alas, with monolithic applications and manual deployments, it was the only choice given that it would take far too long to deploy a new instance.

The cloud thrives on scale-out architectures and automation, meaning new application instances can be added quickly and easily. This allows the elimination of "warm standby servers". Instead, new application or service instances can be deployed when a failure occurs. This is one of several examples of how the cloud can bring enormous cost savings, but *only if you adjust the way you work* (Chapter 29).

A Side-by-Side Comparison

This list is meant to give you a flavor of why selecting a cloud isn't your typical IT procurement—it's not nearly exhaustive. For example, the cloud also *challenges existing financial processes* (Chapter 30). The examples do make clear, though, that applying your traditional procurement and operational processes to a cloud adoption is likely going to put you on the wrong starting point.

The following table summarizes the differences to highlight that cloud is a 180-degree departure from many well-known IT processes. Get ready for some transformation!

Capability	Traditional	Cloud
Budgeting	Predictability	Elasticity
Suitability	Feature Checklist	Vision
Functionality	Snapshot	Evolution
Scope	Component	Platform
Optimization	Local	Global
Alignment	Product to Business	Business to Product
Operational Model	App vs. Infra	Apps and Infra
Compliance	Control	Transparency
Resilience	Redundancy	Automation

Same but Very Different

Despite the stark differences from traditional IT, the major cloud providers' product portfolios might look quite similar to one another. However, having worked not only at two cloud vendors, but also with many cloud customers, I can confidently state that the organizations behind the cloud platforms have very different cultures and operating models. If you have a chance to visit multiple vendors for an executive briefing, you should not just pay attention to the technical content, but also try to understand the organization's culture and underlying assumptions.

Because the cloud is a journey, compare cloud providers not just by their products but also their by their history and cultural DNA.

A telling indicator is the core business that each vendor engaged in before they started to offer cloud services. That history has shaped the vendor's organizing principles and values as well as its product strategy. I won't elaborate on the differences here, because I'd like you to go have a look for yourself (and I also don't want to get into trouble). However, I am sure that after spending a bit of time with each vendor outside of the typical sales pitch will give you a very vivid picture of what I am hinting at.

Because the cloud is a journey more than a destination, it requires a long-term partnership. Therefore, I highly recommend having a look behind the scenes, at the organization and not just the product, to understand the provider's culture and whether it matches your aspirations.

The Cloud in the Enterprise

Cloud providers dealing with enterprises face an interesting dilemma. On one hand, they represent a non-traditional IT model that requires enterprises to transform. However, they still need to help those enterprises on the way. So, the providers make their clouds "enterprise ready" without trying to lose their digital roots. "Enterprise" features such as industry certifications are highly valuable and necessary, but one sometimes wonders whether glitzy customer experience centers overlooking vast control rooms where no real crisis ever seems to be taking place are really needed to engage enterprises.

 When I visit customer experience centers, I feel like going to a fancy casino: I am mightily impressed until I remember where all the money comes from.

Commitment-based pricing models favored by most enterprises stand in con-trast to cloud's elasticity—discounts are given for multi-year agreements that specify a committed minimum spend. Traditionally, such plans compensate for the high cost of enterprise sales; for example, all those folks flying around the world for 60-minute customer meetings and elaborate conferences with well-known musical acts. Isn't the cloud supposed to do away with much of that tradition? Cynics define "enterprise software" as being bloated, outdated, inflexible, and expensive. Let's hope that cloud and traditional enterprise meet somewhere in the middle!

Transforming organizations is challenging in both directions. Whereas tradi-tional enterprises install free baristas because that's what they observed in their digital counterparts, internet-scale companies copy the cheesy customer experience centers that they observe in traditional enterprise vendors. Both initiatives are unlikely to have the intended effect.

Transformation Doesn't Have a SKU

Going to the cloud entails a major lifestyle change for IT and perhaps even the business. Transforming existing organizational structures and processes to embrace the cloud is challenging, especially for wealthy organizations. They're so used to getting it all that they believe everything is just a matter of securing sufficient funding. Such organizations resemble spoiled children who are used to getting any toy they wish for. Usually, their room is so full of toys that they can no longer find anything. I have seen many IT environments that look just like that—you can surely picture the CIO looking for his or her blockchain among all the other IoT, AI, RPA, and AR initiatives.

One critical lesson for such organizations, discussed in more detail in *37 Things*, is that an IT transformation isn't something you can buy with money—it doesn't have a SKU[2]. Rather, transformation forces you to question the very things that helped you become successful in the past. Ironically, the more successful an organization has been, the more difficult this exercise becomes.

Changing Lifestyle

It might help to think of moving to the cloud like moving to a different country. I have moved from the United States to Japan and had a great experience, in large part because I adopted the local lifestyle: I didn't bring a car, moved into a much smaller (but equally comfortable) apartment, learned basic Japanese, and got used to carrying my trash back home (the rarity of public trash bins is a favorite topic of visitors to Japan). If I had aimed for a 3,000 square-foot home with a two-car garage, insisted on driving everywhere, and kept asking people in English for the nearest trash bin, it would have been a rather disappointing experience. And in that case, I should have likely asked myself why I am even moving to Japan in the first place. When in Rome, do as the Romans do (or the Japanese—you get my point).

---

[2]Stock-Keeping Unit, meaning an item you can buy off the shelf.

2. Cloud Thinks in the First Derivative

In economies of speed, the cloud is natural.

Major cloud migrations routinely go hand in hand with a so-called digital transformation, an initiative to help the business become more digital. Even though it's not totally clear what being "digital" means, it appears to imply being able to better compete with so-called "digital disruptors" who threaten existing business models. Almost all of these disruptors operate in the cloud, so even though the cloud alone doesn't make you digital, there appears to be some connection between being "digital" and being in the cloud. Interestingly, the answer lies in mathematics.

Making Things Digital

Before diving into the intricate relationship between cloud computing and first derivatives, I would like to take a brief moment to get on my "digital" soap box. When a company speaks about transforming, it usually aims to become more "digital", referring to the internet giants or *FAANGs*—Facebook, Apple, Amazon, Netflix, and Google.

The issue I take with the term "digital" is that most things became digital three or four decades ago: we replaced the slide ruler with the calculator in the 70s, the cassette tape with the compact disk in the 80s, and the letter with email in the 90s. Oh, and along the way analog watches were replaced by those funny "digital" ones that only show the time when you push a button before being again replaced by digital ones that mimic analog displays. So, making things digital isn't anything particularly new, really.

 We made most things digital decades ago. Now it's about using digital technology to fundamentally change the model.

If we're not in the business of making things digital anymore, what do we refer to when a company wants to become "digital"? We want to use modern— that is, "digital"—technology to fundamentally change the way the business works. A simple example helps illustrate the difference. Microsoft's Encarta was a digital encyclopedia launched in 1993. It initially sold in the form of a CD-ROM, which made it superior to a traditional paper encyclopedia in most every regard: it had more content, was more up to date, had multimedia content, was easier to search, and surely easier to carry. Despite all of these advantages, people don't use Encarta anymore—the product was discontinued in 2009. The reason is now obvious: Encarta was a digital copy of an encyclopedia but failed to fundamentally change the model. The well-known product that did, of course, is Wikipedia. Based on Ward Cunningham's Wiki[1], Wikipedia questioned the basic assumptions about how an encyclopedia is created, distributed, and monetized. Instead of being a relatively static, authoritative set of works created by a small set of experts, it leveraged a global computer network and universal browser access to create a collaborative model. The new model quickly surpassed the "digital clone" and rendered it obsolete.

> Not all changes in model need to be as dramatic as Wikipedia, Uber, or Airbnb. Leanpub, the platform on which I authored this book, changed the book publishing model in a subtle but important way. Realizing that ebooks have a near-zero distribution cost, Leanpub encourages authors to publish books *before* they're finished, making the platform a cross between Kickstarter[a] and book publisher. Such a model is a stark contrast to traditional print publishing, which relies on lengthy editing and quality assurance processes to publish the final book once in high quality.
>
> ---
> [a]https://www.kickstarter.com/

Digital IT

The difference between making things digital and using digital technology to change the model applies directly to corporate IT, which has grown primarily by making digital copies of existing processes. In an insurance business, IT

---
[1]https://wiki.c2.com/

would automate new customer sign-ups, renewals, claims handling, and risk calculation. In manufacturing, it would automate orders, shipping, inventory management, and the assembly line. By speeding up these processes and reducing cost, often by orders of magnitude, IT quickly evolved into the backbone of the business. What it didn't do is change the existing business model. But that's exactly what the Uber's, Airbnb's, and Wikipedia's of the world have done. This shift is particularly dangerous for corporate IT, which has done extremely well creating digital copies, often handling budgets in the billions of dollars and generating commensurate business value. Just like Encarta.

Classic IT sometimes argues that "digital" disruptors are technology companies as opposed to their "normal" financial services or manufacturing business. I disagree. Having worked on one of Google's core systems for several years, I can firmly state that Google is first and foremost an advertising business; advertising is what generates the vast majority of the revenue (and profits). Tesla is making cars, Amazon excels at fulfillment, and Airbnb helps travelers find accommodations. That's "normal" business. The difference is that these companies have leveraged technology to redefine how that business is conducted. And that's what "going digital" is all about.

Change Is Abnormal

Because traditional IT is so used to making existing things digital, it has a well-defined process for it. Taking something from the current "as-is" state to a reasonably well-known future "to-be"state is known as a "project".

Projects are expensive and risky. Therefore, much effort goes into defining the future "to-be" state from which a (seemingly always positive) business case is calculated. Next, delivery teams meticulously plan out the project execution by decomposing tasks into a work breakdown structure. Once the project is delivered, hopefully vaguely following the projections, there's a giant sigh of relief as things return to "business as usual", a synonym for avoiding future changes. The achieved future state thus remains for a good while. That's needed to harvest the ROI (Return on Investment) projected in the up-front business case. This way of thinking is depicted on the left side of the following diagram:

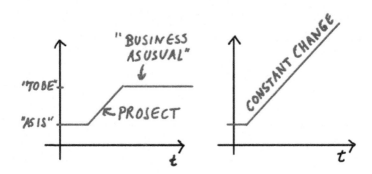

Project thinking (left) vs. constant change (right)

Two assumptions lie behind this well-known way of working. First, you need to have a pretty good idea what you are aiming for to define a good "target state". Second, "change" is considered an unusual activity. That's why it's tightly packaged into a project with all the associated control mechanisms. This way, change is well contained and concludes with a happy ending, the launch party, which routinely takes place before the majority of users have even seen the delivered system.

The Digital World Has No Target Picture

Both assumptions are false in the digital world. So-called digital companies aren't looking to optimize existing processes—they chart new territory by looking for new models. Now, finding new models isn't so easy, so these companies work via discovery and experimentation to figure out what works and what doesn't. Digital companies don't have the luxury of a well-defined target picture. Rather, they live in a world of constant change (indicated on the right side of the diagram).

 Digital companies don't have the luxury of a well-defined target picture. Rather, they live in a world of constant change.

The shift from treating change as an exception to treating is as normal has a fundamental effect on how IT needs to operate. On the left-hand side, the core competence is being a good guesser. Good prediction (or guessing) is needed to define a future target state and to subsequently execute to plan. Organizations benefit from their scale for recovery of the project investment: the bigger they are, the better the returns. They operate based on *Economies of Scale*.

The right-hand side works differently. Here, instead of being a good guesser, companies need to be fast learners so that they can figure out quickly what works and what doesn't. Learning fast reduces the cost of experimentation and allows frequent course corrections. So, instead of scale, they're living by the rules of *Economies of Speed*: not the biggest one succeeds, but the most nimble one.

The two models are almost diametrically opposed. Whereas the left side favors planning and optimization, the right side favors experimentation and disruption. On the left, deviation from a plan is undesired, whereas on the right side it's the moment of most learning. But even more profoundly, the two sides also use a different language.

Absolutes in a Changing World

Because traditional IT is based on the assumption that change is temporary and the normal state is defined by stability, people living in this model think and speak in absolute values. They manage via headcount, time, and budgets: "the project takes 10 engineers for 6 months and costs 1.5 million dollars"; "the server hardware costs 50,000 dollars plus another 20,000 for licenses". Absolute values give them predictability and simplify planning.

For the people who adopted a world of constant change, absolutes aren't as useful. If things are in constant flux, absolutes have less meaning—they change right after having been measured or established.

 Organizations operating in constant change think and speak in relative values because absolutes have little meaning for them.

The following illustration demonstrates how in a static world we look at absolute positions (diagram on the left). When there's movement as indicated on the right-hand side—drawn as vectors because I am not able to animate the book—our attention shifts to the direction and speed of movement.

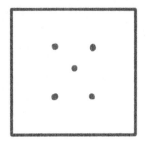 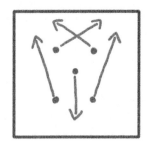

Static view (left) vs. movement (right)

The same is true in IT. Hence, the folks living in the world depicted on the right speak in relative values. Instead of budget, they speak of consumption; instead of headcount, they are more concerned about burn rate (spend per month); instead of fixating on deadlines, they aim to maximize velocity (value delivery per iteration). Those metrics represent rates, i.e., values over time, mathematically known as the *first derivative* of a function (assuming the x axis represents time).

Cloud Speaks Relatives

Because these organizations think in relative terms, or the first derivative, the cloud is a natural fit for their mental model. That's because the cloud operates in a consumption model: the server is no longer $50,000, but $3 *per hour*. Instead of absolute investments, we speak in rates per hour or per second. Hence, the cloud model makes perfect sense for organizations living in the first derivative because both speak the same language. That explains why virtually all of them operate in the cloud.

 The cloud speaks in the first derivative, pricing hardware in rates per time unit, not absolute investment.

It's clear that the cloud providers didn't exactly invent the data center. If all they had done was build a better data center, they'd be traditional IT outsourcing providers, not cloud providers. What the cloud did fundamentally change is allowing IT infrastructure to be procured based on a consumption model that's a perfect fit for a world of constant change.

Cloud computing didn't invent the data center; rather, it pioneered a consumption-based model of IT infrastructure procurement.

Cloud platforms also made provisioning near-instant, which is particularly valuable for folks operating in economies of speed.

Relatives Reduce Stress and Slack

Working with relatives has another significant advantage. No, I am not talking about hiring the in-laws, but about embracing the first derivative, which represents relative values over time. Predictions are necessarily uncertain, especially about the future, as the old adage goes.

So, what happens if the prediction for a project timeline comes out short? We deny reality and embark on a death march. At least the opposite should be alright, then? What if we are about to come in under budget? Well, we need to find ways to spend money quickly and create busywork lest anyone finds out and cuts the budget for next time.

The first derivative, measured in velocity or burn rate, doesn't lead to such project travesties. All we know is that faster progress and a lower burn rate are better, so we're constantly optimizing without burning or slacking. Working with relative figures does indeed reduce stress.

New Meets Old

Traditional organizations adopting the cloud's consumption model can face some unexpected headwind, though. Their IT processes have been built around a traditional up-front planning model for decades. IT departments are asked to estimate their infrastructure sizing and cost for years into the future. Such a process misses the cloud's key capability, *elasticity*, which enables scaling infrastructure up and down as needed. Boxing that capability into a fixed budget number makes about as little as sense as requiring someone to run waving a flag in front of a motor car[2]—a clear sign that an outdated process hinders modern technology.

---

[2]https://en.wikipedia.org/wiki/Locomotive_Acts

A common concern about the cloud that is frequently voiced in traditional organizations is spend control: if your infrastructure scales up and down at will, how do you predict and cap costs? First-derivative organizations think differently. It's not that they have money to give away. Rather, they realize that for a certain hardware cost of x dollars, they can serve n users and generate y dollars in business value. So they don't have a problem paying double for twice as many users and twice as much business benefit! For them, increasing IT spend is a sign of business success (and the cost often won't actually double).

This apparent conflict in thinking between budget predictability and value generation is one of the reasons that the cloud implies an *IT lifestyle change* (Chapter 1). It also hints at why *increasing your run budget may be a good thing* (Chapter 30).

3. Wishful Thinking Isn't a Strategy

Wishes are free but rarely come true.

This guy doesn't work at your favorite cloud provider

When organizations speak about their journey to the cloud, you'll hear a lot of fantastic things like dramatic cost savings, increased velocity, or even a full-on business transformation. However exciting these might be, in many cases they turn out to be mere aspirations—wishes to be a bit more blunt. And we know that wishes usually don't come true. So, if you want your cloud journey to succeed, you'd better have an actual strategy.

Learning from Real Life

We all have aspirations in our life. For many people, the list starts with a baseline of health and a happy family, perhaps an interesting job, and topped off with some nice items like a stately home, a fancy car, and, if you're especially lucky, a nice boat.

However, not all aspirations become reality—many remain just wishes, like my favorite 43-foot powerboat, which remained on my wish list long enough for the British manufacturer to go belly up (better than the boat, I suppose). On the upside, with that much money "saved", I now feel entitled to dream of a fancy sports car! I also learned a useful lesson:

 Wishing for things is free. Making them come true isn't. A clear strategy and concrete goals will increase the odds.

While it's OK and actually encouraged to have ambitions, you need to be careful that these ambitions don't remain wishes. Two things helps us translate wished into reality:

Strategies

A strategy will significantly increase the odds of your wishes coming true. Such strategies come in many different shapes. Some people are lucky enough to inherit money or marry into a wealthy family. Others play the lottery—a strategy that's easily implemented but bears a rather low chance of success. Some work hard to earn a good salary. Others contemplate a bank robbery. While many strategies are possible, not all are recommended. Or, as I remind people: some strategies might get you into a very large house with many rooms. It's called *jail*.

Goals

When implementing a strategy, it isn't always easy to know how you're doing— not having won the lottery yet doesn't have to mean that there was no progress. On the other hand, just reading fancy car magazines might make your wishes more concrete, but it doesn't accomplish much in terms of making them come true.

To know whether you're heading in the right direction and are making commensurate progress, you'll need concrete intermediate goals. These goals will depend on the strategy you chose. If your strategy is to earn money through an honest job, a suitable initial goal can be earning a degree from a reputable educational institution. Setting a specific amount of savings aside per month is also a reasonable goal. If you are eyeing a bank vault, a meaningful goal might be to identify a bank with weak security. Diverse strategies lead to diverse goals.

 One concrete goal derived from my "work hard to be able to buy a boat" strategy was to get a motor boat license as a student—I had time and they don't expire. So, if my boat wish ever comes true, I'll be ready to take the helm.

While goals are useful for tracking progress, they aren't necessarily the end result. I still don't own a boat. Nevertheless, they allow you to make tangible and measurable progress.

A Strategy Helps Wishes Come True

Having a strategy certainly sounds useful, but how do you go about developing one? Clayton Christensen, author of *The Innovator's Dilemma*[1], gives valuable advice on strategy in another book he wrote, *How Will You Measure Your Life?*[2] His guidance applies both to enterprises and personal life, and not just for cars and powerboats. Christensen breaks a strategy down into three core elements:

You need to set priorities
> They tell you which direction to take at the next decision point.

You need to balance your plan with opportunities that might come along
> A course correction might make more sense than holding steady. On the other hand, a strategy that changes every week likely isn't one.

---

[1]Clayton Christensen, *The Innovator's Dilemma*, 2011, Harper Business
[2]Clayton Christensen, *How Will You Measure Your Life?*, 2012, Harper Business

You need to allocate resources along with your strategy
> The strategy is only as good as the execution. Time is one of the most valuable resources in your personal life, so allocate it wisely based on your strategy.

Although large companies have a lot of resources and can afford to have a broad strategy, Christensen's three elements still apply.

- Even the most successful companies have limited resources. A company with unlimited funds, should it exist, would nonetheless be limited by how many qualified people it can hire and how fast it can onboard them. So, they still need to set priorities.
- Ignoring opportunities has been the downfall of many successful enterprises. Most had a viable strategy, or one that was viable within a certain context, to be more precise, but failed to respond to new opportunities. Blockbuster video rental comes to mind—passing on the chance to acquire Netflix to add a mail-order option to the physical stores was the beginning of the end for this once successful business.
- The larger an organization, the bigger the risk of falling into the trap of violating Christensen's last rule: what's shown on the PowerPoint slides might have little to no resemblance with reality. That's why Andy Grove, former CEO of Intel, famously said that "to understand a company's strategy, look at what they actually do rather than what they say they will do."

Strategy = Meaningful Decisions

Setting priorities means putting some things lower on the list than others. If everything is a priority, then nothing ends up being one. Prioritizing forces you to make choices - you can't have it all.

When we were lucky enough to be invited to a 70m luxury yacht, I asked the owner what he wasn't able to get. He responded immediately: a fireplace and draft beer. He was aware of the trade-offs he needed to make despite spending a large sum of money to have this ship custom built.

Hence, a strategy that doesn't require you to make difficult trade-offs likely isn't one. Not wanting to place myself on the same level as Christensen and other big thinkers of our time, I do have a favorite definition of strategy of my own:

 A sound strategy is defined by a series of meaningful decisions.

Meaningful decisions are those where you chose to go left but you could have just as well gone to the right. Choosing to attend university is a meaningful decision: you forgo short-term gains for the opportunity to earn more in the long run. Many viable alternatives would have you go another route: you could earn a certificate, become an apprentice, or simply start your own business. Bill Gates dropped out of university to start his business and has done reasonably well.

The same holds true in IT. Moving your infrastructure to the cloud is a meaningful decision, albeit a rather high level one. Which class of applications to move first and whether to re-architect them is also a meaningful decision that involves clear trade-offs. Some organizations go "all in" and move their entire IT assets to the cloud in one fell swoop, whereas others test the waters first by migrating just a few applications so they can learn how to get the most out of the cloud. The former organization might realize value sooner, but the latter can eventually derive more value. Of course, you could also think about combining the two, but that would imply a *longer path* (Chapter 16).

To highlight the importance of conscious trade-offs, Harvard Business School marketing guru Michael Porter reminds us:

Strategy is defined by what you're not *doing.*

Strategy = Setting the Dials

Linking strategy to meaningful decisions is intuitive but nevertheless a little abstract. I therefore often explain the exercise of setting an IT strategy as follows:

You're looking at a large enclosed box with complex machinery inside. That machinery is your IT, which can do amazing things but also has a lot of moving parts. Your job is to identify the levers and dials on this box and set them so that you can achieve a desirable outcome: reliable operations, low cost, solid security.

The levers tell you what choices you have, but you need to develop an understanding of how they influence the behavior of the box. To make things more challenging, not all levers can be set independently—you can't simply turn all dials to "10"—so you also need to understand how they're interrelated. Deciding the setting for each lever reflects the strategic direction you choose.

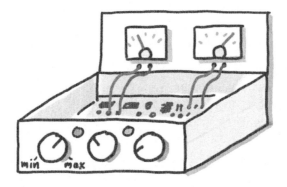

Strategy is like setting dials on a complex circuit

For example, one dial might define how you distribute workloads across multiple clouds. Many organizations will want to turn this dial to "10" to gain ultimate independence from any one cloud provider, ignoring the fact you will now depend on a new set of products and increased overall complexity. That's why setting a strategy is interesting but challenging.

A realistic strategy will need you to change some dial settings over time. You might start with one cloud to gain expertise and also receive vendor support more easily. Leaving that dial on "1" will do. Once you build expertise with one cloud, you structure your applications such that they isolate dependencies on proprietary cloud services from your application code. That would be like turning that dial to "3". Over time, you can consider balancing your workloads across clouds, slowly turning up the dial to about "5". You may not need to shift applications from one cloud to the next all the time, so you're content with leaving the dial there.

A major part of this book is dedicated to giving you decision models that put names and reference architectures behind the box's dials and numbers. For example, the *chapter on multicloud* (Chapter 18) lays out five settings for this dial and guides you how to choose.

If this approach reminds you of complex systems thinking, you are spot on. The exercise here is to influence the system to get it to a desired outcome. However, there are too many interdependencies to simply take it apart and see how it all works. That's the defining difference between a complicated system and a complex one as skillfully defined by Dave Snowden in the Cynefin Framework[3]. You need to use heuristics to set the controls and constantly observe the resulting effect. This means you have to probe first, then sense, and then respond as defined in the framework.

A corollary to this insight is that although you can't completely reverse-engineer what's inside the box, you need to develop an understanding of how things are connected. That implies that you can't manage what you can't understand[4].

Strategy = Creativity + Discipline

Building a meaningful strategy relies on both creativity and decision-making discipline, two traits that are often considered as at odds with each other. One requires you to think big and brainstorm, whereas the other needs you to make conscious trade-offs and lay out a concrete plan. So, you'd want to thoroughly explore options and then carefully select those that you will pursue, making sure to communicate your choices and the ramifications broadly.

 When defining your strategy, you want to expand and contract: explore several options and then carefully select those to pursue.

I refer to this process as *expand and contract*: broaden your view to avoid blind spots and then narrow back toward a specific plan. Many of the decision models in the later chapters in this book (see Part IV) are designed to assist you with this exercise. They define a clear language of choices that help you make informed decisions.

---

[3]https://hbr.org/2007/11/a-leaders-framework-for-decision-making
[4]https://www.linkedin.com/pulse/you-cant-manage-what-understand-gregor-hohpe/

If you look at most creative domains, such as movie making, fashion
design, or industrial design, you will find that creativity and discipline go hand-in-hand there as well. So you can take that hint and
apply it to IT strategy as well.

The Wishing Contest

Given how much is at stake, you'd think that IT is full of well-worked-out
strategies, meticulously defined and tracked via specific and achievable goals
that are packaged into amazing slide decks. After all, what else would upper
management and all the strategy consultants be doing?

Sadly, reality doesn't always match the aspirations. Large companies often
believe that they have sufficient resources to not require laser-sharp focus. Plus,
because business has been going fairly well, the strategy frequently comes down
to "do more of the same, just a bit better". Lastly, large enterprises tend to have
slow feedback cycles and limited transparency, both of which hinder tracking
progress and responding to opportunities.

When spending the past five years discussing and developing cloud strategies
for my employers and my clients, I have repeatedly observed how wishful
thinking can take precedence over developing a clear strategy. Organizations
(or vendors) promise straight-out 30% in cost reduction, 99.99% uptime for even
the oldest applications, and a full-on digital transformation across the whole
organization. Like all wishes, these objectives sound really, really good. That's
a common property of wishes—rarely does someone wish for something crappy
or uninteresting.

That's why wishes are a very slippery slope for organizations. "Outcome based
management" can degenerate into selecting unsubstantiated claims over well-
balanced strategies. The wishing contest can further degrade into a lying contest
where the person making the most outrageous claims will get their projects
initiatives funded. By the time reality hits, the folks having presented their
wishes will have moved on to the next project (or company) or blame lack of
execution for the wishes not having come true.

Be careful to not fall for promises of amazing outcomes. Demand to see a viable path to results, intermediate goals, and conscious trade-offs.

It's OK and in fact useful to have wishes. For example, at least you'll know *why you are going to the cloud* (Chapter 11) in the first place. These objectives must be supplemented by a viable plan on how to achieve them and be somewhat realistic to avoid preprogrammed disappointment. Calibrating your wishes and pairing them up with a viable path is the essence of defining a strategy. That's why strategy is the difference between making a wish and making it come true.

Beware the Proxy

In personal life, when you are looking for ways to get closer to realizing some of your wishes, it's easy to fall for products that are offered as substitute stepping stones. In your pursuit to become an athlete, you are lured by fancy sneakers, perhaps bearing your idol's signature; your path to a fancy lifestyle seems lined with brand-name suits, dresses, and handbags, which might even be adorned with the logo of your favorite sports car. Sadly, buying Michael Jordan branded sneakers isn't any more likely to make you a professional athlete than buying a Ferrari cap makes you an F1 driver. While they might be decent shoes, they are merely a proxy for a real goal like winning the next match or going for a workout every morning.

IT is littered with such proxies. They also have well-known labels and price tags many orders of magnitude higher than even the fanciest sneakers, which can actually run into the thousands of dollars. To make matters worse, IT being far ahead of itself by buying fancy "sneakers" doesn't just make them look silly, it's also *outright dangerous* (Chapter 5).

4. Principles Connect Strategy and Decisions

It's not the destination. It's the turns you took.

Turning wishes into a viable strategy is a necessary precondition for a successful cloud journey and the essence of this book. It's also hard work. A strategy has to be both forward-looking and executable. It has to be concrete but also allow for unforeseen circumstances. It has to be well-thought-through but also easy to grasp. A well-considered set of principles can be useful way to bridge these tensions.

A Strategy You Need

Developing a cloud strategy is significantly more difficult than stating *aspirations* (Chapter 3), another corporate euphemism for wishes. For example, are you going to move a specific class of applications to the cloud first? Will you "lift-and-shift" or re-architect applications to take full advantage of the cloud? Or perhaps use different strategies for different types of applications? If your organization is global, will you migrate by geographic region? Or by business unit? What about continents where cloud infrastructure is still sparse? Will you wait for cloud providers to build out their infrastructure or deploy an on-premises cloud in the meantime? Can you get rid of some applications altogether, replacing them with a SaaS (Software as a Service) offering? There are so many decisions to be made that this book contains an entire chapter on *Moving to the Cloud*. And the inherent trade-offs even lead us to *Pythagoras' Theorem* (Chapter 16).

Decisions Define the Journey

When embarking on a journey, the defining element isn't the destination, but the turns you take along the way. Are you going for the scenic route, stay on the freeway, or take a risky shortcut? All are viable options, and the option you take will depend on your preferences. However, in most cases you'd want to have some consistency in decision making. Perhaps you prefer to take the freeway because you have a long way to go, allowing just a short scenic detour where there's a major sight not too far from the freeway.

The Software Architect Elevator devotes an entire chapter to the connection between architecture and decisions.

 A picture with boxes and lines could depict an architecture, but it could also be abstract art. As an architect, what you're interested in are the decisions that were made, especially the ones that aren't obvious or trivial.

I use the simple drawing that follows to highlight the importance of highlighting decisions. The sketch on the left shows a boilerplate house–hardly what we would call architecture. The one on the right is quite similar but includes two critical decisions related to the roof's angle and overhang:

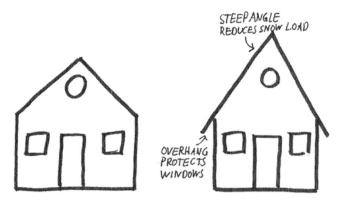

Decisions define architecture

Those decisions define the architecture, despite the sketch remaining crude. For those who think that pointy roofs that help the snow slide down aren't a particularly significant decision, I might point to Japan, a country with surprisingly heavy snowfall in regions such as Shirakawago in the Gifu prefecture. The pointy-roofed houses in this town obtained World Heritage status thanks to their unique design. These houses also highlight that architecture decisions are meaningful only in a given context—you won't find such houses by the beach.

Be Aware of Your Decisions

The first critical step towards a decision-based approach is to be aware when you are making a significant decision. Although it might sound trivial, in the heat of the daily enterprise IT battle, many decisions happen in the form of tacit assumptions, as highlighted in my blog post "Your most important architecture decisions might be the ones you didn't know you made[1]":

 An architecture team that described how they are deciding on the most suitable tool for each function had implicitly made a critical decision without being aware: to follow a best-of-breed strategy.

Most decisions are framed by a previous decision, so it's useful to occasionally "rewind the movie" to revisit which prior decisions led you to the current one. A classic example is people lamenting constraints imposed by prior decisions:

 People stating the desire to use more public transit / bike to work / shop by foot routinely claim to be held back by being far from the station / lack of bike routes / lack of nearby stores. If they had prioritized those items when choosing a place to live, this "constraint" would not have materialized.

Don't play victim to your own past decisions.

Strategy Informs Decisions

The role of architects in complex enterprise settings includes the need for disciplined decision making. I share the following diagram to highlight that organizations can make more consistent decisions by basing them on common principles:

---

[1]https://architectelevator.com/architecture/important-decisions/

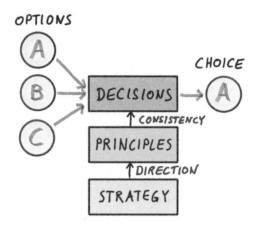

Strategy and principles provide decision consistency

The principles in turn are derived from an overarching strategy. The strategy lays out the overall direction you are heading in and how you want to go about achieving it. In a sense, it sets the frame and defines important boundaries.

 Defining a set of guiding principles is an important first step of any strategy.

Principles translate the strategy into a decision aid. Those decisions, in turn, define your architecture. Hence, one of the first steps when laying out a strategy will be defining a set of guiding principles. Meaningful principles should cause some amount of debate and perhaps disagreement. This way, you are detecting mismatched expectations or conflicting goals early on. Such debates won't be easy, but skipping them will simply defer and multiply the pain (and the associated cost) for later on.

Principles for Defining Principles

Defining meaningful principles isn't an easy task. Principles easily slip back into *wishful thinking* (Chapter 3) by portraying an ideal state rather than something that makes a conscious trade-off. I haven't been able to distill a simple litmus test for good principles, but I have come across enough bad ones that I have compiled a check list for meaningful principles:

- If the opposite of a principle is nonsense, it's likely not a good one. Everyone wants happy customers and a high-quality product, so turning them into a principle won't guide a lot of decisions.
- Principles that include product names or specific architectures (usually in the form of buzzwords) run the risk of being decisions that wanted to be elevated to principles—an unwelcome form of reverse engineering.
- Principles should pass the test of time. No one is a clairvoyant, but it helps to imagine whether the principle is still likely to make sense in a few years' time. A good proxy can be looking back three years and finding poor examples.
- It helps if the list of principles employs parallelism, meaning they apply the same grammatical construct. For example, it's useful if all principles consist of full sentences or just nouns. Mixing the two will make them look awkward.
- Principles should be memorable. Few teams will walk around with the list of principles on a cheat sheet, making principles that no one remembers unlikely to influence many decisions. If you're placing the principles on motivational posters plastered on the office walls, you're likely kidding yourself.
- Although there is no magic count for the number of principles, less than a handful might be sparse, whereas more than a dozen will be difficult to remember.

If you're looking for an academic foundation for using principles, there's a short paper titled Impact of Principles on Enterprise Engineering[2]. The part I found most useful is how principles are positioned as the connecting elements between root causes and outcomes. There's also a whole book titled *Architecture Principles*[3] that includes a catalog of candidate principles (not all of which would pass my test) but otherwise leans a bit heavily on TOGAF-flavored enterprise architecture.

Looking for Inspiration

One company famous for being guided by principles is Amazon, which cherishes its 14 Leadership Principles[4] so much that they accompany employees from the

---

[2]https://www.researchgate.net/publication/43205891_Impact_of_Principles_on_Enterprise_Engineering
[3]Greefhorst, Proper, *Architecture Principles*, 2011, Springer
[4]https://www.amazon.jobs/en/principles

initial interview to performance appraisals. Now, you might wonder whether Amazon's first and most famous leadership principle, *Customer Obsession*, violates the first guideline I mentioned earlier. I'd say it doesn't—the principle goes far beyond just having "satisfied customers". Instead, it mandates that "Although leaders pay attention to competitors, they obsess over customers." There's clearly a trade-off here: you glance left and right at your competition but you have the customer in firm focus. The opposite would also be meaningful and is widely practiced.

To gain some inspiration on how to develop sound principles, I tend to refer to Agile methods, one of the simplest but most profoundly misunderstood approaches in software development. The Agile Manifesto[5] defines four core values that are augmented by 12 principles. Each principle is stated in a short paragraph of one or two sentences, for example:

> *"Welcome changing requirements, even late in development. Agile processes harness change for the customer's competitive advantage."*

> *"Deliver working software frequently, from a couple of weeks to a couple of months, with a preference to the shorter timescale."*

> *"Working software is the primary measure of progress."*

Although the principles aren't entirely parallel in structure, they do place an important emphasis and pass our tests. For example, many organizations loathe late changes because they are expensive and annoying. Such places would adopt the opposite principle.

A related structure can be, not quite coincidentally, found in Kent Beck's classic book *Extreme Programming Explained*[6]. Kent progresses from a core set of values, which relate to our definition of a strategy, to 14 principles, most of which consist of a single noun, elaborated in a short chapter. For example, the principle of *flow* establishes that XP (Extreme Programming) favors "continuous flow of activities rather than discrete phases", in contrast to many earlier software development frameworks. Kent then progresses to derive concrete practices from this set of principles.

---

[5] https://agilemanifesto.org/
[6] Kent Beck, *Extreme Programming Explained*, 2nd edition, 2014, Addison-Wesley

Cloud Principles

Just like architecture, principles live in context. It therefore isn't meaningful to provide a list of principles to be copied and pasted to other organizations. To give some concrete inspiration, I will share a few principles that I have developed with organizations in the past, separating "higher-level", more strategic principles from more narrowly focused ones.

High-Level Principles

A label adorning virtually all cloud strategy documents is "multicloud". Sadly, too many of these documents state that the architects "favor multicloud". If you're lucky, there's a reason attached, which is usually to avoid *lock-in* (Chapter 21). That's all good, but it doesn't really help guide concrete decisions, so it's hardly a very meaningful principle. Should I deploy all applications on all clouds? That might be overkill. Are all clouds equal? Or do I have a primary cloud and another as fallback? That's where things get a lot more interesting.

With one customer, I defined the preference clearly in the following principle:

Multicloud doesn't mean uniform cloud.

> As a central IT group, we give business units a choice of cloud. However, we aren't looking to provide a uniform experience across clouds. Each application should use the cloud's features, especially managed services, if they allow us to deliver software faster and in higher quality.

For more detail on this principle, see *Multicloud: You've Got Options* (Chapter 18). Another principle that I used in the past related to pace of adoption:

We anticipate cloud evolution. Waiting can be a viable strategy.

> The rate at which cloud platforms evolve marginalizes efforts to build heavyweight platforms in house. We therefore carefully evaluate what we build ourselves versus simply waiting a few months for the feature to become part of the cloud platform.

Again, the opposite is also viable: anything that's needed but isn't yet available, we build as quickly as possible. Sadly in large organizations, "as quickly as possible" typically translates into 18 months. By then the cloud providers have often delivered the same capability, likely orders of magnitude cheaper. Strategy takes discipline.

Specific Principles

In other situations, when dealing with a smaller and more nimble organization, we developed more specific principles. Some of these principles were designed to counterbalance prevalent tendencies that made us less productive. We essentially used the principles to gently course correct—that's totally fine as long as the principles don't become too tactical. A good test is how frequently you are able to cite the principles during design discussions.

Use before reuse.

> Don't build things that could be reused some day. Build something that is useful now and refine it when it's actually used by other services.

This principle was intended to counterbalance engineers' well-intentioned tendency to design for the future, occasionally forgetting the present need. The principle vaguely relates to my saying that "reuse is a dangerous word because it describes components that were designed to be widely used but aren't." This principle could apply well to a lot of platform initiatives.

Design from front-to-back.

> Don't build elaborate APIs that mimic the back-end system's design. Instead, build consumer-driven APIs that provide the services in a format that the front-ends prefer.

During a transition we wanted to design interfaces such that they reflect where we are heading, not where we came from. Easy-to-use APIs also have a higher chance of being widely used, so they don't remain "reusable". This principle counterbalances the temptation to speed up API development by leaking details of existing systems that are intended to go away.

To make those principles more punchy and memorable, each of them received a clever slogan:

- Use before reuse: "Avoid gold plating."
- Design from front-to-back: "Customer-centricity also applies to APIs."

We validated the set of 10 principles by asking the team to reconstruct them from collective memory. Only principles that are remembered can have an impact.

One could consider applying a MECE-test (Mutually Exclusive, Collectively Exhaustive) to the set of principles. Although I can see that as a useful intellectual exercise, I don't feel that principles have to live up to that much structure. For example, I am generally fine with principles placing an emphasis (and hence not being collectively exhaustive). However, if your set of principles leaves a giant blind spot, a MECE check can help you identify that.

Dangerous Disconnect: The Hourglass

When defining strategies, one clear and present danger is having a nice set of high-level principles and then jumping into decisions or project proposals without an unambiguous linkage between the two. This problem typically manifests itself in presentations that start by pitching colorful buzzwords, supported by a long list of purported benefits, before suddenly jumping to propose the purchase of a specific tool or the approval of a large project. The logical connection between the two remains very thin. I refer to such presentations or arguments as the "hourglass".

You can detect the hourglass from the following recurring pattern. The talk starts with an elaborate list of benefits and buzzwords. However, as soon as you are enamored with wanting to become digital, cloud native, cloud first, data driven, Agile and Lean, a rather foggy and confusing segment follows (often aided by incomprehensible diagrams). Finally, the thin trickle in the middle leads to a conclusion of a significant headcount and funding request. How the story got from A to B is left as an exercise for the reader.

The IT presentation hourglass

A good strategy brings value by making a strong connection between the desirable outcome for the business and the detailed decision. An hourglass is rather the opposite, so watch out for this common antipattern.

5. If You Don't Know How to Drive...

...buying a faster car is the worst thing you can do.

Window shopping is a popular pastime: it doesn't cost very much and you can look at many exciting things, be it luxury fashion or exotic cars. Sometimes window shopping lures you into actually buying one of these shiny objects only to find out that they weren't really made for the average consumer. Or, to put it another way: the average driver is likely better off with a VW Golf (or perhaps a BMW) than the latest Lamborghini. The same holds true for corporate IT when it goes shopping for cloud[1].

Shiny Objects Can Make You Blind

Favoring a buy-over-build model, IT spends a fair amount of time shopping around for solutions. In the process, enterprises can compare vendor solutions, conduct evaluations, and also learn quite a bit. Of course, looking for new IT solutions is a bit like window shopping for cars, clothing, or real estate. For a moment, you can break away from the constraints of reality and get a taste of the life in luxury: the racy two seater (that doesn't have room for the kids), the fancy dress (that's not washable and a bit too sheer), and the exquisite country home (that's half an hour's drive away from the next store). All these have their lure but ultimately give way to the pressures of reality. And that's generally a good thing, unless you're keen to take out the two seater wearing an evening dress to get milk (I guarantee it will get old).

So, when looking at products, IT or not, we are well advised to separate the "being enamored by shiny objects" from the "let's actually buy something that serves our needs" mode. While the former surely is more fun, the latter is more important.

---

[1] The analogies in this chapter refer to several traditional gender role models. They are intended purely for sake of metaphor and don't indicate any endorsement in either direction by the author.

Capability ≠ Benefit

A critically important but often-neglected step when evaluating products is the translation of a tool's abstract capability into concrete value for the organization. Some systems that can scale to 10,000 transactions per second are as impressive as a car with a top speed of 300 km/h. However, they bring about as much benefit to a typical enterprise as that car in a country that enforces a 100 km/h speed limit. If anything, both will get you into trouble. You either end up with a speeding ticket (or in jail) or stuck with overpriced, highly specialized consultants helping you implement a simple use case in an overly complex tool.

 Not every tool feature translates into concrete value for your organization. Fancy features that you don't need mean you're paying for something that doesn't have any value to you.

Naturally, vendors benefit from us ogling shiny objects. It gives them a shot at selling us that two-seater. A common sales technique for this goes as follows: The salesperson leads us into describing ourselves as more sophisticated/modern/stylish than we really are. The next step, then, is the suggestion to buy a product that's suitable to a person or company of that inflated standing. This technique is nicely illustrated in Bob Cialdini's classic *Influence*[2]: a young woman comes to survey his social habits, which he naturally overstates a fair bit. Next, she builds a rational business case for him to sign up for some form of social club membership that gives discounts for folks who frequently go out. Or, perhaps closer to (enterprise) home: "organizations like yours who are successfully moving to the cloud realize substantial savings by making a larger up-front commitment"—wanna tell them that your cloud migration is going a bit more slowly than anticipated?

The Best Tool Is the One That Suits Your Level

Fancy tools need fancy skills, meaning a product that matches your capabilities is best for you. Or, put another way, if you're a poor driver, about the dumbest thing you can do is buy a faster car. It will only make a crash more likely and

---

[2]Cialdini, Robert B.: *Influence, the new psychology of modern persuasion*, 1984, Quill

more expensive—probably not what you were looking for unless you're angling to be immortalized in YouTube's amazingly popular "supercar fails" channels. It seems that *Schadenfreude* drives viewership, but perhaps not quite to the point of making the economics work out. So, first become a better driver and consider upgrading after you've maxed out your vehicle's capabilities.

The one time I tested my driving skills on the Nürburgring Nord-schleife in a (admittedly underpowered) BMW 1-series rental car, I was passed by a VW Golf and a (surely overpowered) minivan. A faster car wouldn't have helped much except to get me into trouble.[3]

Back in IT the same applies. Transformation takes place by changing an organization's assumptions and operating model. There is *no SKU for transformation* (Chapter 3)—it's not something that you can buy. Better tools help you work in better ways (you probably won't take the Yugo to the Nürburgring), but there's a cycle of continuous improvement in which both tools and capabilities incrementally ratchet up.

Look for products that generate value even if you use only a subset of features, thus giving you a "ramp" to adoption.

When procuring IT tools, organizations therefore shouldn't pick those products that have the longest list of features, but those that can grow with them; for example, by providing value even if you use only a subset of features. I refer to this capability as affording *incremental value delivery*. Or, to quote Alan Kay: "Simple things should be simple, complex things should be possible."

Giant Leaps Don't Happen

As our capabilities improve, isn't it OK to buy a tool one or two sizes ahead of where you are now? It's like buying kids' shoes half a size bigger—they'll be the right size in two months. On the other hand, wanting to have an adult racing cycle when you're just learning how to balance is dangerous.

---

[3]I do get my redemption, however, every time I pass someone riding a much more expensive mountain bike.

The same holds true for IT tools. A unified version control system and some form of continuous integration are a great step forward toward accelerated software delivery even if you still have to work on shortening your release cycles and improving your test coverage. A fully automated build-deploy-Kubernetes-container-Helm-chart-generator setup is likely less helpful—it's a great aspiration and may get you some bragging rights, but it's likely a bit too much to bite off in one setting for traditional IT.

When looking at tools, target a clear progression and keep a balanced view on how far you can jump in one setting. If you're a bit behind, it's ever so tempting to catch up by making one big leap. The reality is, though, that if a small step is difficult to make, a giant jump is guaranteed to end up in utter failure.

 Organizations that have fallen behind are tempted to make one giant leap ahead to catch up. Sadly, this is the most unlikely path to success.

IT's inclination to look too far ahead when procuring tools often isn't the result of ignorance but of excessive friction in approval processes. Because procuring a new product requires elaborate evaluations, business cases, security reviews, and so on, starting with a simple tool and upgrade soon after would be inefficient—you'd just be doing the whole process over again. Instead, teams are looking for a tool that will suit them three years down the road, even if it's a struggle for the first two. Systemic friction is once again the culprit for IT's ailments.

You Can Sell Only What People Don't Already Have

There's a common assumption that products are made and sold to address an unmet customer need. However, I don't find that equation to be quite that simple. In many cases it appears that demand is first created just so it can be subsequently addressed. Allow me to try another analogy from daily life.

Having lived and worked on three continents, I have observed how the fashion and beauty industries set quite different, and often opposing, ideals in different regions. In Asia, it's desirable to be fair skinned (a heavy tan makes you look like a farmer, supposedly), whereas in Europe the number of tanning studios is only barely outdone by fitness centers (being tanned means you can afford an exotic beach vacation or perhaps at least a tanning studio). Asian women often wish they were more full-figured, whereas everyone else seems to be trying to lose weight and become more petite. The list of contrasting goals continues to include high cheekbones (European models tend to have them, Asian models usually don't), wide or narrow noses, round or almond-shaped eyes, and so on.

While body image is always a delicate topic, I've personally come to derive two conclusions from this:

1. Be happy being whoever you are regardless of what's on the billboards.
2. People who sell you stuff will promote an ideal that's rare and difficult, if not impossible, to achieve. See conclusion #1.

Back in IT, we can find quite a few analogies. While your enterprise is proudly making its first steps into the cloud, you are made to believe that everyone else is already blissfully basking in a perimeter-less-multi-hybrid-cloud-native-serverless nirvana. Even if that were the case, it would still be fine to be going at your own pace. You should also be a bit skeptical as to whether there's some amplification and wishful thinking at play. Go out and have a look—you might see some of your peers at the tanning studio.

 Don't fret if you're not on the bleeding edge. There *are* successful businesses that don't run all their applications as microservices in containers being deployed 1,000 times a day. It's OK.

Marketing Isn't Reality

Technology moves fast, but technology adoption is often not quite as fast as the readers of quarterly earnings reports or attendees of semi-annual launch events would like. Transforming IT infrastructure and changing the fundamental operating model may take a sizable enterprise two, three, or even five years. In the meantime, vendors have to announce new things to stay in business.

Hence, we get to see shiny demos that auto-deploy, auto-heal, auto-migrate, and almost auto-procure (lucky for us, not quite yet). Looking ahead at product evolution is quite useful when selecting vendors or products, so marketing serves a valuable function (I have many good friends in marketing and highly appreciate their work). But we mustn't confuse vision with reality. Marketing shares a possible target picture, whereas we are the ones who actually walk the path, and that's usually done by taking one step after another.

Does a Better Knife Make You a Better Cook?

Indulge me to share one last metaphor. I love cooking—it serves as an important therapeutic function that lets the hands and the intuition do their work while my brain cools off. After spending a good bit of time in specialty shops around the globe, Europe is my favorite source for pots and baking supplies. I look to Japan for knives, ceramics, wooden products, and hyper-specialized tools like my *ginger grater cleaner*. Over time, the significant price increase for basic kitchen tools, such as knives, struck me. General inflation aside, a very good German knife used to run some 30–40 Euros. Modern kitchen shops are now full of knives for easily five times that, sometimes running north of 400 Euros. While there's certainly a bit of priming at play (see *Making Decisions* in *37 Things*), another reason given by the stores were changes in cooking habits.

In most Western societies, the domestic role model up until the mid-to-late twentieth century was based on the woman taking care of food and child rearing while men would work in the fields or later in factories and offices. This division of labor led to knives being a tool—a thing that you use to cut your meat or vegetables. And a €30 knife managed that just fine. Men increasingly taking an interest in cooking changed kitchen supplies, especially knives, from being basic tools to being seen as hobby or even vanity items. This change has enabled a completely different product selection and pricing model—the cook is now a modern-age samurai who chooses to wield his 200-times folded carbon steel blade at tomatoes rather than enemies.

Translating my cooking experiences back to IT, I like to ask vendors pitching their shiny tools: will your better knife make me a better cook? Or will it rather put my fingers at risk? I do enjoy a good knife, but my experience tells me that good cooking comes from practice and a good understanding of how to prepare and assemble the ingredients. And you could say the same of good architecture! So, buy a solid IT tool, not a vanity item, and invest in your own skill!

Part II: Organizing for the Cloud

The cloud implies a fundamental IT lifestyle change. That's why getting the most out of it requires changes to the organization, including departmental structures, processes, career schemes, and HR guidelines. Moving to the cloud is thus as much an organizational as it is a technology topic. The relationship between technical and organizational change is one of the core themes of my book *The Software Architect Elevator*[4] and applies directly to cloud transformations.

Even adopting cloud computing as a purely technical move implies an organizational change. After all, you're outsourcing a big portion of your IT responsibilities to a third party. This doesn't mean, though, that all operational concerns disappear—quite the contrary. Organizing for the cloud has a wide-ranging impact on operational and business functions up to financial management.

Culture Changes

My friend Mark Birch, who used to be the regional director for Stack Overflow in APAC, pointedly concluded:

> *There is no Stack Overflow for transformation where you just cut and paste your culture change and compile.*

Organizations are often portrayed by their structure—the classic *org chart*. Many organizations therefore wonder what new kind of structure they should embrace

---

[4]Hohpe, *The Software Architect Elevator*, 2020, O'Reilly

48

when they move to the cloud. Sadly, structural changes alone rarely bring the anticipated results. Rather, changing the way of working, including the written and often unwritten processes, is essential to harvesting the benefits of moving to the cloud.

Organizational Architectures

To not leave this book devoid of references to *The Matrix* movie trilogy, the *Matrix Reloaded* includes a famous scene that has the Merovingian comment on Neo stopping a hail of bullets mid air with, "OK, you have some skill." Successfully migrating applications to or building applications for the cloud also requires some skill, perhaps short of stopping bullets with your bare hands.

Rather, technical teams need to be familiar with the wealth of products and services being offered, account management and permissions schemes, modern application architectures, DevSecOps, and much more. A decade ago, hardly any of these concepts existed. On one hand, that's a great level setter—everyone starts fresh. But it also means that not learning new technologies and new ways of working puts you at risk of quickly being left behind.

Organizations therefore need to decide to what extent they can train existing staff and how they are going to acquire new skill sets. Some organizations are looking to start with a small Center of Excellence, which is expected to carry the change to the remainder of the organizations. Other organizations have trained and certified everyone, including their CEO. The happy medium will vary by organization. So, along with your technical cloud architecture, you'll also want to be defining your organizational architecture.

Organizing for the Cloud

Organizations built for the cloud have learned that...

- *The cloud is outsourcing, but of a special kind* (Chapter 6).
- *The cloud turns your organization on its side* (Chapter 7).
- *Needing new skills doesn't mean hiring different people* (Chapter 8).
- *Hiring a digital hitman is bound to end in mayhem* (Chapter 9).
- *Enterprise Architecture gets a new meaning in the cloud* (Chapter 10).

6. Cloud Is Outsourcing

And outsourcing is always a big deal.

Sweet Ops dreams

Traditional IT relies heavily on outsourcing to third-party providers for software development, system integration, and operations. Doing so afforded IT some perceived efficiencies but also introduced friction, which becomes a hindrance in an environment defined by *Economies of Speed* (Chapter 2). Many enterprises are therefore bringing much of their IT back in house. However, moving to the cloud is outsourcing "par excellence": all of your infrastructure is hosted and operated by someone else. And we're told the more we hand over to the cloud provider to operate, the better off we are. How do these two ideals reconcile?

Don't Outsource Thinking!

Classic IT is a *buy-over-build environment* (Chapter 1) because traditionally IT wasn't a differentiator for the business and thus could be safely outsourced. Outsourcing is most prevalent in data-center facilities and operations, system integration of packaged software, and software development. In these respective areas, I have seen ratios of outsourced to in-house staff of 5 to 1, and sometimes even 10 to 1. In the extreme case, all that's left in IT is a procurement and program management umbrella, which motivated me to author a blog post with the intentionally controversial title Don't Outsource Thinking[1].

Outsourcing is driven by thinking in *Economies of Scale*. Because the outsourcing provider has more people qualified to do the job and is typically much larger (sometimes employing hundreds of thousands of people), it's assumed that the provider can perform the respective task more efficiently. In return for this efficiency, IT departments give up some amount of control as part of the contractual agreement. In an IT world that's perceived as a commodity, lack of control isn't a major concern because the provider would agree to operate based on well-understood and acknowledged *best practices*.

Efficiency versus Agility

Much has changed since. The competitive environment is no longer defined by a company's size, but by its speed and agility. That's why digital disruptors can challenge incumbent businesses despite being orders of magnitude smaller in size. Because these challengers operate at higher velocity, they can realize faster (and cheaper) *Build-Measure-Learn* cycles[2], a critical capability when charting new territory. These companies also understand the *Cost of Delay*[3], the price paid for not having a product on the market sooner.

In these Economies of Speed, the benefits realized by moving fast outweigh the efficiencies to be gained from being large. Traditional IT outsourcing doesn't mesh well with these rules of engagement. Driven by the quest for efficiency gains, outsourcing contracts often span multiple years (sometimes decades!) and are bound by rather rigid contractual agreements that specify each party's

---

[1]https://architectelevator.com/strategy/dont-outsource-thinking/
[2]Ries, *The Lean Startup*, 2011, Currency
[3]Reinertsen, *The Principles of Product Development Flow*, 2009, Celeritas Publishing

obligations in excruciating detail. Changes are cumbersome at best and likely expensive—*change request* is the most feared phrase for anyone who has signed an outsourcing contract.

Bring 'em Home

So, it's no surprise that many IT departments are rethinking their outsourcing strategy. Most companies I worked with were bringing software delivery and DevOps skills back in house, usually only held back by their ability to attract talent. In-house development benefits from faster feedback cycles. It also assures that any learning is retained within the organization as opposed to being lost to a third-party provider. Organizations also maintain better control over the software they develop in house.

One challenge with insourcing is that an IT group that builds software looks quite different from one that *mostly operates third-party software* (Chapter 13). Instead of oversight committees and procurement departments, you'll need product owners who aren't program managers in disguise and architects who can make difficult trade-offs under project pressure instead of commenting on vendor presentations. So, just like outsourcing, insourcing is also a big deal, and one that should be well thought through.

A recurring challenge is the apparent chicken-or-egg problem of *attracting talented staff* (Chapter 8). Qualified people want to work with other highly skilled folks, not in an environment dominated by budgeting and procurement processes. So you'll need a few folks to "break the ice", who are either brave or foolish enough (or more likely both) to sign up for a major transformation. I know because I have been one of those ice breakers—that's the story of *The Software Architect Elevator*[4].

Don't look for talent just on the outside. Chances are you are sitting on unrealized potential: motivated employees who are held back by rigid processes and procedures. Take a good walk around the engine room or invite people to share some of their pet projects. You may find some gems.

---

[4]https://architectelevator.com

Digital Outsourcing

Strangely, though, while traditional companies are (rightly) reeling things back in, their competitors from the digital side appear to do exactly the opposite: they rely heavily on outsourcing. No server is to be found on their premises as everything is running in the cloud. Commodity software is licensed and used in a *SaaS model* (Chapter 13). Food is catered and office space is leased. HR and payroll services are outsourced to third parties. These companies maintain a minimum of assets and focus solely on product development. They're the corporate equivalent of the "own nothing" trend.

Outsourcing à la Cloud

The cloud isn't just outsourcing; it might well pass as the mother of all outsourcings. Activities from facilities and hardware procurement all the way to patching operating systems and monitoring applications are provided by a third party. Unlike traditional infrastructure outsourcing that typically just handles data-center facilities or server operations, the cloud offers fully managed services like data warehouses, pre-trained machine learning models, or end-to-end software delivery and deployment platforms. In most cases, you won't even be able to inspect the service provider's facilities due to security considerations.

So, what makes outsourcing to the cloud so different from traditional outsourcing? Despite being similar in principle, the cloud excels by providing all the important capabilities that traditional outsourcing could not:

Full Control

In a cloud environment, you get exactly the infrastructure that you specify via an API or a visual console. Hence, you have full control over the types and sizes of servers, the network compartments they're part of, which operating system they run, and so on. Instead of being bound by a restrictive order sheet that attempts to harvest efficiencies by restricting choice, the cloud showers you with flexibility. With that flexibility also comes some responsibility— more on that later.

Transparency

The cloud also gives you complete transparency into service levels, system status, and billing details. Except in rather unusual circumstances there is no "blame game" when something goes wrong—the transparency protects both sides.

Short-Term Commitments

Elastic billing is a key tenet of cloud computing. Although cloud providers do encourage (and incentivize) large multi-year commitments, you're essentially paying for usage and can scale down at will. Shifting your workloads to another cloud provider is often more of a technical consideration than a legal one.

Evolution

Terms that are set in stone are a significant downside of traditional outsourcing. Folks who signed an outsourcing contract in 2015 might have felt that provisioning a server within several days was acceptable and that a server with more than 512 GB of RAM would never be needed. Five years later, we complain if a new server takes more than a few minutes to spool up, while memory-hungry applications like SAP HANA happily consume terabytes of RAM in the double-digit range. Updating existing outsourcing contracts to include these shifts will be time consuming and expensive. In contrast, cloud providers release new services all the time—at the time of this writing, Amazon Web Services (AWS) could provision 8-socket bare-metal servers with 24 TB RAM.

Economics

Cloud providers routinely reduce prices for their services. AWS, the longest-running of the major cloud providers, boasts of having slashed prices 70 times between 2006 and 2020. Try that with your outsourcing provider.

So, while the cloud is indeed outsourcing, it redefines what outsourcing actually means. This major shift has become possible through a combination of technical advancements such as software-defined infrastructure and the willingness of a provider to break with a traditional business model.

Once Again, It's the Lines!

Those who have read *37 Things* know that I am proud to reject any purported architecture diagram that contains no lines. Lines are important—more important than the boxes in my view—because they define how elements interact and how the system as a whole behaves. And, after all, that's what architecture is about. So: "no lines, no architecture".

The same is true for the relationship between your organization and your infrastructure. If you were going to draw a simple diagram of you and your (cloud or traditional) outsourcing provider, you'd see two boxes labeled "you" and "them", connected by a line. Using a cloud platform would not look much different:

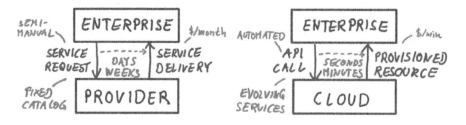

Comparing traditional outsourcing with the cloud

However, what those lines entail makes all the difference. On the left side of the diagram it's lengthy contracts and service requests (or emailing spreadsheets for the less fortunate) that go into a black hole from which the requested service (or something vaguely similar) ultimately emerges. The cloud, in contrast, feels like interacting with a piece of commercial software. Instead of filing a service request, you call an API, just like you would with your ERP package. Or you use the browser interface via a cloud console. Provisioning isn't a black hole; pricing is transparent. New services are announced all the time. You could call cloud platforms a service-oriented architecture for infrastructure.

This simple comparison highlights that organizations that take a static view of the world won't notice the stark differences between the models. Organizations that think *in the first derivative* (Chapter 2), however, will see that the cloud is a lifestyle changer.

Core vs. Non-Core

A fundamental difference between outsourcing to a cloud and outsourcing software delivery hinges on the notion of what in IT is core vs. non-core. In much of traditional IT, operations is king: the quality of IT is defined by its operational excellence. As IT shifted from a cost-driven commodity to becoming a differentiator and innovation driver, though, software delivery moved into the limelight. That's why it should be held in house as you would do with any other core asset. That's also why you *should not consider the cloud an infrastructure topic* (Chapter 12).

Outsourcing a Mess Is a Bigger Mess

There's an old rule in outsourcing: if your IT is a mess, outsourcing will make it only worse. That's so because messy, largely manual IT is able to function only thanks to an extensive *black market* (see *37 Things*). Black markets aren't just inefficient, they also can't be outsourced: Joe in operations who used to pull a few strings for you is no longer in charge.

Knowing that the cloud is outsourcing, you should also expect to get the most out of cloud if you first clean up your house. That means, for example, knowing your application inventory and dependencies. Because the usual state of affairs is that these things aren't known, most cloud providers have devised clever scanning and monitoring tools that aim to figure out what software runs on which server and which other applications it talks to. They're certainly helpful but no substitute for actually cleaning up. It's a bit like someone coming to your house before a move to tell you that you have 35 plates and 53 mismatching forks. You might appreciate the information, but it doesn't really make things better unless you know which forks are family heirloom and which ones came with the Happy Meal.

The Cloud Leverages Economies of Scale

It's noteworthy that although the cloud is a key ingredient into making organizations *successful in Economies of Speed* (Chapter 2), it itself relies heavily on Economies of Scale. Building large data centers and private, global networks takes enormous investment that only a few large hyperscale providers can afford.

 The cloud managed to draw a very precise line between a scale-optimized implementation and a speed-based business model.

It appears that cloud providers managed to draw a very precise dividing line between a scale-based implementation and a democratic, speed-based business model. Perhaps that's the real magic trick of the cloud.

Outsourcing Is Insurance

Anyone who's spent time in traditional IT knows that there's another reason for outsourcing: If something blows up, such as a software project or a data-center consolidation gone wrong, with outsourcing you're further from the epicenter of the disaster and hence have a better chance of survival. When internal folks point out to me that a contractor's day rate could pay for two internals, I routinely remind them that the system integrator rate includes life insurance for our IT managers. "Blame shield" is a blunt term sometimes used for this setup. No worries, the integrator who took the hit will move on to other customers, largely unscathed.

Sadly, or perhaps luckily, the cloud doesn't include this element in the outsourcing arrangement. "You build it, you run it" also translates into "you set it on fire, you put it out." I feel that's fair game.

7. The Cloud Turns Your Organization Sideways

And your customers will like it.

"See, we already transformed our organization."

Traditional IT maintains a fairly strict *separation between infrastructure and application teams* (Chapter 12). Application teams delight customers with functionality, whereas infrastructure teams procure hardware, assure reliable operations, and protect IT assets. The frequent quarrels between the respective teams might hint that maybe not everything is perfect in this setup. The conflict is easy to see because the two groups have opposing goals: application delivery teams are incentivized to release more features, but the infrastructure and operations teams want to minimize change to assure reliability. A move to the cloud puts the final nail into the coffin of this already strained relationship.

The IT Layer Cake

Traditional organizations function by layers. Just like in systems architecture, working in layers has distinct advantages: concerns are cleanly separated, dependencies flow in one direction, and interfaces between units are well defined. That's why layering makes it easy to swap out one layer for another.

However, as is invariably the case with architecture, there are also downsides. For example, layering can cause translation errors and additional latency when traversing layers. Additionally, even simple changes often ripple through multiple layers, slowing development down. Most developers have seen situations in which a simple change like adding a field to the user interface required changes to the UI code, the WAF (Web Application Firewall), the web server, the API gateway, the back-end API, the application server code, the object-relational mapping, and the database layer. So, a layered structure, which is intended to localize change, often runs across end-to-end dependencies.

Interestingly, these effects apply to both technical layers (e.g. from front-end to application to database) and organizational layers (e.g. from UI design to development to QA to operations). For example, swapping out one layer in an organization is called *outsourcing* (Chapter 6).

Optimizing End to End

Layering also adds friction due to *local optimization*. Clean separation of concerns between the layers leads us toward optimizing each individual layer. In organizations, you notice this effect when having to fill out an endless form when requesting something from another team. The form allows that team to be highly optimized internally, but it burdens other teams in ways that aren't measured anywhere. The end result is a collection of highly optimized teams where nothing seems to get done due to excessive friction.

 Layering favors local optimization over end-to-end optimization, often causing friction at the interfaces.

The technical equivalent is a microservices architecture in which all communication occurs via SOAP/XML—most CPU cycles are going to be spent parsing

XML and garbage collecting DOM (Domain Object Model) fragments.

In contrast, optimizing end-to-end focuses on the flow of a change or a request across the whole system. That this works has been demonstrated by the Lean movement in manufacturing, which for about half a century benefited from optimizing end-to-end flow instead of individual processing steps.

 Your customers have an end-to-end view of your organization and won't have much appreciation for handovers between teams.

This is also the view your customers have, e.g. when they contact support or customer service. Your internal structure ("please hold while I transfer you to another department") is merely a convenience for yourself and a rather poor excuse for sub-par customer service.

Pivoting For Low Friction

Cloud computing reduces friction, such as having to wait for delivery and installation of servers. To take advantage of that technical capability, though, you need to think and optimize end to end, cutting across the existing layers. Each transition between layers can be a friction point and introduce delays—service requests, shared resource pools, or waiting for a steering committee decision. Such friction slows down feedback cycles, one of the most critical capabilities in *Economies of Speed* (Chapter 2).

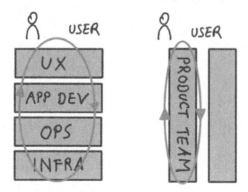

Feedback loops crossing layers (left) increases friction

Hence, a cloud operating model works best if you turn the layer cake on its side. Instead of slicing by UI/application/operations/infrastructure teams, you give each team end-to-end control and responsibility over a functional area. Instead of trying to optimize each function individually, they are optimizing the end-to-end value delivery to the customer.

 Teams previously structured as layers turn into vertical slices representing functional areas or services.

Such teams are often called tribes, product teams, or feature teams. Regardless of the name, minimizing friction is the main driver for such a team structure.

Is Provisioning per Commit Dev or Ops?

Infrastructure automation turns out to be a big booster for loosening up the boundaries between the IT layers. With techniques such as *Infrastructure as Code* and *GitOps*, provisioning and configuring infrastructure becomes as simple as checking a new version of a file into the source-code repository (a "commit" in Git). This has tremendous advantages as the source-code repository has now become the single source of truth for application and infrastructure. Moreover, having a full description of your deployment environment in your source-code repository allows you to automatically *scan these configurations* (Chapter 23) for compliance with security guidelines.

Being able to manage infrastructure via a piece of source code makes a separation between application and infrastructure team rather meaningless—it's an infrastructure task that's done via a development approach. Coincidentally that's one of the key aspects of "DevOps".

Cloud-Enabling Teams

Let's look at what teams in this new structure will look like. As you might expect, some changes are quite significant while others are more subtle.

Cloud Infra Teams

Automated deployments don't imply that there's nothing *left for infrastructure teams to do* (Chapter 31). They are still in charge of commissioning cloud interconnects, deploying common tools for monitoring and security, and creating automation, among many other things. My standard answer to anyone in IT worrying about whether there will be something left to do for them is, "I have never seen anyone in IT not being busy."

As IT is asked to pick up pace and deliver more value, there's plenty to do! Modern operations teams are extracted from frequent feedback loops like provisioning hardware for application teams. Instead, they are helping support change. Essentially, they have been moved into the *first derivative* (Chapter 2).

Engineering Productivity Team

Ironically, embracing the cloud often entails the formation of a new layer, or unit perhaps, which also resides "beneath" the application development teams. Commonly called called *Engineering Productivity Teams* or *Developer Productivity Engineering* (DPE), their role is to maximize the software delivery teams' productivity, e.g. by relieving each team from having to rig up their own software delivery pipeline or run-time components such as log processing. Although on the surface, such a team might look like another layer, there are a couple of defining differences:

- The team's role is to be an enabler, not a gating function. A good productivity team shortens the time to initial deployment and enables teams to deploy frequently. Infrastructure teams were often doing the opposite.
- Rather than focus on undifferentiated work (your customers won't buy more products because of the brand of server you installed), productivity teams contribute to customer-visible business metrics such as the time it takes to implement a new feature.
- The productivity team doesn't absolve applications teams from their operational responsibilities. This critical feedback cycle remains within the application teams, who, for example, manage their own *error budgets*, a key practice of *Site Reliability Engineering* (SRE).
- Names matter. Instead of naming teams by what they do, it's better to express the value they deliver. This team makes developers more productive, and the name reflects that.

Interestingly, the value of software delivery automation also hasn't escaped the cloud providers who now provide numerous tools to speed up the software delivery life cycle, such as fully hosted continuous integration pipelines. Those services simplify the work of engineering productivity teams that now can focus on configuring and integrating fully-operated cloud services. In a sense, cloud providers are no longer just "moving up the stack", but are also *looking sideways* (Chapter 12).

Centers of Excellence (Not Always an Excellent Idea)

A Cloud Center of Excellence (CCoE) or Cloud Center of Competence (CCoC) is part of many large-scale cloud journeys. Borrowing from existing enterprise vernacular (do other teams lack competence?), such teams are designed to house experts who are well versed in the new technology and support the rest of the organization. The appeal is apparent: instead of retraining an entire organization, you seed a small team that can act as a multiplier to transform the rest of the organization. While the idea is legit, I have seen such teams, or perhaps a specific implementation thereof, face several challenges.

First, the idea of transforming an organization from a small central team is analog to the missionary model[1]. Missionaries are sent out to "convert" existing cultures to a new way of thinking. As one astute reader of my blog once pointed out, being a missionary is very hard—some missionaries ended up being food. While IT missionaries are likely to survive, bringing change into teams that work within the confines of existing incentive systems and leadership structures is nevertheless difficult at best.

If converting an entire organization in a missionary model is understood to be difficult, building tools and frameworks is the typical conclusion to increase the team's impact across the organization. Unfortunately, this route often leads teams into the *trap of prescriptive governance* (Chapter 10), which is more likely to disable than enable the organization. People will hardly embrace a new technology because you make it harder for them to use.

While many organizations rightly worry about things spinning out of control if no guard rails are in place, I routinely remind them that in order to steer, you first have to move[2]. So, in my experience, it's best to first get things rolling,

---

[1]https://www.linkedin.com/pulse/transformation-missionaries-boot-camps-shanghaiing-gregor-hohpe/
[2]https://www.linkedin.com/pulse/before-you-can-steer-first-have-move-gregor-hohpe/

perhaps with fewer constraints and more handholding than desired, and then define governance based on what has been learned.

Last, many CCoE teams that manage to move the organization toward a new way of working fall victim to their own success by becoming a bottleneck for inbound requests. This effect is nicely described in the article *Why Central Cloud Teams Fail*[3]. Note that the authors sell cloud training, giving them an incentive to propose training the whole organization, but the point perhaps prevails.

In summary, a CCoE can be useful to "start the engine" but just like a *two-speed architecture* (Chapter 19), it isn't a magic recipe and should be expected to have a limited lifespan.

Team Topologies

The book "Team Topologies"[4] by Matthew Skelton and Manuel Pais presents a suitable vocabulary and visualization for flow-optimized team structures:

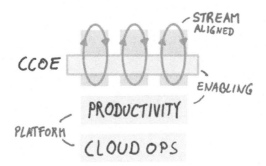

Enabling and platform teams support fast feedback cycles

Borrowing from their book's nomenclature, cloud infrastructure teams become *platform teams*, i.e. teams that enable the *stream-aligned* product teams to work autonomously. CCoEs are *enabling teams* that cut across stream-aligned teams to try out options and make informed suggestions on tooling, practices, and frameworks. The most effective engineering productivity teams, in my experience, act in a combination of platform and enabling team.

The new team structure looks as shown in the diagram (stream and enabling teams are rotated by 90 degrees vs. *Team Topologies* to maintain consistency

[3]https://acloudguru.com/blog/engineering/why-central-cloud-teams-fail-and-how-to-save-yours
[4]Skelton, Pais, *Team Topologies: organizing business and technology for fast flow*, 2019, IT Revolution Press

with the previous figure). *Just like with cloud* (Chapter 6), the big difference isn't in the structure but in how the different pieces interact. The new model enables short feedback loops as opposed to injecting delays and gating steps.

Organizational Debt

Changes to organizational structures, processes, and HR schemes are complex and will take time, even in the best cases. As a result, the technical changes, while also not simple, can often be implemented more quickly than the organizational changes.

Pushing the technical change while neglecting (or simply not advancing at equal pace) the organizational change is going to accumulate organizational debt. Just like technical debt, "borrowing" from your organization allows you to speed up initially, but the accumulating interest will ultimately come back to bite you just like overdue credit card bills. Soon, your technical progress will slow down due to organizational resistance. In any case, the value that the technical progress generates will diminish—an effect that I call the value gap[5].

---

[5]https://aws.amazon.com/blogs/enterprise-strategy/is-your-cloud-journey-stuck-in-the-value-gap/

8. Retain/Re-Skill/Replace/Retire

The four "R"s of migrating your workforce.

WMAF = Workforce Migration Acceleration Framework

When IT leaders and architects speak about cloud migrations, they usually refer to migrating applications to the cloud. To plan such a move, several frameworks with *varying numbers of R's* (Chapter 16) exist. However, an equally large or perhaps even bigger challenge is how to migrate your workforce to embrace cloud and work efficiently in the new environment. Interestingly, there's another set of "R's" for that.

Migrating the Workforce

New technology requires new skills. Not just new technology skills like formulating Helm charts, but also new mindsets that debunk existing beliefs as described in "Reverse Engineering the Organization" in *37 Things*. For example, if an organization equates "fast" with "poor quality"—they do it "quick and dirty"—they will consciously or unconsciously resist higher software delivery velocity. Therefore, *change management* is a major part of any cloud journey. Organizations are made up of people, so people are a good starting point for this aspect of your cloud journey.

The 4 "Rs" of People Transformation

When it comes to preparing your workforce for the cloud journey, just like with applications, you have several options:

Retain

> Although cloud computing permeates many aspects of the organization, not all jobs will fundamentally change. For example, you might be able to keep existing project managers, assuming that they haven't degenerated into pure budget administrators. Retaining staff might also include providing additional training; for example, on Agile methods or a shift from projects to products.

> Interestingly, even though applications built for the cloud are different, developers often fall into the *Retain* category because they are already used to adopting new technology. Chances are they have already tinkered with cloud technology before your organization went "all in". The most important aspect for developers is that they don't see cloud computing just as a new set of tools but understand the fundamental shifts, such as *making everything disposable* (Chapter 23).

Re-Skill

> Other roles might remain by title but require completely different skill sets. This is often the case in infrastructure and operations for which processes that were once manual are now automated. This doesn't mean folks will be out of work (after all, *automation isn't about efficiency* (Chapter 31)), but the nature of the work is changing substantially. Instead of (semi-)manually provisioning servers or

other IT assets, tasks now focus on building automation, baking golden virtual machine images, and creating more transparency through monitoring.

Re-skill should be the first choice in any organizational transformation because, as I like to say, "the best hire is the person you didn't lose." Existing staff is familiar with the organization and the business domain, something a new person might still have to acquire over several months. Also, the hot job market for IT talent has hurt the signal-to-noise ratio for recruiting, meaning you have to sift through more candidates to find good ones.

Replace

Not every person can be re-skilled. In some cases, the jump is simply too big, whereas in others the person isn't willing to start from scratch. Although it might be easy to peg this on the individual, for folks who have excelled in a particular task for several decades, having the intellectual rug pulled out from under their feet can be traumatizing.

Its worth considering that being replaced isn't always bad in the long run. So-called "out of date" skill sets often end up being in high demand due to dwindling supply. For example, many COBOL programmers make a very good living!

Naturally, replacing also implies the organization finding and onboarding a new person with the desired skill set, which isn't always easy. More on that in a moment.

Retire

Some roles are no longer needed and hence don't need to be replaced. For example, many tasks associated with data-center facilities, such as planning, procurement, and installation of hardware are likely not going to be required in a cloud operating model. Folks concerned with design and planning might instead evaluate and procure cloud providers' services, but this function largely disappears after an organization completes the move to the cloud. In many IT organizations, such tasks were outsourced to begin with, softening the impact on internal staff.

In real life, just like on the technical side of cloud migration, you will have a mix of "migration paths" for different groups of people. You'll be able to retain and re-skill the majority of staff and might have to replace or retire a few. Choosing will very much depend on your organization and the individuals. However, having a defined and labeled list of options will help you make a meaningful selection.

You Already Have the People

Categorizing people is a whole different game than categorizing applications—this isn't about shedding the "legacy"! When looking for new talent your first major mistake might be to look only outside the organization. You're bound to have folks who showed only mediocre performance but who were simply bored and would do a stellar job once your organization adjusts its operating model.

In a famous interview[1], Adrian Cockcroft, now vice president of cloud architecture strategy at AWS, responded to a CIO lamenting that his organization doesn't have the same skills as Netflix with, "Well, we hired them from you!" He went on to explain that, "What we found, over and over again, was that people were producing a fraction of what they could produce at most companies." So, have a close look to see whether your people are being held back by the system.

 In my talks and workshops I routinely show a picture of a long row of Ferraris stuck in a traffic jam (or perhaps a cruising event) and ask the audience how fast these cars can go. Most people correctly estimate them to have a top speed north of 300 km/h. However, how fast are they going? Maybe 30. Now, the critical question is would putting more horsepower in the cars make them go faster? The answer is easy: no. Sadly, that's what many organizations are attempting to do by claiming they "need better people".

You might also encounter the inverse: folks who were very good at their existing task but are unwilling to embrace a new way of working. It's similar to the warning label on financial instruments: Past performance is no guarantee of future results.

---

[1]https://dzone.com/articles/tech-talk-simplifying-the-future-with-adrian-cockc

Training Is More Than Teaching

One technique that can be a better indicator than past performance is training. Besides teaching new techniques, a well-run training that challenges students as opposed to just having them copy and paste code snippets (many of us have sadly seen those) can easily spot who latches on to new tools and concepts and who doesn't. I therefore recommend debriefing with the instructor after any training event to get input into staffing decisions. Training staff also gives everyone a fair shot, ensuring that you don't have a blind spot for already existing talent.

Training can also come in the form of working side by side with an expert. This can be an external or a well-qualified internal person. Just like before, you'd want to use this feedback channel to know who your best candidates are.

Some organizations feel that having to (re-)train their people is a major investment that puts them at a disadvantage compared to their "digital" competitors who seem to employ only people who know the cloud, embrace DevOps, and never lose sight of business value. However, this is a classic "the grass is greener" fallacy: The large tech leaders invest an enormous amount into training and enablement, ranging from onboarding bootcamps over weekly tech talks and brown bags, to self-paced learning modules. They are happy to make this investment because they know the ROI is high.

Top Athletes Don't Compete in the Swamp

Many organizations are looking to bring in some super stars to handle the transition. Naturally, they are looking for top athletes, the best in their field. The problem is, as I described in a blog post[2], that the friction that's likely to exist in the organization equates to everyone one wading knee-deep in the mud. In such an environment a superstar sprinter won't be moving a whole lot faster than the rest of the folks. Instead, they will grow frustrated and soon leave.

 On my team we often reminded ourselves that for each task we have two goals: first, accomplish the task, but also to improve the way it's done in the future.

---

[2]https://www.linkedin.com/pulse/drain-swamp-before-looking-top-talent-gregor-hohpe/

So, you need to find a way to dry up the mud before you can utilize top talent. However, once again you're caught in a chicken-or-egg situation: draining the swamp also requires talent. You might be fortunate enough to find an athlete who is willing to also help remove friction. Such a person might see changing the running surface as an even more interesting challenge than just running.

More likely, you'll need to fix some of the worst friction points before you go out to hire. You might want to start with those that are likely to be faced first by new hires to at least soften the blow. Common friction points early in the onboarding process include inadequate IT equipment such as laptops that don't allow software installs and take 15 minutes to boot due to device management (aka "corporate spyware"). Unresponsive or inflexible IT support is another common complaint.

 I was once forced to take a docking station along with my laptop because all equipment comes in a single, indivisible bundle. When returning equipment I ran into issues because some of the pieces I didn't want in the first place were tucked away in some corner.

HR onboarding processes also run the risk of turning off athletes before they even enter the race. One famous figure in Agile software development was once dropped off the recruiting process by a major internet company because he told them to just "Google his name" instead of him submitting a resume. I guess they weren't ready for him.

Organizational Anti-Corruption Layer

You can't boil the ocean, so you also don't need to dry up all the mud at once. For example, you can obtain an exception for your team to use non-standard hardware. However, you must dam off the part that's dry from the rest of the swamp lest it floods again.

I call this approach the *Organizational Anti-Corruption Layer*, borrowed from the common design pattern[3] for working with legacy systems. In organizations, this pattern can for example be applied to headcount allocation:

---

[3]https://domainlanguage.com/ddd/reference/

When working in a large organization, I had all team members officially report to me so that shifting resources between subteams would not affect the official org chart and spared us from lengthy approval processes.

You can build similar isolation layers for example for budget allocation.

Up Your Assets

One constant concern among organizations looking to attract desirable technical skills is their low (perceived) employer attractiveness. How would a traditional insurance company/bank/manufacturing business be able to compete for talent against Google, Amazon, and Facebook?

The good news is that, although many don't like to hear it, likely you don't need the same kind of engineer that the FAANGs (Facebook, Apple, Amazon, Netflix, Google) employ. That doesn't imply that your engineers are not as smart—they simply don't need to build websites that scale to one billion users or develop globally distributed transactional databases. They need to be able to code applications that delight business users and transform the insurance/banking/manufacturing industry. They'll have tremendous tools at their fingertips, thanks to the cloud, and hence can focus on delivering value to your business.

 In a past job, I was quite successful in hiring qualified candidates because our team didn't require them to speak the local language (German). Additionally, many of the "digital brand-name" competitors had very few actual engineering positions in their sales and consulting offices, which also required extensive travel.

Second, large and successful organizations typically have a lot more to offer to candidates than they believe. At a large and traditional insurance company, we conducted an exercise to identify what we can offer to desirable technical candidates and were surprised how long the list became: from simple items like a steady work week and paid overtime (not every software engineer prefers to sleep under their desk), we could offer challenging projects on a global scale, access to and coaching from top executives, assignments abroad, co-presenting at conferences with senior technologists, and much more. It's likely that your organization also has a lot more to offer than it realizes, so it's a worthwhile exercise to make such a list.

Re-Label?

In many organizations, I have observed a "fifth R": the re-labeling of roles. For example, all project managers underwent SCRUM training and were swiftly renamed into SCRUM masters or product owners. Alternatively, existing teams are re-labeled as "tribes" without giving them more end-to-end autonomy. With existing structures and incentives remaining as they are, such maneuvers accomplish close to nothing besides spending time and money. Organizations don't transform by sticking new labels on existing structures. So, don't fall into the trap of the fifth R.

9. Don't Hire a Digital Hitman

What ends poorly in the movies rarely goes well in IT.

"Your mission: eliminate servers. This message will self-destruct in 3...2..."

When looking to transform, traditional organizations often look to bring in a key person who has worked for so-called *digital companies* (Chapter 2). The idea is simple: this individual knows what the target picture looks like and will lead the organization on the path to enlightenment. As a newcomer, this person can also ruffle some feathers without tarnishing the image of the existing management. He or she is the digital hit(wo)man who will do the dirty work for us. What could possibly go wrong?

Movie Recipes

It's well known that Hollywood movies follow a few, proven recipes. A common theme starts with a person leading a seemingly normal if perhaps ambitious life. To achieve their ambitious goal this person engages someone from the underworld to do a bit of dirty work for them. To at least initially save the character's moral grounds, the person will justify their actions based on a pressing need or a vague principle of greater good. The counterpart from the underworld often comes in form of a hitman, who is tasked with scaring away, kidnapping, or disposing of a person who stands in the way of a grand plan. Alas, things don't go as planned and so the story unfolds.

A movie following this recipe fairly closely is *The Accountant* with Ben Affleck. Here, the CEO of a major robotics company hired a hitman to dispose of his sister and his CFO who might have gotten wind of his financial manipulations. Independently, the company also hired an accountant to investigate some irregularities with their bookkeeping. As it turns out, the accountant brings a lot more skills to the table than just adding numbers. After a lot of action and countless empty shells, things... (spoiler alert!) don't end well for the instigator.

The Digital Hit(wo)man

Back in the world of IT and digital transformation, we can quickly see the analogy: a business leader is under pressure from the board to change the organization to become faster and "more digital"; there is some amount of handiwork involved, such as re-skilling, re-orgs or, de-layering. But it's in the name of greater good—saving the company. Wouldn't it be easiest to recruit some sort of digital hit(wo)man, who can clean the place up and then disappear as quickly as they came?

The natural candidate wouldn't be as good looking as Ben Affleck and wouldn't bring a trailer full of firearms. To be precise, the movie accountant is also the one who chases the hitman. For that part, you better watch the movie, though. Digital IT hit(wo)men would come with credentials such as having held a major role at a brand-name digital company, having led a corporate innovation center, or having run a start-up incubator. He or she would be full of energy and promise, and they would have one or the other magic trick up their sleeve.

Crossing Over into the Unknown

Sadly, though, hiring the IT hit(wo)man is more likely to end up as in the movie than in a successful transformation. The key challenge in hiring someone from a different world (under or otherwise) is that you won't know the world into which you're crossing over. For example, you wouldn't know how to pick a good candidate, because the whole premise is that you need someone who has a very different background and brings completely different skills. You also won't understand the unwritten rules of engagement in the other world.

 When hiring someone from a different world, you're not qualified to make the hiring decision.

Although as an IT leader you may not have to worry about someone else outbidding you to turn your own hitman against you, you may still hit a few snags, such as:

- The transformation expert you are hiring may feel that it's entirely reasonable to quit after a half a year because that's how things work where they're from.
- They may simply ignore all corporate rules—after all they are here to challenge and change things, right? But perhaps that shouldn't include blowing the budget half way through the year and storming into the CEO's office every time they have what they think is a good idea.
- They may also feel that it's OK to publicly speak about the work they're doing, including all of your organization's shortcomings.

As a result, some of the stories involving a digital hit(wo)man don't fare much better than in the movies. While luckily the body count generally stays low, there's carnage in other forms: large sums of money spent, many expectations missed, results not achieved, egos bruised, and employees disgruntled.

Asking Trust-Fund Kids for Investment Advice

A digital hit(wo)man usually worked in a digital environment, so they understand well what it looks like and how it works. What most of them didn't have to do, though, is build such an environment from scratch or, more difficult yet, transform an existing organization into a digital one. Therefore, they might not be able to lay out a transformation path for your organization because they have never seen the starting point. That likely ends up being a frustrating experience both for them and for you.

 Folks coming from a digital company know the target picture but they don't know the path, especially from your starting point.

Asking someone who grew up in the Googles of the world how to become like them is a bit like asking trust-fund kids for investment advice: they may tell you to invest a small portion of your assets into a building downtown and convert it into luxury condos while keeping the penthouse for yourself. This may in fact be sound advice, but tough to implement for someone who doesn't have $50 million as starting capital.

The IT equivalents of trust-fund investment advice can take many forms, most of which backfire:

- The new, shiny (and expensive) innovation center might not actually feed anything back into the core business. This could be because the business isn't ready for it or because the innovation center has become completely detached from the business.
- The new work model may be shunned by employees or it might violate existing labor contract agreements and hence can't be implemented.
- The staff might lack the skills to support a shiny new "digital" platform that was proposed.

So, perhaps instead of a hit(wo)man you need an organizational horse whisperer. That's a less-exciting movie, but organizational transformations can also be slow and draining.

Who to Look for?

Transforming a complex organization without any outside help is going to be difficult—you won't even know much about what you are aiming for. It's like reading travel brochures to prepare for living abroad. So how do you go about finding a good person to help you? As usual, there isn't an easy recipe, but my experience has shown that you can improve the odds by looking for a few specific traits:

Stamina

First of all, don't expect a digital hitman who carries silver bullets to instantly kill your legacy zombies. Look for someone who has shown the stamina to see a transformation through from beginning to end. In many cases, this would have taken several years.

Enterprise Experience

You can't just copy and paste one company's culture onto another— you need to plot a careful path. So, your candidate may be extremely frustrated with your existing platforms and processes and quickly leave. Look for someone who has had some exposure to enterprise systems and environments.

Teacher

Having worked for a so-called "digital" company doesn't automatically qualify a person as a transformation agent. Yes, they'll have some experience working in the kind of organization that you're inspired by (or compete against). However, that doesn't mean they know how to take you from where you are to where you want to be. Think about it this way: not every native speaker of a specific language is a good teacher of that language.

Engine Room

Knowing how a digital company acts doesn't mean the person knows the kind of technology platform that's needed underneath. Yes, "move to the cloud" can't be all wrong, but it doesn't tell you how to get there, in which order, and with which expectations. Therefore, find someone who can ride the Architect Elevator at least a few floors down.

Vendor Neutral

Smart advice is relatively easy to come by compared to actual implementation. Look for someone who has spent time inside a transforming organization as opposed to looking on from the outside. Likewise, watch out for candidates who are looking to drive the transformation through product investment alone. If the person spews out a lot of product names you might be looking at a sales person in disguise. Once hired, such a person will chummy up to vendors selling you transformation snake oil. This is not the person you want to lead your transformation.

What Do They Look for?

Naturally, qualified candidates who can lead an organization through a transformation will have plenty of opportunities. And although they will likely look for a commensurate compensation package, they usually can't be bought with money alone (see "Money Can't Buy Love" in *37 Things*). These folks will look for a challenge but not for a suicide mission—your transformation isn't Mission Impossible and the hero won't come out alive. So they'd want to be assured that the organization is willing to make difficult changes and that top-management support is in place. Realistically, the candidates will interview your organization as much as you will interview them.

It Sure Ain't Easy, but It's Doable

If you feel that these suggestions will narrow down the set of available candidates even further, you are probably right. Finding a good person to drive the transformation is hard—unicorns don't exist. That's perhaps the first important lesson for any transformation: you have to put wishful thinking aside and brace for harsh reality.

10. Enterprise Architecture in the Cloud

Keeping your head in the cloud but the feet on the ground.

"You said we need to aim for the cloud..."

For several years I ran *Enterprise Architecture* at a major financial services firm. When I joined the organization, I had little idea what Enterprise Architecture actually entailed, which in hindsight might have been an asset because the organization wanted someone with a Silicon Valley background to bring a fresh take. The results are well known: I concluded that it's time to redefine the architect's role as the connecting element between the IT engine room and the business penthouse, a concept which became known as *The Software Architect Elevator*[1].

Of course I could not have done any of this without a stellar team. Michele was one architect who did great work in the engine room but regularly popped his

---

[1]Hohpe, *The Software Architect Elevator*, 2020, O'Reilly

head into the penthouse to help chart the IT strategy. He's now running his own architecture team supporting a cloud journey. Here are some of his insights on how cloud and enterprise architecture intersect.

By Michele Danieli

Enterprises turn to the cloud to reap substantial benefits in agility, security, and operational stability. But the way the cloud journey starts can vary greatly. In many organizations, so-called shadow IT bypasses corporate restrictions by deploying in the cloud; others require extreme scale that's only available in the cloud; some see a unique opportunity for reinventing the IT landscape with no ties to the past; or perhaps a new IT strategy foresees the orderly migration of resources to the cloud. Each starting point also impacts the role the Enterprise Architecture team plays during the cloud journey.

Enterprise Architecture

Most IT departments in large enterprises include a team labeled "Enterprise Architecture" (EA), typically as part of a central IT governance team. Although interpretations vary widely, enterprise architect teams bring value by providing the glue between business and IT architecture (see "Enterprise Architect or Architect in the Enterprise?" in *The Software Architect Elevator*). As such a connecting element, they translate market needs into technical components and capabilities. Bridging the two halves across a whole enterprise requires both breadth of expertise and the ability to cut through enormous complexity.

Migrating Enterprise Architecture

Like many IT functions, EA is also affected by the organization's move to the cloud. Interestingly, the starting point of the cloud initiative impacts the way sponsors and project teams see the new role of EA:

- Business units seeing the cloud as a way to overcome excessive friction inside the central IT department will stay away from EA, except perhaps for guidance on connectivity or security constraints.
- Software and product engineering teams will believe they can figure it all out without much help from EA.
- Infrastructure and operations teams will seek support from EA to map applications onto the newly designed infrastructure.
- If cloud migration is an enterprise strategy, EA will be asked to develop a comprehensive view of the current infrastructure, application, and process inventory to be used as input to strategic planning.

In any scenario, EA departments in cloud-enabled enterprises should focus their guidance on the *why* and *what* of the initiative, leaving the implementation details (the *how*) to other teams. This means departing from prescriptive roles, as they often exist in the form of design authorities and other governance bodies, and becoming cloud advocates in the boardroom and sparring partners in the engine room.

 Enterprise architects in the cloud enterprise should depart from prescriptive roles to become cloud advocates in the boardroom and sparring partners in the engine room.

Filling this mandate translates into three concrete tasks that are material to the cloud journey's success:

Inform Business Leadership
Business leadership gets bombarded with buzzwords, usually accompanied by unsubstantiated promises. EA teams can help them separate hype from reality.

Link Business, Organization, and IT
There are many paths to the cloud. EA teams can help navigate cloud decisions with a holistic architecture view that includes the business and the organization.

Establish Guidelines and Enable Adoption
EA can foster knowledge sharing by translating individual experiences into common technical guidelines. Also, EA can develop running services that make following the guidelines easy.

Let's look at each task in detail.

Inform Business Leadership

Although cloud computing can do amazing things, it also attracts a lot of hype. Business and IT management, therefore, needs a solid understanding of how the cloud will affect their enterprise. Although cloud providers and external consultants give support, enterprise architects articulate the *drivers* (Chapter 11) for moving to the cloud, balancing strategic aspects like *lock-in* (Chapter 21) or the *economics* (Chapter 30) of a cloud operating model. This strategic dialog calibrates the expectations regarding direction, value, and costs over the long term. Without it, business leadership is bound to be disappointed by the move to the cloud.

Link Business, Organization, and IT

Developing a cloud enterprise is a lot more than using cloud technologies. It requires understanding how cloud computing will impact the organization as much as how to transform the existing landscape of applications and IT services. Cloud providers support transformation with services like the AWS Cloud Adoption Framework[2] or Pivotal Labs[3]. Despite originating from different perspectives, both programs recognize the importance of a holistic view across business, people, and IT. Enterprise architects complement the vendor expertise with insider knowledge.

EA helps the organization identify the different aspects of moving to the cloud and plotting viable *adoption paths* (Chapter 16). They contribute to a decision framework for *hybrid* (Chapter 19) and *multicloud* (Chapter 18) selection, complementing developers' application and technology views with a broader perspective.

Cloud transformation will require change, and change bears cost and risks. Gaining business support is easier if such change is linked to specific business benefits. For example, automation and containerization can enable growth in new regions with lower cost and faster time to market. Increased elasticity absorbs workload fluctuations (e.g., seasonal patterns) to maintain a seamless customer experience. It is the role of EA to articulate such connections.

---

[2]https://aws.amazon.com/professional-services/CAF
[3]https://tanzu.vmware.com/labs

Establish Guidelines and Enable Adoption

EA must help operationalize the cloud strategy. Because applications in a typical enterprise portfolio aren't equally portable to the cloud, enterprise architects should help establish the criteria and guidelines that can be used to assess an application's cloud readiness, using frameworks like *FROSST* (Chapter 27).

 My current EA team is defining applications' cloud readiness across application structure, build and run processes, technologies, and delivery model.

Instead of restricting technology decisions with rigid standards, cloud EA should translate needs into mechanisms and running services. Engineers consume services, not abstract principles.

 At my current employer, the cloud security community translated security principles into building blocks, released in the enterprise code repository.

Lastly, rather than cite abstract principles such as loose coupling, architects should model the actual impact of lock-in at the time of service design.

The Enterprise IT Cast of Characters

How can EA perform these important but challenging tasks within the IT organization? Understanding the organization helps EA find the appropriate positioning and engagement model.

Enterprise IT has to tackle the complexity of concurrently managing business, technical, operational, financial, and compliance aspects across several layers. Enterprises split this complexity across specific roles and processes, each carrying slightly different perspectives:

- Product Owners – Shape the product vision by acting as the interface between business and IT; they care about team productivity and product quality.

- Software Developers – Translate a product vision into working software; they need tools that maximize productivity and match product requirements.
- Infrastructure Engineers – Set up and keep infrastructure up and running and secure; they care about fast provisioning and non-functional qualities.
- Service Managers – Are responsible for application or technical services; they guarantee the service level and security to internal customers.
- Infrastructure Managers – Are responsible for the infrastructure decisions across a wide range of areas; they care about operational stability, costs, and security.
- Enterprise Architects – Coordinate work across different architectural domains, looking at long term strategy and compliance with operating models.
- Technology Providers – Provide technologies and software running, on premises or in a hosted environment; they care about business growth.

This list isn't meant to be exhaustive. Several other roles contribute to delivering solutions, such as domain architects, User Experience (UX) designers, quality engineers, and project managers. These actors play a critical role in the flow from product vision to running services, and connect application and infrastructure domains.

Although these roles and their needs existed before, shifting to a cloud operating model changes the way these players interact. In traditional IT, long-term investments in vendor products, long procurement lead times, and mature but constrained technology options (both in infrastructure and software) limited the pace of change and innovation. Hence, much time was spent carefully selecting software and managing the technology life cycle. In this context, EA was needed to lay out a multi-year roadmap and ensure convergence from the present to the defined future state.

Virtuous Cycles

The cloud gives enterprises more options to choose from, which can also be adopted at a faster pace and with lower investment. At the same time, the cloud elevates the roles of developers, operations engineers, and product owners because it *turns your organization sideways* (Chapter 7). Traditional organization charts don't reflect this dynamic well.

I visualize this new organizational model as a circle connecting three vertices: product owners, developers, and infrastructure engineers. This Value Delivery Loop is depicted in the following diagram:

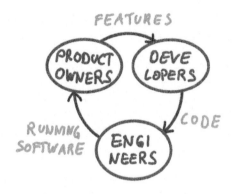

The Value Delivery Loop

The faster this loop spins, the more value it delivers to the business and the more confidence the team gains: product owners and developers working in shorter sprints; developers pushing to production more often; engineers setting up stable environments faster. To operate fast, the loop depends on efficient IT services. Any disturbance is seen as reducing output and is therefore unwelcome.

To the parties in the loop, enterprise-wide IT standards that constrain technical choices are considered friction. Such standards are often holdovers from a legacy operating model that doesn't suit the way modern teams work. For example, they might prescribe manual approval steps that interfere with the level of automation engineers desire and reduce team velocity.

The loop operates in a context shaped by business leadership, IT stakeholders (infrastructure managers, service managers) and external parties (cloud service providers). This outer network defines and manages infrastructure services, thus shaping the capabilities available to the teams in the inner loop.

The outer context supports the business strategy with investments in new technologies such as machine learning or collaborative workplaces. It also defines mechanisms to support market growth, expansion into new regions, and reduced IT cost. It thus shapes the IT strategy based on business needs, including selecting providers while ensuring security and compliance.

Although IT strategy doesn't move as fast as the inner loop, it also speeds up in a modern enterprise. Ideas flow more quickly from business to development who return continuous feedback thanks to more flexible adoption of technologies. Instead of defining multi-year plans, teams now probe and explore technologies and solutions, consuming IT services provided by cloud providers. Consolidation of technologies into the enterprise landscape can follow more frequently a bottom-up path, thanks to lowered barriers and quickly measurable outcomes.

Modern enterprise architects need to fit into this context to avoid becoming purely ceremonial roles. Does that mean that they are giving way to product owners, developers, engineers, and cloud providers' own architects? Not at all.

Bringing Value to the Cloud Enterprise

Enterprise architects must position themselves as the interface between strategic context and the inner delivery loop. This is a two-way street: they feed the delivery teams' learnings into the IT strategy while channeling the strategy to delivery teams with particular attention to security and costs.

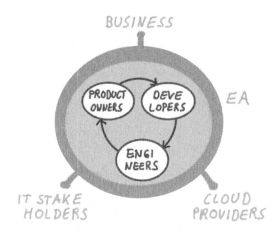

Enterprise architects as connecting element

In this role, cloud enterprise architects connect different levels of abstraction and ride the elevator from the executive board down to the engine room many times. They discover and foster Economies of Scale in the way teams adopt cloud, advise projects on aspects like security or resilience, and help teams adopt technical and organizational best practices based on provider know-how.

When a central IT group migrated specific applications like machine learning to the cloud but retained core business systems on premises with traditional infrastructure, some projects started to explore the cloud on their own, leading to fragmented decisions and lack of experience sharing. Our EA team set out to translate these early experiences into shared capabilities by creating a compelling vision (going as far as creating an internal brand name and logo) and driving implementation with the infrastructure manager to a broadly available cloud platform.

Connecting delivery and strategy allows EA to move from conceptualization to action. In some cases, the team can even act as a technical product owner, stimulating engineering teams to work and think differently. For such a model to succeed, EA teams need to be pragmatic, descriptive instead of prescriptive.

Concrete activities for such modern EA teams can include:

- Convincing business leadership on the need for a longer architecture planning horizon
- Working across teams to build an environment that enables cloud adoption; for example, via shared services
- Supporting engineers in building services that benefit the widest audience

To succeed in this role of flywheel for the cloud transformation, enterprise architects need to not only develop specific skills in cloud architecture and technologies, but also reposition themselves as an enabler rather than a governing function.

In conclusion, EA's role in the cloud enterprise isn't to design the cloud infrastructure (cloud architects and engineers will do that) nor to select cloud technologies for a specific project (developers and engineers will do that) nor to model applications for available cloud services (solution architects and developers will do that). EA teams detail where and why the business will benefit from the cloud, taking a broad perspective on business, applications, and technology.

 Enterprise architects neither design the cloud infrastructure nor do they select cloud technologies. They detail where and why the business will benefit from cloud computing.

Even though the role isn't fundamentally different from the past, the wheel spins ever faster and thus requires a more pragmatic and undogmatic approach to strategy. It also requires leaving the ivory tower behind to work closely with developers, engineers, and infrastructure managers in the engine room.

Part III: Moving to the Cloud

Understanding that the cloud is an entirely different affair from traditional IT procurement is a good precondition for laying out a cloud strategy. Now, it's time to tackle the shift of on-premises resources to a cloud operating model.

In with the New...

The center of such a strategy will be the migration of existing on-premises applications to the cloud. However, simply moving your IT assets from your premises to the cloud is more likely to yield you another data center than a cloud transformation. You therefore need to shed existing assumptions—leaving things behind is a critical element of any cloud migration. Some of the things to be left behind are the very assumptions that made IT big and powerful, such as operating servers and packaged applications.

Too Much Buzz Makes You Deaf

Widespread "advice" and buzzwords can muddy the path to cloud enlightenment a good bit. My favorite one is the notion of wanting to become a "cloud native" organization. As someone who's moved around the world a good bit, I feel obliged to point out that "being native" is rather the opposite of "migrating". Hence, the term doesn't just feel unnecessarily exclusionary, but also constitutes an oxymoron. Moreover, in many countries' history, the natives didn't fare terribly well during migrations.

Measuring Progress

So, it's better to put all that vocabulary aside and focus on making a better IT for our business. Your goal shouldn't be to achieve a certain label (I'll give you any label you'd like for a modest fee...), but to improve on concrete core metrics that are relevant to the business and the customer such as uptime or release frequency.

Plotting a Path

Most cloud migration frameworks give you options: for example, you can re-architect applications or just lift-and-shift them as is. Most of these publications assume, though, that this migration is a one-step process: you decide the path for each application and off they go. I have never seen things take place as easily as that. Applications are interdependent, and migrations often take multiple passes of preparing, shifting, optimizing, and re-architecting workloads. So, a migration strategy is more than dividing applications into buckets.

Cloud service providers and third parties provide many resources that help you with the mechanics of a cloud migration. For example, AWS[4], Microsoft Azure[5], and Google Cloud[6] each published an elaborate Cloud Adoption Framework. This chapter isn't looking to replicate advice that's already presented in a well-structured format. Rather, it's intended to fill in the gaps by alerting you to common pitfalls and highlighting important nuances:

- Be clear *why you're going to the cloud in the first place* (Chapter 11).
- Remember that *no one wants a server* (Chapter 12).
- Realize that *you shouldn't run software that you didn't build* (Chapter 13).
- Don't let internal processes turn your cloud into *a non-cloud* (Chapter 14)!
- Make sure you have the right team and a good plan for your *move to the cloud* (Chapter 15).
- Dig out your high school course notes to *apply Pythagoras to your cloud migration* (Chapter 16).
- Making progress is good, but what counts is *value delivered* (Chapter 17).

---

[4]https://aws.amazon.com/professional-services/CAF/
[5]https://azure.microsoft.com/en-us/cloud-adoption-framework/
[6]https://cloud.google.com/adoption-framework

11. Why Exactly Are You Going to the Cloud, Again?

It's good to know where you want to go.

"Next time we'll be more careful with that last-minute deal."

Cloud adoption has become synonymous with modernizing IT to the point where asking why one is doing it will be seen as ignorance at best or heresy at worst. Alas, there are many paths to the cloud, and none are universally better than others. The objective, therefore, is to select the one that best suits your organization. To know how you want to go to the cloud requires you to first become clear on why you're going in the first place.

There are Many Good Reasons to Come to the Cloud

Luckily, the list of common motivations for IT to move to the cloud isn't infinitely long, as the following compilation shows. You might find a few unexpected entries. One all-too-common motivation is intentionally omitted: FOMO—the *fear of missing out.*

Cost

If you want to get something funded in an IT organization that's seen as a cost center, you present a business case. That business case demonstrates a return on the investment through cost reduction. So, it's not a big surprise that cost is a common but also somewhat overused driver for all things IT, including the cloud. That's not all wrong—we all like to save money—but, as happens so often, the truth isn't quite as simple.

Cloud providers have favorable Economies of Scale but nevertheless invest heavily in global network infrastructure, security, data-center facilities, and modern technologies such as machine learning. Hence, one should be cautious to expect drastic cost reduction simply by lifting and shifting an existing workload to the cloud. Savings, for example, come from using managed services and the cloud's elastic "pay as you grow" pricing model that allows suspending compute resources that aren't utilized. However, realizing these savings requires transparency into resource utilization and high levels of deployment automation—*cloud savings have to be earned* (Chapter 29).

 The cloud's major savings potential lies in its elastic pricing model. Realizing it requires transparency and automation, though.

Organizations looking to reduce cost should migrate workloads that have uneven usage profiles and can thus benefit from the cloud's elasticity. Analytics solutions have yielded some of the biggest savings I have seen: running interactive queries on a cloud-provider-managed data warehouse can be two or three orders of magnitude cheaper than rigging up a full data warehouse yourself when it's only sporadically used. Ironically, migrating that same warehouse to the cloud won't help you much, because you're still paying for underutilized hardware. It's the fully managed service and associated pricing model that makes the difference.

Another common migration vector is data backup and archiving. On-premises backup and archiving systems tend to consume large amounts of operational costs for very infrequent access. Such data can be stored at lower cost in the commercial cloud. Most providers (e.g., AWS Glacier) charge for retrieval of your data, which is a relatively rare event.

Uptime

No one likes to pay for IT that isn't running, making uptime another core metric for the CIO. The cloud can help here, as well: a global footprint allows applications to run across a network of global data centers, each of which features multiple availability zones (AZs). Cloud providers also maintain massive network connections to the internet backbone, affording them improved resilience against distributed denial-of-service (DDoS) attacks. Set up correctly, cloud applications can achieve 99.9% availability or higher, which is often difficult or expensive to realize on premises. Additionally, applications can be deployed across multiple clouds to further increase availability.

Organizations moving to the cloud to increase uptime should look at fully managed solutions that routinely come with 99.9% Service-Level Agreements (SLAs). Load balancing existing solutions across multiple instances can yield even better uptimes as long as the workloads are architected to do so. Run-time platforms with built-in resilience, such as container orchestration or serverless platforms, are good destinations for modern applications.

Alas, cloud computing isn't a magic button that makes brittle applications suddenly available 24/7 with zero downtime. Even if the server keeps running, your application might be failing. Hence, *adjustments to application architecture and the deployment model* (Chapter 28) might be needed to achieve high levels of availability.

Scalability

Assuring uptime under heavy load requires scalability. Cloud platforms tout instant availability of compute and storage resources, allowing applications to scale out to remain performant even under increased load. Many cloud providers have demonstrated that their infrastructures can easily withstand tens of thousands of requests per second, more than enough for most enterprises. Conveniently, the cloud model makes capacity management the responsibility of the cloud provider, freeing your IT from having to maintain unused hardware inventory. You just provision new servers when you need them.

Organizations looking to benefit from the cloud for scale might want to have a look at *serverless compute* (Chapter 26), which handles scaling of instances transparently inside the platform. However, you can also achieve massive scale with regular virtual machine instances; for example, for large batch or number crunching jobs.

Performance

Many end users access applications from the internet, typically from a browser or a mobile application. Hosting applications with a cloud provider can provide shorter paths and thus a better user experience compared to applications hosted on premises. Global SaaS applications like Google's Gmail are proof of the cloud's performance capabilities. Performance is also a customer-relevant metric, unlike operational cost reduction, which is rarely passed on to the customer.

One enterprise ran a promotion for customers who download and install a mobile app. Following common IT guidelines, they hosted the app image on premises, meaning all downloads took place via their corporate network. The campaign itself was a huge success, sadly causing the corporate network to be instantly overloaded. They would have been much better off hosting that file in the cloud.

Organizations looking to improve application performance might benefit from highly scalable and low-latency data stores or in-memory data stores. For applications that can scale out, provisioning and load balancing across multiple nodes is also a viable strategy. Many applications will already use cloud Content Delivery Networks (CDNs) to reduce website load times.

Velocity

Speed isn't just relevant when the application is running but also on the path there; that is, during software delivery. Modern cloud tools can greatly assist in accelerating software delivery. Fully managed build tool chains and automated deployment tools allow your teams to focus on feature development while the cloud takes care of compiling, testing, and deploying software. Once you realize that *you shouldn't run software that you didn't build* (Chapter 13), you are going to focus on building software and the velocity with which you can do it.

 Writing this book involved automated builds: a GitHub workflow triggered a new PDF generation each time I committed or I merged a change into the `main` branch.

Most cloud providers (and hosted source control providers like GitHub or Git-Lab) offer fully managed Continuous Integration/Continuous Delivery (CI/CD) pipelines that rebuild and test your software whenever source code changes. *Serverless compute* (Chapter 26) also vastly simplifies software deployment.

Security

Security used to be a reason for enterprises *not* to move to the cloud. However, attack vectors have shifted to exploit hardware-level vulnerabilities based on microprocessor design (Spectre[1] and Meltdown[2]) or compromised supply chains. Such attacks render traditional data-center "perimeter" defenses ineffective and position large-scale cloud providers as the few civilian organizations with the necessary resources to provide adequate protection. Several cloud providers further increase security with custom-developed hardware, such as AWS' Nitro System[3] or Google's Titan Chip[4]. Both are based on the notion of an in-house hardware root of trust that detects manipulation of hardware or firmware.

Cloud providers' strong security posture also benefits from a sophisticated operating model with frequent and automated updates. Lastly, they provide numerous security components such as Software-Defined Networks (SDNs), identity-aware gateways, firewalls, Web Application Firewalls (WAFs), and many more, which can be used to protect applications deployed to the cloud.

There likely isn't a particular set of products that automatically increases security when migrating to the cloud. However, it's safe to say that when used

---

[1]https://en.wikipedia.org/wiki/Spectre_(security_vulnerability)
[2]https://en.wikipedia.org/wiki/Meltdown_(security_vulnerability)
[3]https://aws.amazon.com/ec2/nitro/
[4]https://cloud.google.com/blog/products/gcp/titan-in-depth-security-in-plaintext

appropriately, operating in the cloud might well be more secure than operating on premises.

Insight

The cloud isn't all about computing resources. Cloud providers offer services that are impractical or impossible to implement at the scale of corporate data centers. For example, large-scale machine learning systems or pre-trained models inherently live in the cloud. So, gaining better analytic capabilities or better insights—for example, into customer behavior or manufacturing efficiency—can be a suitable motivator for going to the cloud.

Customers looking for improved insight will benefit from open-source machine learning frameworks such as TensorFlow, pre-trained models such as Amazon Rekognition[5] or Google Vision AI[6], or data warehouse tools like Google BigQuery or AWS Redshift.

Transparency

Classic IT often has limited transparency into their operational environments. Simple questions like how many servers are provisioned, which applications run on them, or what is their patch status are often difficult and time consuming to answer. Migrating to the cloud can dramatically increase transparency thanks to uniform automation and monitoring.

Organizations looking to increase transparency should use automation for infrastructure deployment and configuration. They should also consider a careful setup of billing and account hierarchies.

It's easy to see that there are many good reasons to want to go to the cloud. It's also apparent that different motivations lead to different adoption paths. Choosing multiple reasons is totally acceptable and, in fact, encouraged, especially for large IT organizations.

Priorities and Trade-Offs

Despite all of the great things that cloud platforms provide, it can't solve all problems all at once. Even with the cloud, if a strategy sounds too good to be

---

[5]https://aws.amazon.com/rekognition/
[6]https://cloud.google.com/vision

true, it probably is. As we learned earlier, *a strategy that doesn't force trade-offs likely isn't one* (Chapter 3).

Working off a catalog of potential goals enables a balanced discussion about which problems to address first, and which ones to defer until later. Perhaps you want to focus on uptime and transparency first and tackle cost later, knowing well that *savings have to be earned* (Chapter 29).

Setting Clear Expectations

Clearly communicating goals is as important as setting them. An IT team that's aiming for uptime improvements while management was promised cost savings is headed for trouble. Working off a baseline list and showing what's in and what's out (or comes later) can be a great help here.

A cloud strategy document should therefore start with the objectives, the indicators that tell us whether we are making progress, and how the priorities are expected to shift over time. That way, we don't mistake initial successes as the end goal. It's called a cloud *journey* for a reason: you'll be on the road for a while.

The Cloud with Training Wheels

Interestingly, many of the benefits listed earlier, scalability perhaps aside, don't actually hinge on moving your applications to the public cloud. Adopting a cloud operating model combined with popular open-source tools can achieve a large subset of the presented benefits on premises in your own data center. The downside is that you'll need to build, or at least assemble, much of it yourself. It could be a useful testing ground, though, for whether your organization is able to adjust to the new operating model. Think of it as "the cloud with training wheels".

12. No One Wants a Server

Cloud computing is not an infrastructure topic.

"This server is rock solid! Not like this fluffy cloud stuff."

When traditional enterprises embark on a cloud journey, they usually create a project because that's how things get done in IT. When they look for a project owner, the infrastructure team appears to be the obvious choice. After all, the cloud is all about servers and networks, right? Not necessarily—running the cloud from the infrastructure side could be your first major mistake. I'll explain why.

You Build It, They Run It

Most IT organizations separate teams by infrastructure operations and application delivery. Often, these respective suborganizations are labeled "change" for application delivery and "run" for operations, which include infrastructure. So, you build (change) a piece of software and then hand it over to another team to run it.

It isn't difficult to see that such a setup provides the respective teams with conflicting objectives: the operations team is incentivized to minimize change, whereas the "change" team is rewarded for delivering new features. Often, the resulting applications are "handed" (or, more accurately, thrown) over to the operations team, letting them deal with any production issues, letting the "change" team essentially off the hook. Naturally, operations teams learn quickly to be very cautious in accepting things coming their way, which in turns stands in the way of rapid feature delivery. And so the unhappy cycle continues.

Servers + Storage = Infrastructure

When traditional IT organizations first look at the cloud, they mostly look at things like servers (in the form of virtual machines [VMs]), storage, and networking. Recalling that AWS' Simple Storage Service (S3) and Elastic Compute Cloud (EC2) were the first modern-era cloud services offered back in 2006, a focus on these elements appears natural.

In enterprise parlance, servers and storage, translate into "infrastructure". Therefore, when looking for a "home" for their cloud migration effort, it seems natural to assign it to the infrastructure and operations team; that is, the "run" side of the house. After all, they should be familiar with the type of services that the cloud offers. They are also often the ones who have the best overview of current data-center size and application inventory, although "best" doesn't mean "accurate" in most organizations.

 Driving the cloud journey from the infrastructure group could be your first major mistake.

Unfortunately, as simple as this decision might be, in many cases it could be the first major mistake along the cloud journey.

Serving Servers

To understand why running a cloud migration out of the infrastructure side of the house should be taken with caution, let's look at what a server actually does. In my typical unfiltered way, I define a server as an expensive piece of hardware that consumes a lot of energy and is obsolete in three years.

 A server is a piece of expensive hardware that consumes a lot of energy and is obsolete in three years.

Based on that definition, it's easy to see that most business and IT users wouldn't be too keen on buying servers, whether it's on premises or in the cloud. Instead of buying servers, people want to run and use applications. It's just that traditional IT services have primed us that before we can do so, we first need to order a server.

Time Is Money

Being able to programmatically provision compute resources is certainly useful. However, focusing purely on hardware provisioning times and cost misses the real driver behind cloud computing. Let's be honest, cloud computing didn't exactly invent the data center. What it did was revolutionize the way we procure hardware with elastic pricing and instant provisioning. Not taking advantage of these disruptive changes is like going to a gourmet restaurant and ordering french fries—you'd be eating but entirely missing the point.

Being able to provision a server in a few seconds is certainly nice, but it doesn't do much for the business unless it translates into business value. Server provisioning time often makes up a small fraction of the time in which a normal code change can go into production (or into a test environment). Reducing the overall time customers have to wait for a new feature to be released, the *time to value*, is a critical metric for businesses operating in *Economies of Speed* (Chapter 2). Velocity is the currency of the digital world. And it needs much more than just servers.

Increasing the velocity with which you can deploy software reduces the time to value for the business and the hardware cost. It's a win-win.

Rapid deployment is also a key factor for elastic scaling: to scale out across more servers, running software needs to be deployed to those additional servers. If that takes a long time, you won't be able to handle sudden load spikes. This means that you have to keep already configured servers in standby, which drives up your cost. Time is money, also for software deployment.

The Application-Centric Cloud

Organizations that look at the cloud from an infrastructure point of view, seeing servers, storage, and network, will thus miss out on the key benefits of cloud platforms. Instead, organizations should take an application-centric view on their cloud strategy. You might think that this is a somewhat narrow view because a large portion of what IT runs wasn't actually built in house. Park that thought for a minute or, more precisely, until the *next chapter* (Chapter 13).

An *application-centric approach to cloud computing* (Chapter 24) will look quite different from an infrastructure-oriented approach. It focuses on speeding up software delivery, primarily by reducing friction. Reduced friction and increased delivery speed comes from automation, such as a fully automated tool chain, Infrastructure as Code (IaC), and cloud-ready applications that scale horizontally. Coupled with modern techniques like Continuous Integration (CI), Continuous Delivery (CD), and Lean development, such tooling can transform the way an enterprise thinks about software delivery. For more insight into why automation is so important, see *Automation Isn't About Efficiency* (Chapter 31).

Looking Sideways

Naturally, cloud providers realize this shift and have come a long way since the days when they offered only servers and storage. Building an application on EC2 and S3 alone, while technically totally viable, feels a little bit like building a web application in HTML 4.0—functional, but outdated. A minority of Amazon's

175-plus cloud services these days is purely related to infrastructure. You'll find databases of all forms, content delivery, analytics, machine learning, container platforms, serverless frameworks, and much more.

Although there are still minor differences in VM-level cloud services between the providers, the rapid commoditization of infrastructure has the cloud service providers swiftly moving up the stack from Infrastructure as a Service (IaaS) to middleware and higher-level run times. "Moving up the stack" is something that IT has been doing for a good while; for example, when moving from physical machines to virtual ones in the early 2000s. However, once this process reaches from IaaS and PaaS (Platform as a Service) to FaaS (Functions as a Service), aka "Serverless", there isn't much more room to move up any further.

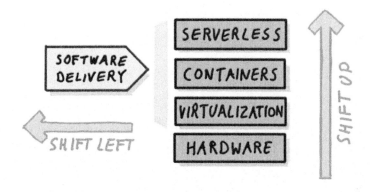

After moving up, look sideways!

Instead, as illustrated in the diagram, IT and cloud providers start to look "sideways" at the software development life cycle and tool chain: Getting new features into production quickly is the core competency for competing in the digital world that's based on rapid build-measure-learn cycles. Tool chains are an application's *first derivative*[1]—they determine an application's rate of change.

Modern tool chains are quite sophisticated machines. A common strategy is to "shift left" aspects like quality and security. Rather than being tacked on at the end of a software project life cycle, where they tend to get squeezed and it's often too late to make significant improvements anyway, these concerns become part of the CD tool chain. This way, any deviations can be detected automatically and early in the process because tests are executed on every code change or every

---

[1]Hohpe, *The Software Architect Elevator*, 2020, O'Reilly

deployment. Following this principle, modern tool chains thus include steps like these:

- Code-level unit tests
- Static code analysis for vulnerabilities (sometimes referred to as SAST [Static Application Security Testing])
- Dependency analysis; for example, detecting the use of outdated or compromised libraries
- License scans to detect license "pollution" from third-party libraries
- Tracking of code quality metrics
- Penetration testing

Gone are the days when delivery tool chains were cobbled-together one-offs. Modern tool chains—run in containers—are easily deployed, scalable, restartable, and transparent.

The shift to looking sideways is also incorporated in modern *serverless* (Chapter 26) products like AWS Lambda or Google Cloud Functions, which blend run time and deployment. These platforms not only abstract away infrastructure management, they also improve software deployment: you essentially deploy source code or artifacts directly from the command line, passing any run-time configuration that is needed.

Don't Build Yet Another Data Center

Driving a cloud migration from the infrastructure perspective has another grave disadvantage: you're likely to transport your current way of managing infrastructure into the cloud. That happens because the infrastructure and operations teams are built around these processes. They know that these processes work, so why not keep them to minimize risk?

Naturally, these teams will also have a certain sense of self-preservation, so they'll be happy to keep their existing processes that emphasize control and manual check points over end-to-end automation.

 Carrying your existing processes into the cloud will get you another data center, not a cloud.

Moving to the cloud with your old way of working is the cardinal sin of cloud migration: you'll get yet another data center, probably not what you were looking for! Last time I checked, no CIO needed more data centers. In the worst case, you need to face the possibility that you're not getting a cloud at all, but an *Enterprise Non-Cloud* (Chapter 14).

"It Runs in the Cloud" Doesn't Make the Mark

Knowing that the real value lies in quickly deploying and scaling applications also implies that a statement like "app XYZ can run in the cloud" doesn't carry much meaning. Most applications running on an operating system from this century can be run on a server in the cloud somehow.

A cloud strategy's objective should therefore not be limited to getting existing applications to run in the cloud somehow. Rather, applications should measurably benefit from running in the cloud; for example, by scaling horizontally or becoming resilient thanks to a globally distributed deployment. Hence, my snarky retort to such a claim is to state that my car can fly—off a cliff. Don't hurl your applications off a cliff!

13. Don't Run Software You Didn't Build

Running other people's software is actually a bad deal.

Does your IT feel a bit overloaded?

The answer to common concerns about cloud computing often lie in taking a step back and looking at the problem from a different angle. For example, several modern cloud platforms utilize *containers* (Chapter 25) for deployment automation and orchestration. When discussing container technology with customers, a frequent response is: "Many of my enterprise applications, especially commercial off-the-shelf software, don't run in containers, or at least not without the vendor's support." Fair point! The answer to this conundrum, interestingly, lies in asking a much more fundamental question.

Enterprise IT = Running Someone Else's Software

Enterprise IT grew up running other people's software. That's because enterprise IT favors *buying over building software* (Chapter 6), and in most cases rightly so: there's little to be gained from writing your own payroll or accounting software. Also, to address a broad market (and to cater to organizations' *fear of code*—see *37 Things*), enterprise packages are often highly configurable, reducing the need for custom development.

Over time, running other people's software has thus become the fundamental premise of IT. IT's main responsibility consisted of procuring software and hardware, installing the software on the hardware, configuring and integrating, and then operating it, the latter often being *outsourced* (Chapter 6). Although you might think that this setup lets others do the heavy lifting while IT "merely integrates", this setup isn't nearly as great as it looks on paper.

First, it has led to a state in which IT is quite overloaded with countless applications, sometimes resembling the image at the beginning of this chapter. It's impressive how much load your IT cart can handle, but nevertheless it's time to shed some ballast.

The Unfortunate IT Sandwich

Worse yet, because traditional IT often also outsources operations, it ends up in a somewhat awkward place, "sandwiched" between commercial software vendors on one side, and the third-party operations provider on the other. And to make it ever more fun (for those watching, not those in the middle of it) the business would beat down on IT why they couldn't have the desired features and why the system is down again, squeezing the sandwich from both sides, as illustrated in the following graphic (not shown: blood, sweat, and tears running out from IT):

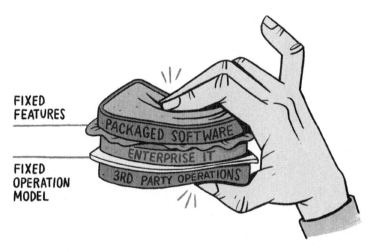

FIXED
FEATURES

FIXED
OPERATION
MODEL

The IT sandwich getting a squeeze

Stuck in the middle, IT would shell out money for licenses and hardware assets but lack control over either the software features or their own infrastructure. Instead of a sandwich, an image of a vice might also come to your mind. Aren't we glad the cloud came and showed us that this isn't a particularly clever setup?

Running Others' Software Is a Bad Deal!

Looking at it this way, it's not difficult to see that running software built by others is actually a pretty bad deal:

You pay for hardware

The only thing that IT owns are expensive assets, which depreciate quickly. To make it worse, software vendors' sizing requirements are often padded because they'd rather have you buy more hardware than explain performance issues later on.

Installation is cumbersome

Although many folks want to make us believe that the benefit of packaged software is easy and safe installation and configuration, the reality often looks different. When we faced installation issues once, the vendor's response was that it's due to our environment. Isn't getting other people's software to run in our environment the very purpose of installation?

If something breaks, you're guilty until proven innocent

Yup, it's like that porcelain shop: you break, you pay. In this case, you pay for support. And if something breaks you have to convince external support that it's not due to your environment. All the while business is beating down on you, asking why stuff isn't running as promised.

You can't make changes when you need them

And despite all this effort, the worst part is that you don't have control on either end. If you need a new feature in the software you are running, you'll have to wait until the next release—that is, if your feature is on the feature list. If not, you may be waiting a looooong time. Likewise, operations contracts are typically fixed in scope for many years. No Kubernetes for you.

Running software you didn't build isn't actually all that great. It's amazing how enterprise IT has become so used to this model that it accepts it as normal and doesn't even question it.

 Enterprise IT has become so used to running other people's software that it doesn't realize what a bad deal it is.

Luckily, the wake-up call came with the cloud and the need to *question our basic assumptions* (Chapter 1).

Software as a Service

The world of cloud has brought us new options to rethink our operational model. A Software as a Service (SaaS) model hands over most of the responsibilities to the software vendor: the vendor runs the applications for you, applies patches, upgrades, scales, and replaces faulty hardware (unless they run on a cloud, which they likely should be). Now that sounds a lot better!

Salesforce CRM was really the first major company to lead us on that virtuous route back around 2005, even before the modern cloud providers started offering us servers in an Infrastructure as a Service (IaaS) model. Of course, it's by far no longer the only company following this model: you can handle your communications and documentation needs in the cloud thanks to Google G Suite[1] (which started in 2006 as "Google Apps for Your Domain"), HR and performance management with SAP SuccessFactors[2], ERP with SAP Cloud ERP[3], service management with ServiceNow[4], and integrate it all with Mulesoft CloudHub[5] (note: these are just examples; I have no affiliation with these companies and the list of SaaS providers is nearly endless).

Anything as a Service

Service-oriented models aren't limited to software delivery. These days you can lease an electric power generator by the kWh produced or a train engine by the passenger mile traveled. Just like SaaS, such models place more responsibility on the provider. Whereas in the traditional product model operational issues are the customer's problem, the service model places them into the provider's scope.

For example, if a train engine doesn't run, in the traditional model, the customer—that is, the train line—takes the loss, and in many cases even has to pay extra for service and repairs. In a service model, the engine manufacturer doesn't get to charge the customer in case of operational issues. Instead, the manufacturer takes the hit because the customer won't pay for the passenger kilometers that could not be achieved. This feedback loop motivates the provider to correct any issue quickly:

---

[1]https://gsuite.google.com
[2]https://www.successfactors.com
[3]https://www.sap.com/sea/products/erp/erp-cloud.html
[4]https://www.servicenow.com/
[5]https://www.mulesoft.com/platform/saas/cloudhub-ipaas-cloud-based-integration

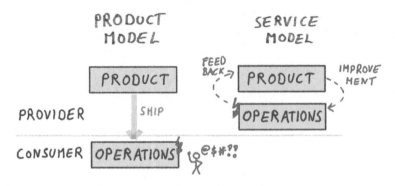

SaaS: Feedback leads to better quality

The same is (or at least should be) true for SaaS: if you pay per transaction, you won't pay for software that can't process transactions.

 SaaS is like applying DevOps to packaged software: It places the end-to-end responsibility with those people who can best solve a problem.

Naturally, you'd be happier with running software (or a running train). However, the feedback loop established through value-based pricing ultimately leads to a higher-quality product and more reliable operations, aligning the incentives for a well-running system across provider and consumer. The same principle applies in a DevOps model for software development: engineers will invest more into building quality software if they receive the pager call in case of production issues.

But What About...

When considering SaaS, enterprise IT tends to pull from its long repertoire of "buts", triggered by a major shift in operating model:

Security
    As described earlier, the days when running applications on your premises meant that they were more secure are over. Attack vectors like compromised hardware and large-scale denial-of-service attacks by nation-state

attackers make it nearly impossible to protect IT assets without the scale and operational automation of large cloud providers. Plus, on-premises often isn't actually on your premises—it's just another data center run by an outsourcing provider.

Latency

Latency isn't just a matter of distance, but also a matter of the number of hops and the size of the pipes (saturation drives up latency or brings a service down altogether). Most of your customers and partners will access your services from the internet, so often the cloud, and therefore the SaaS offering, is closer to them than your ISP and your data center.

Control

Control is when reality matches what you want it to be. In many enterprises, manual processes severely limit control: someone files a request, which gets approved, followed by a manual action. Who guarantees the action matches what was approved? A jump server and session recording? Automation and APIs give you tighter control in most cases.

Cost

Although cloud platforms don't come with *a magic cost reduction button* (Chapter 29), it does give you better cost transparency and more levers to control cost. Especially hidden and indirect costs go down dramatically with SaaS solutions.

Integration

One could write whole books about integration—oh, wait[6]! Naturally, a significant part of installing software isn't just about getting it to run, but also to connect it to other systems. A SaaS model doesn't make this work go away completely, but the availability of APIs and prebuilt interfaces (e.g., Salesforce and GSuite[7]) makes it a good bit easier. From that perspective, it's also no surprise that Salesforce acquired Mulesoft, one of the leading Integration as a Service vendors.

What About the Software You Do Build?

Naturally, there's going to be some software that you do want to build; for example, because it provides a competitive advantage. For that software, delivery

---

[6]https://www.enterpriseintegrationpatterns.com
[7]https://www.salesforce.com/campaign/google/

velocity, availability, and scalability are key criteria. That's exactly why you should look for an *application-centric cloud* (Chapter 24)!

Strategy = Setting the Vector

Not all of your on-premises software will disappear tomorrow. And not all other software will run in containers or on a serverless platform. But strategy is a direction, not current reality. The key is that every time you see yourself running software that you didn't build, you should ask yourself why you're carrying someone else's weight.

14. Don't Build an Enterprise Non-Cloud!

Be careful not to throw the cloud baby out with the enterprise bathwater.

This fancy looking sports car is unlikely to meet your expectations

Many enterprises that moved to the cloud have found that not all of their expectations have been met, or at least not as quickly as they would have liked. Although an *unclear strategy* (Chapter 3) or *inflated expectations* (Chapter 11) can be culprits, in many cases the problems lie closer to home. The migration journey deprived the enterprise of exactly those great properties that the cloud was going to bring them.

Enterprise-Flavored Cloud

When enterprises move to a commercial cloud provider, they don't just grab a credit card, sign up, and deploy away. They have to abide by existing policies and regulations, need to ensure spend discipline, and often have special data encryption and residency requirements. Therefore, almost every IT department has a cloud transformation program underway that attempts to marry existing ways of working with the operating model of the cloud. Now, because the amazing thing about the cloud is that it *rethinks the way IT is done* (Chapter 1), we can imagine that this translation process isn't trivial.

 Enterprises don't just grab a credit card, sign up for a cloud provider, and deploy away.

When I work with large organizations on their cloud strategy, several recurring themes come up:

- Onboarding process
- Hybrid cloud
- Virtual Private Cloud (VPC)
- Legacy applications
- Cost recovery

Each of them makes good sense. Let's take a closer look.

Onboarding

Enterprises have special requirements for cloud accounts that differ from start-ups and consumers:

- They utilize central billing accounts to gain cost transparency instead of people randomly using credit cards.
- They need to allocate cloud charges to specific individual cost centers.
- They negotiate discounts based on overall purchasing power or "commits", stated intents to use a certain volume of cloud resources.
- They may limit and manage the number of cloud accounts being shared in the organization.
- They may require approvals from people whose spending authority is sufficiently high.

Most of these steps are necessary to connect the cloud model to existing procurement and billing processes, something that enterprises can't just abandon overnight. However, they typically lead to a semi-manual sign-up process for project teams to "get to the cloud". Likely, someone must approve the request, link to a project budget, and define spend limits. Also, some enterprises have restrictions on which cloud providers can be used, sometimes *depending on the kind of workload* (Chapter 18).

Cloud developers might need to conduct additional steps, such as configuring firewalls so that they are able to access cloud services from within the corporate network. Many enterprises will require developer machines to be registered with device management and be subjected to endpoint security scans (aka "corporate spyware").

Hybrid Network

For enterprises, *hybrid cloud* (Chapter 19) is a reality because not all applications can be migrated overnight. This will mean that applications running in the cloud communicate with those on premises, usually over a combination of a cloud interconnect, which connects the VPC with the existing on-premises network, making the cloud look like an extension of the on-premises network.

Virtual Private Cloud

Enterprises aren't going to want all of their applications to face the internet, and many also want to be able to choose IP address ranges and connect servers with on-premises services. Many enterprises are also not too keen to share servers with their cloud tenant neighbors. Others yet are limited to physical servers by existing licensing agreements. Most cloud providers can accommodate this request, for example with dedicated instances[1] or dedicated hosts (e.g., AWS[2] or Azure[3]).

Legacy or Monolithic Applications

The majority of applications in the enterprise portfolio are going to be third-party commercial software. Applications that are built in house often are

---

[1]https://aws.amazon.com/ec2/pricing/dedicated-instances/
[2]https://aws.amazon.com/ec2/dedicated-hosts/
[3]https://azure.microsoft.com/en-us/services/virtual-machines/dedicated-host/

architected as single instances (so-called "monoliths"). These applications cannot easily scale out across multiple server instances. Re-architecting such applications is either costly or, in case of commercial applications, not possible.

Cost Recovery

Lastly, preparing the enterprise for a commercial cloud, or the commercial cloud for enterprise, isn't free. This cost is typically borne by the central IT group so that it can be amortized across the entire enterprise. Most central IT departments are cost centers that need to recover their cost, meaning any expenditure has to be charged back to business divisions, which are IT's internal customers. It's often difficult to allocate these costs on a per-service or per-instance basis, so IT often adds an "overhead" charge to the existing cloud charges, which appears reasonable.

There may be additional fixed costs levied per business unit or per project team, such as common infrastructure, the aforementioned VPCs, jump hosts, firewalls, and much more. As a result, internal customers pay a base fee on top of the measured cloud usage fee.

Remembering NIST

The US Department of Commerce's National Institute of Standards and Technology (NIST) published a very useful definition of cloud computing in 2011 (PDF download[4]). It used to be cited quite a bit, but I haven't seen it mentioned very much lately—perhaps everyone knows by now what the cloud is and the ones who don't are too embarrassed to ask. The document defines five major capabilities for cloud computing (edited for brevity):

On-Demand Self-Service
　　A consumer can unilaterally provision computing capabilities, such as server time and network storage, as needed automatically without requiring human interaction.
Broad Network Access
　　Capabilities are available over the network and accessed through standard mechanisms.

---

[4]https://nvlpubs.nist.gov/nistpubs/Legacy/SP/nistspecialpublication800-145.pdf

Resource Pooling

> The provider's computing resources are pooled to serve multiple consumers using a multitenant model, with different physical and virtual resources dynamically.

Rapid Elasticity

> Capabilities can be elastically provisioned and released to scale rapidly outward and inward with demand.

Measured Service

> Cloud systems automatically control and optimize resource use by leveraging a metering capability (typically pay-per-use).

So, after going back to the fundamental definition of what a cloud is, you might start to feel that something doesn't 100% line up. And you're spot on!

The Enterprise Non-Cloud

Putting the enterprise "features" that I mentioned earlier next to the NIST capabilities, you realize that they largely contradict:

- Lengthy sign-up processes contradict on-demand self-service because they routinely require manual approvals and software installs—corporate IT processes send their regards.
- Your corporate network isn't going to be quite as broad as the internet, and firewalls and loads of other restrictions make network access far from being universal.
- Dedicated instances aren't as widely pooled and have poorer economies of scale. Your network interconnect is also dedicated.
- Traditional applications don't benefit from rapid elasticity, because they don't scale out and deployment often isn't automated.
- A high baseline cost charged from corporate IT makes the cloud a lot less "measured" and often burdens small projects with prohibitive fixed costs.

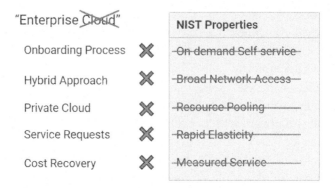

The enterprise non-cloud

That's bad news: despite all good intentions your enterprise didn't get a cloud! It got yet another good, ol' corporate data center, which is surely not what it was looking for.

 Many "enterprise clouds" no longer fulfill the fundamental capabilities of a cloud.

What Now?

So, how do you make sure your enterprise cloud remains deserving of the label? Although there's no three-step recipe, a few considerations can help:

Calibrate Expectations

Realization is the first step to improvement. So, being aware of these traps helps avoid them. Also, it behooves us to temper rosy visions of *cost savings* (Chapter 29) and digital transformation. Moving all of your old junk to a new house means you'll be living with the same junk, just in a fancier environment. Likewise, carrying your enterprise baggage into the cloud won't transform anything.

Bring the Cloud to You, Not Vice Versa

The cloud *isn't a classic IT procurement* (Chapter 1), but a fundamental change in IT operating model. Therefore, you should be cautious not to transport your existing operating model to the cloud, because that will lead to the results cited earlier. Instead, you need to bring some elements of the cloud operating model to your environment. For example, you can replace cumbersome manual processes with automation and self-service so that they benefit both on-premises systems and those running in the cloud.

Measurable Goals

A cloud migration without clear measurable goals risks getting off track and becoming lost in shiny new technology toys. Instead, *be clear why you're going to the cloud* (Chapter 11): to reduce cost, to improve uptime, to launch new products faster, to secure your data, to scale more easily, or to sound more modern. Prioritizing and measuring progress helps you stay on track.

Segmentation

Enterprise IT loves harmonization, but one cloud size won't fit all applications. Some applications don't need to undergo all firewall-compartment-peering-configuration-review-and-approval steps. Perhaps some applications—for example, simple ones not holding customer data—can just go straight to the cloud, just as long as billing isn't on Jamie's credit card.

When You're in the Cloud, Use the Cloud!

Cloud migrations navigate in treacherous waters. Many enterprises are falling into the trap of wanting to *avoid lock-in at all cost* (Chapter 21) and look to achieve that by not using cloud-provider-managed services because most of them are proprietary. This means no DynamoDB, Athena, SQS, BigQuery, Spanner, and so on. You might still have a cloud, but one that predates the NIST definition from 2011. If you embrace the cloud, you should also embrace managed services.

Enterprises embarking on a cloud journey often focus on the great new things they will get. But equally important is leaving some of your enterprise baggage behind.

15. Cloud Migration: How Not to Get Lost

Get the right crew and watch where you're going.

"Just three more servers ahead, then a sharp left."

Despite a steady supply of tooling and frameworks, cloud migrations are hardly ever fun. And while it's all too easy to take comfort in not having to do them very often, that very fact makes migrations particularly risky. Tahir had the opportunity to refine his approach over the course of several migrations, so let's learn from his battle scars.

———————————————————

By Tahir Hashmi

Cloud migrations are the kind of task that's great when it's done but that you hope you'd never have to do again. Today's constant rate of change makes that an unlikely proposition, though. I have myself gone through five migrations in my last three jobs, averaging one migration every two years! Cloud providers' tools and frameworks are a major help in such an undertaking, but ultimately it's up to you to navigate your existing environment and find a path that matches your circumstances and ambitions.

 Migration is not a "business-as-usual" activity. Your team won't have any habits or a rhythm for it like they have for regular sprints.

Whether migrating from your on-premises infrastructure to the cloud or migrating between clouds, systematically breaking the task down into three main phases—planning, execution and validation—can reduce the inherent stress and uncertainty.

Phase 1: Planning and Staffing

The first order of business in a migration is to get a picture of what the migration is going to look like and how it would proceed. Here's a short checklist of things to plan for ahead of the migration:

1. **Size up the migration**. Define the scope of the migration, both in size (e.g., how many applications or computing resources) and complexity (e.g., to what extent applications will change during the migration).
2. **Clarify the motivations and goals**. A *clear set of goals* (Chapter 11) is critical for success in the cloud and the same is true for the migration.
3. **Define success metrics**. During the cloud migration journey, *success metrics* (Chapter 17) are the GPS device that lets you track progress and correct your course.
4. **Get stakeholder buy-in**. Every stakeholder should have a clear idea of how they are going to benefit from the migration so that they can assist rather than resist.

The Migration Triumvirate

Despite proven processes and methodologies, the key to the success of any complex undertaking remains with the people performing the job. Not having the right people could easily derail a migration into millions of dollars of cost overruns or, worse, stalling the whole effort.

Having the "right" people doesn't just relate to skills but also to clear functions and responsibilities for each. Irrespective of the size of the migration, the following roles are critically important:

1. **Executive sponsor** – Responsible for securing resources and budget, and being accountable for the success of the migration
2. **Chief architect** – Makes the key technology decisions and sets the migration's technology goals
3. **Program manager** – Handles communication and schedules, to keep things moving during the execution phase

These three roles don't necessarily translate into three people. Whereas for small migrations the same person could play all three roles, large migrations may require multiple people to tackle one role. Regardless of the number of people allocated, having all roles in place is critical to enable them to work together as parts of the migration machinery. A deficiency in one role would also render the others ineffective.

To understand the interdependency, we can draw on the analogy of a motor vehicle. The executive sponsor is the accelerator (and brakes) who provides the necessary resources and budget (fuel flow) to keep things moving at the right pace. The chief architect is the steering wheel, who makes sure the migration vehicle is following the desired trajectory. The program manager is the transmission assembly who controls how the productive power is converted into actual migration velocity, carefully matching the movements of the various parts.

The teams performing the actual migration are organized into "working groups". They are the wheels that produce actual motion as the rubber meets the road, as indicated in the following diagram:

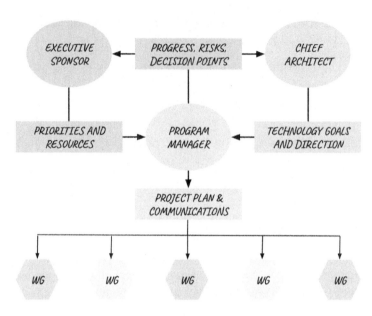

Parts of the migration machinery

Executive Sponsor

As the person responsible for getting the necessary approvals, or "green light" for the migration, the executive sponsor interacts with stakeholders ranging from a team leader for very small migrations, to the board of directors and shareholders for enterprise-wide initiatives. Along with the approvals, the executive sponsor also needs to secure the required budget and manpower allocation.

As shown in the preceding diagram, the executive sponsor provides the resources and priorities to the program manager and continuously tweaks these based on the migration's progress, new risks identified, and new decision points being brought up.

Chief Architect

A chief architect is the executive sponsor's technology partner and plays two key roles in the team:

1. Being the ultimate source of knowledge about the existing systems and their properties

2. Being the ultimate arbiter of technical decision making and setting the standards for migration

The chief architect has the right mix of seniority and tenure in the company to know things that aren't obvious: why certain things are the way they are, or from where to get the necessary information.

 Involving the chief architect early and deeply provides teams with a common understanding of what needs to be done and how.

Just like the executive sponsor, the chief architect reviews the ongoing progress, newly identified risks, and new decision points to update finer details of technology goals and direction along the executive sponsor.

Program Manager

A program manager is the "third pillar" of a the migration leadership, handling several important tasks:

- Keeping track of the migration schedule and deliverables
- Applying influence where needed to get the execution going across various teams
- Coordinating the flow of information between various parties
- Publishing regular updates on the migration progress
- Highlighting risks and important decision points to the executive sponsor and chief architect

These tasks might seem superfluous at first glance. However, because a migration is not a business-as-usual activity, no one has any habits or rhythm that gets them through the migration like the ones that get them through regular project sprints. Also, because the team must put in effort far ahead of the outcome of eventual migration, even highly motivated teams can face impulsive stalling, de-prioritization, or cold feet.

 I attempted a couple of small migrations with highly motivated teams but without a program manager. They achieved their objectives, but with participant burnout and huge cost and time overruns.

Migration not being business-as-usual also causes effort estimates to be highly inaccurate. Crunching and slogging to meet those estimates won't sustain the migration velocity. Rather, coordinating dependent tasks and updating the work schedule becomes a vital, full-time activity.

Finding a Good Program Manager

The program manager plays a pivotal role, like the transmission of a vehicle that converts the power from the executive sponsor and the directional steering from the chief architect into the wheels—the working groups. Look for the following qualities in potential program management candidates:

- Well known and well regarded in the company; someone who people would not easily ignore
- Have a persuasive communication style; neither too emotionally charged nor too detached
- Have deep knowledge of the organization and know all the right people to contact to get things done
- Have a track record for informational transparency; they often need to be the bearer of bad news
- Able to "talk shop" with the engineers as well as business people; do not feign ignorance of technology-speak or money-talk

Partnerships

In addition to the internal staffing for the three "pillar" roles, you're also going to involve partners from the Cloud Service Provider (CSP) that is going to house your workloads after the migration. Their role, at the minimum, is to review your choice of infrastructure on their platform. However, they may also assist with the planning and execution phase. Most often, though, the hands-on execution is done through trusted third parties recommended by the CSP.

Engaging external partners can help minimize the time your teams spend on throw-away effort so that they can focus on long-term design and operations concerns. Partners can also help reduce "unknown unknowns" and convert "known unknowns" into "knowns", reducing your migration risk.

Phase 2: Execution

It's all about execution, but jumping in head-first is risky.

Discovery

Gathering information about the existing environment helps formulate a mapping of existing components to the new environment. Components that no one knew existed and thus don't get provisioned in the destination environment are a major risk for migrations. Teams therefore utilize migration tools that can capture the entire inventory of machines and applications running on them along with their key resource limits and utilization (e.g., CPU, network). Your team would add uptime/performance expectations to decide the mapping to the destination environment.

The outcome of discovery is the tech plan describing what the destination environment would be like and a sequence of high-level tasks to get there.

Automation and Federation

Provisioning and validating the new cloud environment can be time consuming. However, this process can be accelerated along two dimensions: using automation instead of manual deployments and federated instead of centralized execution.

Automated vs. Manual Deployments

Automation involves building software to provision, deploy, and verify components in the new environment. This approach works well if applications or components adhere to architectural conventions or standards.

Automation works a bit like a flywheel. Initially the progress is slow as the migration toolkit is being built. Subsequent migrations become increasingly faster and more reliable as the level of automation increases. Still, take care to not get caught in a big up-front design—get the flywheel turning right from the start.

Manual approaches work better for small migrations or where the heterogeneity in the tech stack hinders the encoding of migration tasks.

Federated vs. Centralized Execution

For environments in which teams are capable of individually maintaining and running their infrastructure, federation gives each team the freedom of how to deliver the migration outcomes. Federation achieves velocity by parallelizing the setup and configuration efforts. It is, however, important to define integration standards and goals at the outset to maintain overall tractability of the migration.

The best way to run a federated migration program is to define clear phases of delivery and their cut-off dates. The program manager needs to carefully track each team's progress through these phases and call out any teams that may be lagging. Federation pushes greater responsibility down to individual teams. Teams that don't manage their own infrastructure might be better off with centralized execution.

Accelerating migration through automation and federation

Organizations that have standardized their technology stack and have decentralized operations can combine automation and federation to achieve even faster migration velocity.

Training

Whether migrating from an on-premises environment to the cloud or migrating between clouds, a change in the operational practices and tooling can have a debilitating impact on teams if they are not sufficiently trained for the new environment.

A hand-off "warranty period" after the migration can help mitigate this problem by pairing the personnel that performed the migration with the team owning the migrated component. They jointly manage the component for a week or two in a business-as-usual scenario and exercise some of the operational runbooks in artificially induced incidents or failure scenarios.

During this "warranty period" teams must have easy and fast access to help. Being able to reach out to the CSP's experts and on-call handlers is crucial and should be arranged immediately from the beginning.

Phase 3: Validation

The chances that a large migration project exactly yields the anticipated results are low. A well-planned validation structure helps to continuously correct course and arrive at a result that is in line with expectations.

 Two large-scale migrations that I was involved with did not meet their goals. In one case, this uncomfortable situation was discovered quite a while after the migration was complete.

It is helpful to classify the validation into broad segments:

Environment Validation

Environment validation ensures that things work as expected, conducted during the warranty period mentioned in the previous section. It also ensures that the migrated components perform their business functions as they are expected to. Lastly, the environment must be comprehensively stress tested to check whether it meets the performance and scale expectations.

Cost Validation

Almost all cloud migrations have a cost structure or Total Cost of Ownership (TCO) objective. Cloud infrastructure billing is fine grained and usage based. Along with that, there are multiple cost-saving instruments offered by CSPs, and these instruments intersect with one another. This makes it significantly more complicated to *forecast a cloud budget* (Chapter 32), especially when moving from fixed-server environments to an on-demand model that fluctuates with the business volume.

Benchmarking the actual cost of operation against the projected cost helps detect deviations early and adjust the project budget and funding. It also uncovers any faulty assumptions in the initial cost projections so that the value proposition of the migration exercise can be reevaluated.

Business Goal Validation

Finally, the team must validate the migration's business goals, such as improving agility, enhancing the security posture, or providing better system availability. Business goal validation should be started early in the migration journey and performed frequently, based on measurable targets (e.g., number of deployments per day as a measure of agility) or certification programs (e.g., receiving a security certification).

End Up Where You Need to Be

 I seldom end up where I wanted to go, but almost always end up where I need to be. —Douglas Adams

Cloud migration can be an anxiety-inducing, business-critical undertaking. The main challenges lie in delivering the migration smoothly without business disruption, delays, or cost overruns. The key is to course-correct early and often as the migration progresses.

16. Cloud Migration per Pythagoras

It's time to dig out your schoolbooks.

"Its all a matter of simple geometry."

Choosing the right path to the cloud isn't always easy. Just moving all the old junk into the cloud is more likely to yield you *another data center* (Chapter 12) than a cloud transformation, whereas re-architecting every last application will take a long time and not be cost effective. So, you'll need to think a bit more carefully about what to do with your application portfolio. Decision models help you make conscious decisions, and sometimes even third-grade geometry lessons can help you understand the trade-offs.

Moving Up or Moving Out

I have long felt that organizations looking to move their workloads to the cloud can benefit from better decision models. When people read about models they often imagine something quite abstract and academic. Good models, however, are rather the opposite. They should be simple but evocative so that they both help us make better decisions and allow them to communicate those decisions in an intuitive way.

One of my more popular blog posts, coauthored with Bryan Stiekes, titled Moving Up or Out[1], presented such a model. The model plots application migration options on a simple two-dimensional plane, as demonstrated in the following diagram:

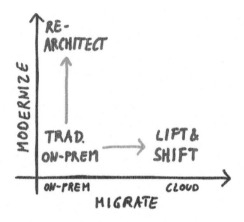

Moving applications up or out

The plane's horizontal axis represents moving "out" from on premises to the cloud, represented by a vector to the right. Alternatively, you can modernize applications to operate further "up" the stack, further away from servers and hardware details, for example by utilizing PaaS, serverless, or SaaS services.

So, a completely horizontal arrow implies a lift-and-shift approach, moving applications as they are without any modernization. A vertical arrow would imply a complete re-architecting of an application (e.g., to run on a serverless framework) while remaining in place in an on-premises data center.

Combinations aren't just allowed but actually encouraged, so the blog post advises architects to visually plot the direction they suggest for each application or class of applications on such a matrix: out, up, or a combination thereof. It's a good example of a simple decision model that allows architects to make conscious decisions and to communicate them broadly in the organization.

---

[1]https://cloud.google.com/blog/topics/perspectives/enterprise-it-can-move-up-or-out-or-both

Not All IT Is Binary

Although the model plots simple axes for "up"/"modernize" and "out"/"migrate", each direction is made up from multiple facets and gradations:

Up

Moving an application "up the stack" can occur along multiple dimensions:

Platform: IaaS ⇒ PaaS ⇒ FaaS
The metaphor of "moving up" stems from the notion of the *IT Stack* that's rooted in hardware (such as servers, storage, and networks) and is then increasingly abstracted initially through virtual machine (VM)-level virtualization and then via containers (OS-level virtualization) and ultimately *serverless platforms* (Chapter 26).

Sometimes, this progression is also labeled as Infrastructure as a Service (IaaS; i.e., VMs), Platform as a Service (PaaS; i.e., container orchestration[2]), and Functions as a Service (FaaS; i.e., *serverless* (Chapter 26)). Higher levels of abstraction usually increase portability and reduce operational toil. While this nomenclature focuses on the run-time platform itself, applications that take advantage of the respective abstraction level will also look different.

Structure: Monolith ⇒ Microservices
Another way to show how far up an application is along the vertical axis can be expressed by the application's deployment and run-time architecture. Traditional applications are often *monoliths*, single pieces of software. Even though that model has served us well for several decades because it's easy to manage and all of the pieces are in one artifact, monoliths make independent deployment and independent scaling difficult. The push for more delivery velocity gave way to the idea of breaking applications into individual, independently deployable and scalable services—*microservices.*

Deployment: Manual ⇒ Automated
A third way of moving up is to replace manual provisioning, deployment,

---

[2]There is a lot of debate about how similar or different PaaS and container orchestration platforms are, largely fueled by product marketing considerations. Let's stay clear of this mud fight and consider them at roughly the same level of abstraction even though they're not entirely synonymous.

and configuration with *automated methods* (Chapter 31), which give you
fast and repeatable deployments.

One of the nicest, ideology-free summaries I have seen on moving up the
stack is by former colleague Tom Grey in his blog post 5 principles for cloud-
native architecture[3] (The title receives a passing score thanks to "architecture"
compensating for the term "native").

Out

Moving out is a bit simpler as it indicates moving applications from running
on premises to running in the cloud. Gradations on this axis also exist because
single applications may run in a hybrid model in which some components (e.g.,
the front end), are running in the cloud, whereas others (such as a legacy back
end) still run on premises. Hence, "moving out" isn't binary either. You are
welcome to fine tune the model for your use by adding "hybrid" in the middle
of the horizontal axis. A *later chapter* (Chapter 19) details many ways in which
to move along this axis.

Migration Triangles

Although the title plays off the tough career management principle used by some
consulting firms ("if you can't keep moving up, you have to get out"), in our case
up-and-out or out-and-up is definitely allowed and highly encouraged. That's
when our simple two-dimensional model shows its strength.

Plotting the migration path on the up-or-out plane also makes it apparent
that migrations usually aren't a one-shot type of endeavor. So, rather than
just putting applications into a simple bucket like "re-host" or "re-architect",
the visual model invites you to plot a multistep path for your applications,
highlighting that a cloud journey is indeed a journey and not a single decision
point.

---

[3]https://cloud.google.com/blog/products/application-development/5-principles-for-cloud-native-
architecture-what-it-is-and-how-to-master-it

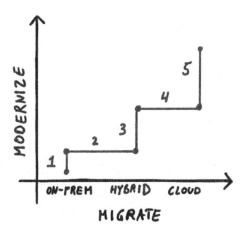

Plotting migration paths

In the example in the diagram, an application might undergo a sensible five-step process:

1. A small amount of modernizing is required to allow a portion of the application (e.g., the front end) to move to the cloud. This could involve developing new or protecting existing APIs, setting up an API gateway, and so on.
2. Subsequently, a portion of the application can be migrated, whereas the legacy back end stays on premises, leading us into a hybrid state.
3. Further modernization—for example, porting the back end from a proprietary application server that isn't compatible with cloud licensing to an open-source alternative such as Tomcat—prepares the remainder of the application for migration.
4. The remainder of the application is migrated.
5. Now fully in the cloud, the application can be further modernized to use managed database services, cloud monitoring, and so forth to increase stability and reduce operational overhead.

Why not do everything at once? Time to value! By moving a piece first, you immediately benefit from scalability thanks to Content-Delivery and protection from cloud WAFs (Web Application Firewalls). The whole *next chapter* (Chapter 17) is dedicated to optimizing your path to value.

Remember Pythagoras?

Once you plot different sequences of migration options on sheets of paper, you might feel like you're back in trigonometry class. And that thought is actually not as far fetched as it might seem. One of the most basic formulas you might remember from way back when is *Pythagoras' Theorem*. He concluded some millennia ago that for a right triangle (one that has one right angle), the sum of the squares of the sides equals the square of the hypotenuse: $c^2 = a^2 + b^2$.

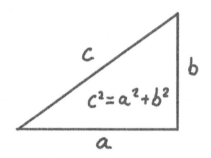

Pythagoras' Theorem

Without reaching too deep into high school math, this definition has a couple of simple consequences[4]:

1. Each side is shorter than the hypotenuse
2. The hypotenuse is shorter than the sum of the sides

Let's see how these properties help you plan your cloud migration.

Cloud Migration Trigonometry

Just like in geometry, the sides of the triangle are shorter, meaning that simply moving out to the cloud horizontally across is going to be faster (shorter line "a")

---

[4]These properties apply to all triangles, but in our up-or-out plane, we deal with right triangles, so it's nice to be able to fall back on Pythagoras.

than trying to re-architect applications while migrating them (the hypotenuse, labeled "c"):

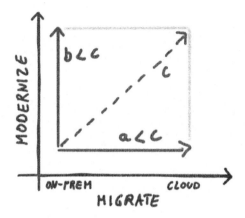

Each side is shorter than the hypotenuse

However, migrating first and then re-architecting makes for a longer path than taking the hypotenuse. Hence it might be considered less "efficient"—spelled with air quotes here as efficiency can be a dangerous goal also. The same holds true for re-architecting first and then migrating out—in either case, the sum of the sides is larger than the hypotenuse:

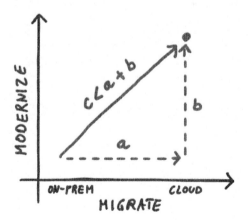

The hypotenuse is shorter than the sum of the sides

However, if generating value is your key metric and you factor in the cost of delay, this path might still be the most beneficial for your business.

What About All the R's?

Many models for choosing application migration paths are based on a series of words starting with "R", such as rehost, replatform, re-architect, and retire. Interestingly, multiple versions exist, at least two with five (by Gartner from 2010[5] and Microsoft from 2019[6]) and one with six (by AWS from 2016[7]). Not all lists use the same vocabulary, and Gartner also apparently updated the terms in 2018 (*Re-architect* became *Refactor*), adding to the confusion.

Here's a brief attempt at a summary, yielding 10 terms grouped into 8 concepts, indicating where the terms appear (A = AWS, G = Gartner, M = Microsoft):

Rehost [A/G/M]
    Moving the whole VM from on premises to the cloud, essentially changing the physical "host" but nothing else.

Replatform [A]
    Shifting the application as is, but changing the operating system or middleware (the platform on which the application resides), usually motivated by licensing restrictions or outdated operating systems not available in the cloud.

Repurchase/Replace [A/G/M]
    Replacing the application with another commercially available (or open-source) one, preferably in a SaaS model.

Refactor/Re-architect [A/G/M]
    Completely redoing the application's deployment architecture; for example, by breaking a monolith into microservices, replacing one-off components with cloud services, or extracting application state into a NOSQL data store.

Revise [G]
    Updating legacy applications to prepare them for a subsequent *rehost*.

Rebuild [G/M]
    Perhaps the more drastic version of *refactor*, implying that the application is rebuilt from scratch. Just like with buildings, there is likely a gray area between remodeling and rebuilding.

---

[5]https://www.gartner.com/en/documents/1485116/migrating-applications-to-the-cloud-rehost-refactor-revi
[6]https://docs.microsoft.com/en-us/azure/cloud-adoption-framework/digital-estate/5-rs-of-rationalization
[7]https://aws.amazon.com/blogs/enterprise-strategy/6-strategies-for-migrating-applications-to-the-cloud/

Retire [A]

Getting rid of the application. This usually happens because sweeping the application portfolio reveals unused or orphaned applications.

Retain [A]

Keeping the application where it is, as it is, on premises.

Or, if you prefer to pivot this matrix, here is the list of "R"s that I was able to extract from each of the online resources:

- **Gartner 2010**: Rehost, Revise, Re-architect, Rebuild, Replace
- **Gartner 2018**: Rehost, Refactor, Revise, Rebuild, Replace
- **AWS 2016**: Rehost, Replatform, Repurchase, Refactor/Re-architect, Retire, Retain
- **Microsoft 2019**: Rehost, Refactor, Re-architect, Rebuild, Replace

In case you are wondering how many more "R"s folks may come up with, Wiktionary[8] lists 200 pages of words beginning with "re". Although the "R's" are undeniably catchy, the semantics behind them are a tad fuzzy. It will be difficult to lock down the semantics in any case, but the primary danger is folks walking out of a meeting mumbling "replatform" to themselves but meaning different things. In that case, you need another "R": *reconcile*.

Looking Inside Decision Models

Sketching paths on our simple chart admittedly also has fuzzy semantics: "up" can mean re-architecting or just automating deployment. However, the abstract model conveys this fact more clearly than a set of seemingly precise words. Also, visual models make communicating your strategy to a wide range of stakeholders easier than reciting lengthy variations of verbs starting with "R".

There's another major difference between the up-or-out model and the "R"s: the "R"s try to create a certain commonality or symmetry across the options that you have. However, a decision model's main purpose is to help you choose, so it should highlight the differences. The order of the "R"s implies a gradation (roughly the "angle" at which you move across the up-or-out plane), but folding all options into a single dimension doesn't quite seem to fit the underlying decision space.

---

[8]https://en.wiktionary.org/wiki/Category:English_words_prefixed_with_re-

Bucketizing

A decision model narrows down the available decision space but it doesn't make the decision for you. You still need to place your applications into the appropriate bucket to send it on the appropriate path. Which applications should take which path? Often, the degree of control you have over the application is a bigger determinant than the application's technical architecture. Hence, I recommend dividing your application portfolio into three main categories:

- **Applications that you didn't build**, including most commercial off-the-shelf applications.
- **Applications that someone built for you**, e.g. those developed by a system integrator.
- **Applications that you built** in house.

This categorization will help you make a first cut across the application inventory. For example, it'll be difficult to move commercial applications up the stack in a *re-architect* fashion. And if you remember that *you shouldn't run applications that you didn't build* (Chapter 13), you can make this someone else's problem.

The Decision Is up to You

Models like these sketches exist to help you make better decisions and communicate them more easily and more broadly. They are particularly useful if there are no simple "left-or-right" answers. The models don't tell you what to do, but help you get to a better answer. If you need to move applications out quickly, for example to vacate an existing data center by the time the contract is up, picking the short side of the triangle to move out first will be best, even though you are ultimately taking a longer path. If you have time and resources, following the hypotenuse is actually less effort than making two hops. However, keep in mind that you will likely make several *Optimization Rounds* (Chapter 29) to reduce cost.

So, get your rulers, pencils, and grid paper and draw some cloud migrations!

17. Value Is the Only Real Progress

CTRL-F Value.

"We're halfway there!"

When I reviewed board meeting presentation drafts, the first thing I would do is search for the word "value" (using the keyboard shortcut CTRL-F). If the word wasn't found, I would send the slides back—what good would it be for the board to discuss something that doesn't have an apparent (or at least articulated) value? The word "value" doesn't have many synonyms, so it's unlikely that the choice of words led to false negatives. The same rule should apply to cloud migrations.

Measuring Progress

Despite sophisticated tooling, cloud migrations aren't instant. Hence, it's natural to want to track progress. Most cloud migration efforts do so by the number of virtual servers or workloads migrated. That's sensible at first glance because the goal is usually to migrate a specific percentage of the workload by a certain date.

Analogously, if you have a 500 km road trip ahead of you, it's also sensible to count kilometers covered so far. Unless, of course, road conditions vary widely: if the first half of your trip is a windy mountain road before you reach the German Autobahn for the second half, being 200 km in can actually be more than half way. So, the number of kilometers travelled or the number of workloads migrated, although easily measured, might not be the most suitable metric for real progress made.

The Proxy Metric

IT metrics like counting migrated workloads are what I call *proxy metrics* . A proxy metric is a stand-in for your real objectives. Proxy metrics are tempting because they're easy to measure and track. But they are also dangerous because they can lure you into believing that you're making progress when you're not actually moving the needle on your overall objective, such as providing value to the business.

 The number of applications migrated is a dangerous proxy metric for real cloud success because your end customers won't care.

Your cloud strategy's objective should be to improve metrics that are visible and meaningful to the business or the customer. Visible metrics can still be "technical" in nature. For example, users will appreciate improvements to system availability, performance, or security. They'll also appreciate faster feature delivery. However, they have a much harder time getting excited about "70% of network routing configured" or "30% of servers migrated"—those servers might be for test environments that end users never touch.

There are cases when the number of servers migrated isn't a proxy metric, but a real one. That might be the case, for example, when you're looking to vacate an existing data center before its contract expires. However, such migrations are often a piece of the puzzle for a larger initiative, which is driven and measured by bigger goals.

The Value Gap

Following IT-internal proxy metrics can lead to a common and dangerous phenomenon during cloud migrations: the *value gap*. As detailed in my Enterprise Strategy Blog Post[1], IT leaders might be headed for a value gap when support from the business and other stakeholders wanes despite solid technical migration progress. This can happen when initial technical progress was welcomed by stakeholders and also showed noticeable improvement; for example, in cost or uptime. Soon after, though, the business no longer seems to recognize value commensurate with the technical progress and investment.

The reason for this dangerous gap, which has even caused some businesses to contemplate moving their workloads back to their on-premises data centers, is that the organizational change (see *The Cloud Turns Your Organization Sideways* (Chapter 7)) often cannot keep pace with the technical progress. Alas, without adopting new ways of thinking and working, all the amazing tech that the cloud brings is unable to deliver the anticipated value. Those organizations are either unaware of or unable to implement the *lifestyle change* (Chapter 1) that goes along with migrating to the cloud.

Pushing along the technical migration is unlikely to overcome the value gap—you'll make progress as measured by your IT proxy metrics, but you won't be closing the value gap. Although avoiding proxy metrics doesn't magically keep you out of the value gap (or, rather, trap), it helps you not be blindsided by the technical progress you're making.

Playing Battleship

Now, when you're just at the beginning of your cloud journey, generating and measuring business value isn't easy. First you have to get going and take care of many technical tasks. It's therefore totally okay to start with technical metrics

---

[1]https://aws.amazon.com/blogs/enterprise-strategy/is-your-cloud-journey-stuck-in-the-value-gap/

like the number of servers or the capacity of storage volumes migrated. However, you should soon start to check whether the business value generated (and made visible) is tracking the technical metrics. The best way to do so is to gradually start using business metrics. So, your metrics will evolve over time along with your migration, transitioning from technical IT metrics to business-relevant value-oriented metrics.

 Your migration metrics should transition from IT-internal metrics to business-relevant metrics as your migration progresses.

I compare this approach to playing the game Battleship, the one in which you have to detect your enemy's ships by launching torpedoes in the form of little pegs placed on a grid. In the beginning, when the playing field is pretty empty, you follow a relatively simple approach and can't expect immediate results. As soon as you score a few hits, you shift to a more refined strategy of exploring the neighboring fields. So, in your cloud journey, it's also okay to start with a few well-placed probes to better understand your environment and become more strategic as things progress. The Battleship analogy can be a good way to make this evolution plausible to stakeholders.

Is it fair to depict working with your IT as playing a game in which the other party's ship positions are completely hidden? Given the *low levels of transparency* (Chapter 11) in a typical IT environment, the metaphor is sadly closer to reality than we might like.

The Value Graph

When working for the Singapore Government IT ("GovTech"), we looked to improve our architecture discipline with simple but evocative models. A particularly useful model was the so-called *value graph*. The simple graph plots a project's value delivered over the effort invested. Although intended to be more qualitative than quantitative it nevertheless leads to valuable discussions about how soon business value can be delivered. The following sketch shows three popular versions, rarely drawn out like this but routinely ingrained into people's minds:

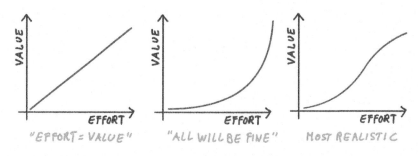

Plotting value over effort

The first fallacy is to equate value delivered with effort (left): "we are halfway through the migration so we have delivered half the value." No, you haven't—you just spent half the money. Equally popular is the infamous "hockey stick" (middle): "we had a slow start but we're going to make up for it later." Yeah, right...

Most commonly, you'd expect some S-curve (right): you need some preparation at the beginning, after which you can harvest low-hanging fruit and make rapid progress. At some point, you'll need to tackle the more difficult applications, causing the curve to flatten. At that point you'll have delivered significant value already, though. For more details, see the related LinkedIn article[2].

Influencing the Curve

How can you change the value curve, assuming that you've overcome the temptation to use the linear or hockey stick versions? Your main interest is going to be to increase the slope of the curve—in other words, to deliver value sooner. Three main factors will help you achieve that:

1. Have a clear definition of how you will measure value. You can't optimize for something that isn't well defined or understood. Naturally, when selecting meaningful metrics, it helps to have a clear view on *why you're going to the cloud in the first place* (Chapter 11).
2. Create sufficient transparency to identify those applications that con-tribute to the chosen metric. The simplest way to achieve this is by ques-

---

[2]*Building a smart(er) nation: Simple models lead to better decisions,* LinkedIn, https://www.linkedin.com/pulse/building-smarter-nation-simple-models-lead-better-decisions-hohpe/

tionnaires or manual reviews. Your *enterprise architecture team* (Chapter 10) should be able to help with such a mapping.

3. Group applications to be migrated such that they best align with the value metrics you are after.

As a concrete example, if improving poor application performance is the key value proposition for moving to the cloud, you'll likely have to migrate entire applications from front end to back end. Otherwise, you'd be introducing additional latency between a front end in the cloud and a back end on premises. If you picture your application portfolio along two dimensions, you'll be migrating a whole vertical slice as shown on the left side of the illustration:

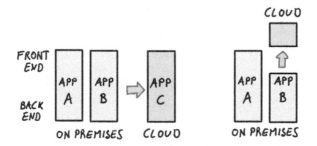

Migration choices determine value delivered

However, if availability is your main objective, you might move only those components that are prone to failure and implement automatic restarts, as shown on the right. While admittedly a "Band-Aid" approach, it will deliver value quickly and give you time to migrate the remaining components.

This simple example shows that the number of applications is a poor substitute for a value-driven migration approach. The chapter *"Hybrid Cloud: Slicing the Elephant* (Chapter 19)" describes many ways of grouping (and slicing) applications for migration.

Adding Value to Pythagoras

The *previous chapter* (Chapter 16) presented an evocative model for visualizing migrations. Would we be able to combine the value chart with the up-or-out migration paths from that chapter? Could adding this dimension make for an uplifting counterpart to Charles Joseph Minard's map of Napoleon's March[3],

---

[3]https://en.wikipedia.org/wiki/Charles_Joseph_Minard

which is frequently lauded by Ed Tufte[4] as one of the best statistical graphics ever drawn?

Perhaps not aiming quite that high, a simple version could plot the value delivered as the size of the dot over the path:

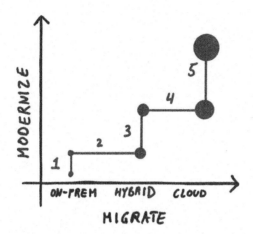

Plotting value on the migration path

This map would show us that the first step isn't intended to deliver value but is rather a preparatory task for the subsequent migration into a hybrid environment in Step 2. The real payoff, though, comes later in steps 4 and 5. Is Mr. Tufte going to approve? You be the judge!

[4]https://www.edwardtufte.com/tufte/posters

Part IV: Architecting the Cloud

IT discussions are routinely dominated by product names and buzzwords. "To implement <buzzword>, we are evaluating <product A> and <product B>" is a common part of IT discussions, only outdone by the second version, "To become <buzzword>, we are evaluating <product C> and <product D>." I'll leave you to assign the words *Agile, Lean, digital, anti-fragile, zero trust, DevOps, IaC,* and *cloud native* to the respective sentences.

A successful cloud migration depends on a lot more than just buzzwords. Selecting the right vendor and the right services might help, but putting those pieces together in a meaningful way that supports the business objectives is what cloud strategy and cloud architecture are all about.

 I frequently compare being an architect to being a restaurant's star chef: picking good ingredients is useful, but how it's put together is what earns the restaurant its reputation. And, as anyone who has tried to re-create their favorite restaurant dish can attest, there's usually a lot more involved than is apparent from the end product.

Cloud Architecture

Unfortunately, many vendor certifications fuel the notion that cloud architecture is mostly about selecting services and memorizing the respective features. It feels to me a bit like becoming a certified LEGO artist by managing to recite all colors and shapes of LEGO bricks (do they make a blue 1x7?).

So, let's look under the covers and take a true architect's point of view. Yes, this will include popular concepts like multi-hybrid and hybrid-multi-cloud, but perhaps not in the way it's described in the marketing brochures. There is no "best" architecture, just the one that's most suitable for your situation and your objectives. Hence, defining your cloud architecture requires a fair amount of thinking—something that you definitely should not outsource[5]. That thinking is helped by decision models presented in this chapter.

The Architect Elevator Approach

The Architect Elevator[6] defines a role model of an architect who can connect the business strategy in the corporate penthouse with the technical reality in the engine room. Instead of simply promising benefits, when such an architect looks at a collection of vendor products, they reverse engineer the key assumptions, constraints, and decisions behind those offerings. They will then map that insight to the enterprise's context and balance the trade-offs of putting these products together into a concrete solution.

Classic IT is built on the assumption that technical implementation decisions are derived from a clear definition of business needs, making architecture a one-way street. The cloud turns this assumption, like many others, on its head, favoring high-level decision makers who understand the ramifications of technical choices made in the engine room. After all, those technical decisions are the critical enablers for the enterprise's ability to innovate and compete in the market. Thus, it is the elevator architect's role not only to make better decisions but also to communicate them transparently to upper management. Clear decision models that skip jargon and buzzwords can be an extremely useful tool in this context.

Decision Models

One could fill an entire book on cloud architecture, and several people have done so (I was lucky enough to write the foreword for *Cloud Computing Patterns*[7]).

[5]https://architectelevator.com/strategy/dont-outsource-thinking/
[6]http://architectelevator.com
[7]Fehling, Leymann, Retter, Schupeck, Arbiter, *Cloud Computing Patterns*, Springer 2014

Cloud service providers have added more architecture guidance (Microsoft Azure maintains a nice site with cloud architecture patterns[8]).

This part is not looking to repeat what's already been written. Rather, it invites you to pick a novel point of view that shuns the buzzwords and focuses on meaningful decisions. To help you become a better informed and more disciplined decision maker, several decision models and frameworks guide you through major decision points along your cloud journey:

- There are many flavors of *multicloud* (Chapter 18) and you should choose carefully which one is best for you.
- *Hybrid cloud* (Chapter 19) requires you to separate your workloads into cloud and on-premises. Knowing your options helps you choose the best path.
- Architects like to look under the covers, so here's how different vendors *architect their hybrid-cloud solutions* (Chapter 20).
- Many architects see their main job as battling lock-in. But life's not that simple: *don't get locked up into avoiding lock-in!* (Chapter 21)
- The cloud changes many past assumptions that drove popular architecture styles. Hence, we may see *the end of multitenancy* (Chapter 22).
- Architects concern themselves with non-functional requirements, also known as "ilities". The cloud brings us a *new "ility": disposability* (Chapter 23), and in an environmentally conscious fashion.

---

[8]https://docs.microsoft.com/en-us/azure/architecture/patterns/

18. Multicloud: You've Got Options

But options don't come for free.

While most enterprises are busily migrating existing applications to the cloud or perhaps building new cloud-ready applications, analysts and marketing teams haven't been sitting idle, concocting slogans like *multi-hybrid-cloud computing*. Or perhaps it was *hybrid-multi*? I am not sure myself.

Are enterprises already falling behind before even finishing their migration? Should they "leapfrog" by going straight for multicloud nirvana? Do people actually mean the same thing when they say "multicloud"? It's time to bust another buzzword and bring things back to earth and to business value. We'll find that, again, there are meaningful decisions to be made.

Multi-Hybrid Split

The initial promise of a multi-hybrid cloud approach sounds appealing enough: your workloads can move from your premises to the cloud and back, or even between different clouds whenever needed; and all that ostensibly with not much more than the push of a button. Architects are born skeptics and thus inclined (and paid) to take a look under the covers to better understand the constraints, costs, and benefits of such solutions.

The first step in dissecting the buzzwords is to split the *multi-hybrid* combo-buzzword into two, separating *hybrid* from *multi*. Each has different driving forces behind it, so let's try two simple definitions:

- **Hybrid** – Splitting workload(s) across the cloud and on premises. Generally, these workloads interact to do something useful
- **Multi** – Running workloads with more than one cloud provider

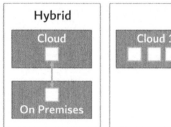 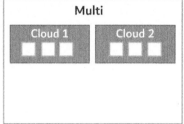

Hybrid and multicloud

As simple as these terms might seem, a disproportionate level of confusion remains. For example, some folks want us to think that multi and hybrid are very similar ("on premises is just another cloud"), whereas others (including myself) highlight the *different constraints of operating on premises versus the public cloud* (Chapter 20).

From an architect's point of view, which focuses on decisions, there's one major difference between the two: *hybrid cloud is a given for most enterprises* (Chapter 19), at least during the transition, whereas a multicloud strategy is an explicit choice you make. Many enterprises are very successfully running on a single cloud, optimizing cost along the way; for example by minimizing the skill sets they need and harvesting volume discounts.

Therefore, as an architect you want to understand what multicloud choices you have and the decision trade-offs that are involved. A buzzword-sanitized decision framework helps you get there.

Multicloud Options

The best starting point is taking a step back from the technical platform and examining common usage scenarios. We can then examine the value each one yields and the trade-offs it implies. After participating in several initiatives that would fall under the general label of "multicloud", I believe that they can be broken down into the following five distinct scenarios:

1. *Arbitrary*: Workloads are in more than one cloud but for no particular reason.
2. *Segmented*: Different clouds are used for different purposes.

3. *Choice*: Projects (or business units) have a choice of cloud provider.
4. *Parallel*: Single applications are deployed to multiple clouds.
5. *Portable*: Workloads can be moved between clouds at will.

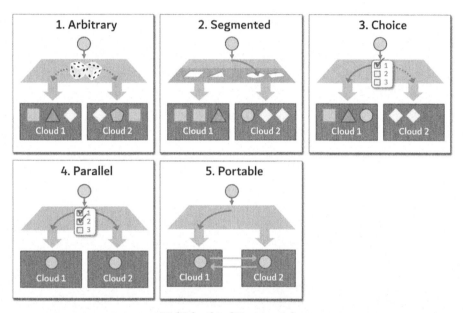

Multicloud architecture styles

A higher number in this list isn't necessarily better—each option has its advantages and limitations. Rather, it's about finding the approach that best suits your needs and making a conscious choice. The biggest mistake could be choosing an option that provides capabilities that aren't needed, because each option has a cost, as we will soon see.

Multicloud architecture isn't a simple one-size-fits-all decision. The most common mistake is choosing an option that's more complex than what's needed for the business to succeed.

Breaking down multicloud into distinct flavors and identifying the drivers and benefits for each is a nice example of how elevator architects see nuances where many others see only left or right. Coupled with simple vocabulary, it enables an in-depth conversation void of technical jargon that gets everyone on the same page. That's what *The Architect Elevator*[1] is all about.

Multicloud Scenarios

Let's look at each of the five ways of doing multicloud individually, with a particularly keen eye on the key capabilities it brings and what aspects to watch out for. We'll summarize what we learned in a decision table.

Arbitrary

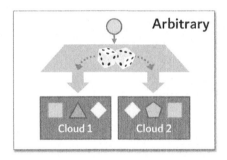

Some stuff in any cloud

If enterprise has taught us one thing, it's likely that reality rarely lives up to the slide decks. Applying this line of reasoning (and the usual dosage of cynicism) to multicloud, we find that a huge percentage of enterprise multicloud isn't the result of divine architectural foresight, but simply poor governance and excessive vendor influence.

This flavor of multicloud means running workloads with more than one cloud provider, but not having much of an idea why things are in one cloud or the other. Often the reasons are historic: you started with one cloud and then added another vendor thanks to a substantial service credit, all the while some developers loved a third cloud so much that they ignored the corporate standard.

Strategy isn't exactly the word to be used for this setup. It's not all bad, though: at least you're deploying *something* to the cloud! That's a good thing because before you can steer, you first have to move[2]. So, at least you're moving. You're gathering experience and building skills with multiple technology platforms, which you can use to settle on the provider that best meets your needs. So, while *arbitrary* isn't a viable target picture, it's a common starting point.

---

[1]Hohpe, *The Software Architect Elevator*, 2020, O'Reilly
[2]https://www.linkedin.com/pulse/before-you-can-steer-first-have-move-gregor-hohpe/

Segmented

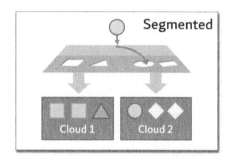

Different clouds for different needs

Segmenting workloads across different clouds is also common, and a good step ahead: you choose different clouds for specific types of workloads. Companies often land in this scenario because they want to benefit from a particular vendor's strength in one area. *Different licensing models* (Chapter 29) may also lead you to favor different vendors for different workloads. A common incarnation of the *segmented* scenario is running most large workloads on the primary provider and using analytics services of another.

You may decide on cloud providers by several factors:

- Type of workload (legacy vs. modern)
- Type of data (confidential vs. openly available)
- Type of service (compute vs. analytics vs. collaboration software)

Understanding the *seams* between your applications avoids excessive egress charges when half your application ends up on the left, and the other half on the right. Also, keep in mind that vendor capabilities are rapidly shifting, especially in segments like machine learning. *Snapshot comparisons* (Chapter 1) therefore aren't particularly meaningful and may unwittingly lead you into this scenario just to find out a few months later that your preferred vendor is now offering comparable functionality.

Also, I have observed enterprises slipping from *segmented* back into *arbitrary* when sales teams use their foothold to grow their slice of the pie. If you use a very specific service from another vendor, its (pre-)sales folks will surely try to pitch their other services, as well—that's their job, after all.

Decision discipline is the backbone of any sound strategy, so you have to remain friendly but firm in such situations. Another slippery slope back into the *arbitrary* model are *résumé-driven architectures* (Chapter 25), so wear your shades and stay away from too shiny objects. Otherwise you might end up in situations where 95% of your applications run in one country and a few percent on another cloud thousands of miles away—a real example, which incurs latency and egress cost, and unnecessarily duplicates the required skill sets.

When comparing clouds, avoid the trap of optimizing for each individual service. A cloud platform should be evaluated as a whole, including how services interoperate with one another and with cross-cutting concerns like access management or monitoring. It comes down to one of the most important lessons in enterprise architecture:

 The sum of local optima is rarely the global optimum. Optimize globally, not locally!

Choice

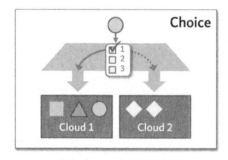

Freedom of choice

Many might not consider the first two examples as *true* multicloud. What they are looking for (and pitching) is the ability to deploy your workloads freely across cloud providers, thus *minimizing lock-in* (Chapter 21) (or the perception thereof), usually by means of building abstraction layers or governance frameworks. Again, there are multiple flavors, separated by the finality of the cloud decision. For example, should you be able to change your mind after your initial choice and, if so, how easy do you expect the switch to be?

The least complex and most common case is giving your developers an initial choice of cloud provider but not expecting them to keep changing their mind. This *choice* scenario is common in large organizations with shared IT service units. Central IT is generally expected to support a wide range of business units and their respective IT preferences. Freedom of choice might also result from the desire to remain neutral, such as in public sector, or a regulatory guideline to avoid placing "all eggs in one basket", often seen in financial services or similar critical services.

A *choice* setup typically has central IT manage the commercial relationships with the cloud providers. Some IT departments also develop a common tool set to create cloud provider account instances to assure central spend tracking and corporate governance.

The advantage of this setup is that projects are free to use proprietary cloud services, such as managed databases, based on their preferred trade-off between minimizing lock-in and operational overhead. As a result, business units get an unencumbered, dare I say *native*, cloud experience. Hence, this setup makes a good initial step for multicloud.

Parallel

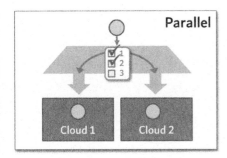

A single app in multiple clouds

While the previous option gives you a choice among cloud service providers, you are still bound by the service level of a single provider. Many enterprises are looking to deploy critical applications across multiple clouds in their pursuit of higher levels of availability than they could achieve with a single provider.

Being able to deploy the same application in parallel to multiple clouds requires a certain set of decoupling from the cloud provider's proprietary features. This can be achieved in a number of ways; for example:

- Managing cloud-specific functions such as identity management, deployment automation, or monitoring separately for each cloud, isolating them from the core application code through interfaces or pluggable modules.
- Maintain two branches for those components of your application that are cloud-provider specific and wrap them behind a common interface. For example, you could have a common interface for block data storage.

- Using open-source components because they will generally run on any cloud. While this works relatively well for pure compute (hosted Kubernetes is available on most clouds), it may reduce your ability to take advantage of other fully managed services, such as data stores or monitoring. Because managed services are one of the key benefits of moving to the clouds in the first place, this is an option that will need careful considerations.
- Utilize a multicloud abstraction framework, so that you can develop once and deploy to any cloud without having to deal with any cloud specifics. However, such an abstraction layer might prevent you from benefiting from a particular cloud's unique offering, potentially weakening your solution or increasing cost.

While absorbing differences inside your code base might sound kludgy, it's what Object-Relational Mapping (ORM) frameworks have been successfully doing for relational databases for more than a decade.

The critical aspect to watch out for is complexity, which can easily undo the anticipated uptime gain. Additional layers of abstraction and more tooling also increase the chance of a misconfiguration, which causes unplanned downtime. I have seen vendors suggesting designs that deploy across each vendor's three availability zones, plus a disaster recovery environment in each, times three cloud providers. With each component occupying 3 x 2 x 3 = *18 nodes*, I'd be skeptical as to whether this amount of machinery really gives you higher availability than using nine nodes (one per zone and per cloud provider).

Second, seeking harmonization across both deployments may not be what's actually desired. The higher the degree of commonality across clouds, the higher the chance that you'll deploy a broken application or encounter issues on both clouds, undoing the resilience benefit. The extreme example are space probes or similar systems that require extreme reliability: they use two separate teams to avoid any form of commonality.

 Higher degrees of harmonization across providers increases the chance of a common error, undoing potential increases in system uptime.

So, when you're designing for availability, keep in mind that the cloud provider's platform isn't the only outage scenario—human error and application software issues (bugs or run-time issues such as memory leaks and overflowing queues) can be a bigger contributor to outages.

Portable

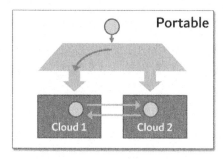

Shifting at will

The perceived pinnacle of multicloud is free portability across clouds, meaning that you can deploy your workloads anywhere and also move them as you please. The advantages are easy to grasp: you can avoid vendor lock-in, which, for example, gives you negotiation power. You can also move applications based on resource needs. For example, you may run normal operations in one cloud and burst excessive traffic into another.

The core mechanisms that enable this capability are high levels of automation and abstraction away from cloud services. Whereas for parallel deployments you could get away with a semi-manual setup or deployment process, full portability requires you to be able to shift the workload any time, so everything better be fully automated.

Multicloud abstraction frameworks promise this capability. However, nothing is ever free, so the cost comes in form of complexity, lock-in to a specific framework, restriction to specific application architectures (e.g., containers) and platform underutilization (see *Don't Get Locked-Up Into Avoiding Lock-in* (Chapter 21)).

Also, most such abstractions generally don't take care of your data: if you shift your compute nodes across providers willy-nilly, how are you going to keep your data in sync? And if you manage to overcome this hurdle, egress data costs may come to nib you in the rear. So, although this option looks great on paper (or PowerPoint), it involves significant trade-offs.

Chasing Shiny Objects Makes You Blind

As highlighted in *"If You Don't Know How to Drive* (Chapter 5)", when chasing shiny objects, you can easily fall into the trap of believing that the shinier, the better. Those with enterprise battle scars know all too well that polishing objects to become ever more shiny has a cost. Dollar cost is the apparent one, but you also need to factor in additional complexity, managing multiple vendors, finding skill sets, and assuring long-term viability (will we just go serverless?). Those factors can't be solved with money. Put into stronger words:

 Excessive complexity is nature's punishment for organizations that are unable to make decisions.

If you want all options all the time, chances are that you'll drown in complexity and don't get any of them. It's therefore paramount to understand and clearly communicate your primary objective. Are you looking to better negotiate with vendors, to increase your availability, or to support local deployment in regions where only one provider or the other operates a data center?

Also, remember that cloud providers continuously reduce prices, increase availability, and deploy new regions. Hence, *doing nothing* (Chapter 29) can be an unexpected, albeit quite effective strategy for addressing these issues. Lastly, *avoiding lock-in* (Chapter 21) is an abstract meta-goal, which, while architecturally desirable, needs to be translated into a tangible benefit. Don't justify one buzzword with another one!

Multicloud ≠ Uniform Cloud

When advising enterprises on a multicloud strategy, I routinely remind them to stay away from building a uniform cloud experience across all providers. Each cloud provider has specific strengths in its product offering but also in its product strategy and corporate culture. Attempting to make all clouds look the same doesn't actually benefit your internal customers. Instead, it incurs a heavy burden; for example, because they won't be able to use an inexpensive managed service from cloud provider X. Or they might be working with an external vendor that's familiar with the original cloud but not with the abstraction layer woven over it. I call this the *Esperanto effect* (Chapter 20): yes, it'd be nice if we all spoke one universal language. However, that means we all have to learn yet one more language and many of us speak English already.

Choosing Wisely

The following table summarizes the multicloud choices, their main drivers, and the side effects to watch out for:

Style	Key Capability	Key Mechanism	Consideration
Arbitrary	Deploying to the cloud	Cloud skill	Lack of governance; traffic cost
Segmented	Clear guidance on cloud usage	Governance	Drifting back to "Arbitrary"
Choice	Support project needs/preferences	Common framework for provisioning, billing, governance	Additional layer; lack of guidance; traffic cost
Parallel	Higher availability (potentially)	Automation, abstraction, load balancing/failover	Complexity; underutilization
Portable	Shift workloads at will	Full automation, abstraction. Data portability	Complexity; framework lock-in; underutilization

As expected: TANSTAAFL—*there ain't no such a thing as a free lunch.* Architecture is the business of trade-offs. Therefore, it's important to break down the options, give them meaningful names, understand their implications, and communicate them broadly.

19. Hybrid Cloud: Slicing the Elephant

Enterprises can't avoid hybrid cloud, but they can choose their path.

A hybrid-cloud setup is a reality for enterprises. A sound cloud strategy goes beyond the buzzword, though, and makes a conscious choice of what to keep on premises and what to move into the cloud. Again, it turns out that simple but evocative decision models help Elevator Architects make better and more conscious decisions on their journey to the cloud.

Hybrid Is a Reality. Multi Is an Option.

Unlike *multicloud* (Chapter 18), hybrid-cloud architectures are a given in any enterprise cloud journey, at least as a transitional state. The reason is simple: despite magic things like AWS Snowmobile[1] you're not going to find all your workloads magically removed from your data center one day—some applications will already be in the cloud, whereas others will still be on premises.

 No CIO will wake up one morning to find all of their workloads in the cloud.

And once you split workloads across the cloud and on premises, more likely than not, those two pieces will need to interact, as captured in our definition from the previous chapter:

 Hybrid cloud architectures split workloads across the cloud and on-premises environments. Generally, these workloads interact to do something useful.

---

[1]https://aws.amazon.com/snowmobile/

Accordingly, the core of a hybrid-cloud strategy isn't *when* but *how*, specifically how to slice, meaning which workloads should move out into the cloud and which ones remain on premises. That decision calls for some architectural thinking, aided by taking the Architect Elevator a few floors down.

Two Isolated Environments Don't Make a Hybrid

First, we want to sharpen our view of what makes a "hybrid". Having some workloads in the cloud while others remain on our premises sadly means that you have added yet another computing environment to your existing portfolio—not a great result.

 I haven't met a CIO who's looking for more complexity. So, don't make your cloud yet another data center.

Therefore, unified management across the environment is an essential element to calling something hybrid. Consider the analogy of a hybrid car:

> The difficult part in making a hybrid car wasn't sticking a battery and an electric motor into a petrol-powered car. Getting the two systems to work seamlessly and harmoniously was the critical innovation. That's what made the Toyota Prius a true *hybrid* and such a success.

Because the same is true for hybrid clouds, we'll augment our definition:

 Hybrid cloud architectures split workloads across the cloud and on-premises environments, *which are managed in a unified way.* Generally, these workloads interact to do something useful.

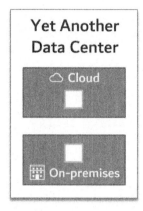
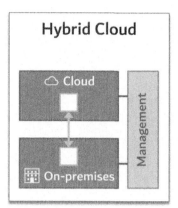

A hybrid cloud unifies management

With this clarification, let's come back to cloud strategy and see what options we have for slicing workloads.

Hybrid splits: 31 Flavors?

The key architectural decision of where to split your workloads between on premises and the cloud is related to the notion of finding *seams* in an IT system, first described (to my knowledge) by Mike Feathers in his classic book *Working Effectively with Legacy Code*[2]. Seams are those places where a split doesn't cross too many dependencies. A good seam minimizes rework, like introducing new APIs, and it avoids run-time problems, such as degraded performance.

I don't think there are quite 31 ways to split workloads. Still, cataloging them is useful in several ways:

- **Improved transparency** – A common vocabulary gives decision transparency because it's easy to communicate which option(s) you chose and why.
- **More choice** – The list allows you to check whether you might have overlooked some options. Especially for environments in which regulatory concerns and data residency requirements still limit some cloud migrations, a list of options allows you to see whether you exhausted all possible options.

[2]Feathers, *Working Effectively With Legacy Code*, 2004, Pearson

- **Lower risk** – Lastly, the list helps you consider applicability, pros, and cons of each option consistently. It can also tell you about what to watch out for when selecting a specific option.

Therefore, our decision model once again helps us make better decisions and communicate them such that everyone understands which route we take and why.

Ways to Slice the Cloud Elephant

I have seen enterprises split their application portfolios in at least eight common ways, divided into three categories of applications, data, and operational considerations, as illustrated here:

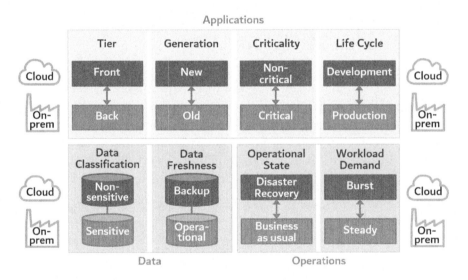

Eight ways to split a hybrid cloud

This list's main purpose isn't as much to find new options that no one has ever thought of—you might have seen more. It's much rather a collection of well-known options that makes for a useful sanity check. Let's have a look at each approach in more detail.

Tier: Front vs. Back

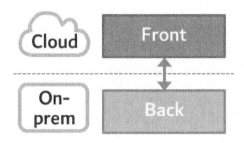

Separating by tier

Moving customer or ecosystem-facing components, aka "front-end systems" / "systems of engagement" to the cloud while keeping back-end systems is a common strategy. Even though you won't see me celebrating two-speed architectures (see "Architects Live in the First Derivative" in *The Software Architect Elevator*[3]), multiple factors make this approach a natural fit:

- Front-end components are exposed to the internet, so routing traffic straight from the internet to the cloud reduces latency and eases traffic congestion on your corporate network.
- The wild traffic swings commonly experienced by front-end components make elastic scaling particularly valuable.
- Front-end systems are more likely to be developed using modern tool chains and architectures, which make them well suited for the cloud.
- Front-end systems are less likely to store personally identifiable or confidential information because that data is usually passed through to back-ends. For environments in which enterprise policies restrict such data from being stored in the cloud, front-end systems are good candidates for moving to the cloud.

Besides these natural advantages, architecture wouldn't be interesting if there weren't some things to watch out for:

- Even if the front end takes advantage of elastic scaling, most back ends won't be able to absorb the corresponding load spikes. So, unless you em-

---

[3]Hohpe, *The Software Architect Elevator*, 2020, O'Reilly

ploy caching or queuing or can move computationally expensive tasks to
the cloud, you may not improve your application's end-to-end scalability.
- Similarly, if your application suffers from reliability issues, moving just
  one half to the cloud is unlikely to make those go away.
- Many front ends are "chatty" when communicating with back-end systems or specifically databases because they were built for environments
  where the two sit very close to each other. One front-end request can issue
  dozens or sometimes hundreds of requests to the back end. Splitting such
  a chatty channel between cloud and on-premises is likely to increase end-
  user latency.

Although the excitement of "two speed IT" wore off, this approach can still be
a reasonable intermediary step. Just don't mistake it for a long-term strategy.

Generation: New vs. Old

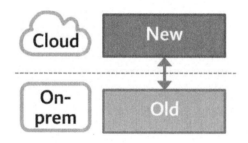

Separating by generation

Closely related is the split by *new* vs. *old*. As just explained, newer systems are
more likely to feel at home in the cloud because they are generally designed
to be scalable and independently deployable. They're also usually smaller and
hence benefit more from lean cloud platforms such as *serverless* (Chapter 26).

Again, several reasons make this type of split compelling:

- Modern components are more likely to use modern tool chains and
  architectures, such as microservices, Continuous Integration (CI), and
  automated tests and deployment. Thus, they can take better advantage
  of cloud platforms.

- Modern components often run in containers and can therefore utilize higher-level cloud services like managed container orchestration.
- Modern components are usually better understood and tested, reducing the migration risk.

Again, there are a few things to consider:

- Splitting by *new* vs *old* may not align well with the existing systems architecture, meaning it isn't hitting a good *seam*. For example, splitting highly cohesive components across data-center boundaries will likely result in poor performance or increased traffic cost.
- Unless you are in the process of replacing all components over time, this strategy doesn't lead to a "100% in the cloud" outcome.
- "New" is a rather fuzzy term, so you'd want to precisely define the split for your workloads.

Following this approach, you'd want your cloud to be *application centric* (Chapter 24). Overall this is a good approach if you are building new systems—ultimately *new* will replace *old*.

Criticality: Non-Critical vs. Critical

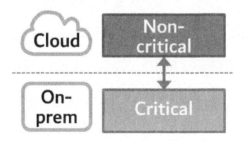

Separating by criticality

Many enterprises prefer to first dip their toe into the cloud water before going all out (or "all in" as the providers would see it). They are likely to try the cloud with a few simple applications that can accommodate the initial learning curve and the inevitable mistakes. "Failing fast" and learning along the way makes sense:

- Skill set availability is one of the main inhibitors of moving to the cloud—stuff is never as easy as shown in the vendor demos. Therefore, starting small and getting rapid feedback builds much needed skills in a low-risk environment.
- Smaller applications benefit from the cloud self-service approach because it reduces or eliminates the fixed overhead common in on-premises IT.
- Small applications also give you timely feedback and allow you to calibrate your expectations.

Although moving non-critical applications out to the cloud is a good start, it also has some limitations:

- Cloud providers generally offer better uptime and security than on-premises environments, so you'll likely gain more by moving *critical* workloads.
- Simple applications typically don't have the same security, uptime, and scalability requirements as subsequent and more substantive workloads. You therefore might underestimate the effort of a full migration.
- While you can learn a lot from moving simple applications, the initial direct ROI of the migration might be low. It's good to set the expectations accordingly.

Overall it's a good "tip your toe into the water" tactic that certainly beats a "let's wait until all this settles" approach.

Life Cycle: Development vs. Production

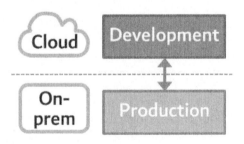

Separating by life cycle

There are many ways to slice the proverbial elephant (eggplant, for vegetarians like me). Rather than just considering splits across run-time components, a whole different approach is to split by application life cycle. For example, you can run your tool chain, test, and staging environments in the cloud while keeping production on premises; for example, if regulatory constraints require you to do so.

Shifting build and test environments into the cloud is a good idea for several reasons:

- Build and test environments rarely contain real customer data, so most concerns around data privacy and locality don't apply.
- Development, test, and build environments are temporary in nature, so being able to set them up when needed and tearing them back down leverages the elasticity of the cloud and can cut infrastructure costs by a factor of three or more: the core working hours make up less than a third of a week's 168 hours. Functional test environments may even have shorter duty cycles, depending on how quickly they can spin up.
- Many build systems are failure tolerant, so you can shave off even more dollars by using preemptible[4]/spot[5] compute instances.
- Build tool chains are generally closely monitored by well-skilled development teams that can quickly correct minor issues.

You might have guessed that architecture is the business of trade-offs, so once again we have a few things to watch out for:

- Splitting your software life cycle across cloud and on-premises results in a test environment that's different from production. This is risky because you might not detect performance bottlenecks or subtle differences that can cause bugs to surface only in production.
- If your build chain generates large artifacts you may face delays or egress charges when deploying those to your premises.
- Your tool chain can also be an attack vector for someone to inject malware or Trojans. You therefore need to protect your cloud tool chain well.

This option may be useful for development teams that are restrained from running production workloads in the cloud but still want to utilize the cloud.

[4]https://cloud.google.com/preemptible-vms/
[5]https://docs.aws.amazon.com/AWSEC2/latest/UserGuide/using-spot-instances.html

Data Classification: Non-Sensitive vs. Sensitive

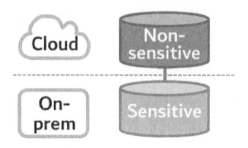

Separating by data classification

The compute aspect of hybrid cloud architectures is comparatively simple because code can easily be redeployed into different environments. Data is a different story: data largely resides in one place and needs to be migrated or synchronized if it's meant to go somewhere else. If you move your compute and keep the data on premises, you'll likely incur a heavy performance penalty. Therefore, it's the data that often prevents the move to the cloud.

As data classification can be the hurdle for moving apps to the cloud, a natural split would be to move non-sensitive data to the cloud while keeping sensitive data on premises. Doing so has some distinct advantages:

- It complies with common internal regulations related to data residency because sensitive data will remain on your premises and isn't replicated into other regions.
- It limits your exposure in case of a possible cloud data breach. While keeping data on premises won't guarantee that no breach occurs, ironically the reputational damage of a data breach on premises can be lower than a breach that's happening in the cloud. In the former case, the organization can be accused of giving their customers' data into someone else's hands, which can be perceived as careless. Oddly enough, incompetence (or sheer bad luck) on premises is more easily shrugged away because "that's the way everyone does it."

However, the approach is rooted in assumptions that don't necessarily hold true for today's computing environments:

- Protecting on-premises environments from sophisticated attacks and low-level exploits has become a difficult proposition. For example, CPU-level exploits like *Spectre and Meltdown* (Chapter 11) were corrected by some cloud providers before they were announced—something that couldn't be done on premises.
- Malicious data access and exploits don't always access data directly but often go through many "hops". Having some systems in the cloud while your sensitive data remains on premises doesn't automatically mean that your data is secure. For example, one of the biggest data breaches, the Equifax Data Breach[6] that affected up to 145 million customer records, had data stored on premises.

So, although this approach may be suitable to getting started in face of regulatory or policy constraints, use it with caution as a long-term strategy.

Data Freshness: Back-Up vs. Operational

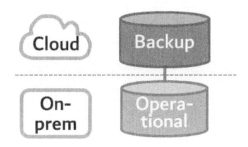

Separating by data freshness

Not all of your data is accessed by applications all the time. In fact, a vast majority of enterprise data is "cold", meaning it's rarely accessed. Cloud providers offer appealing options for data that's rarely accessed, such as historical records or backups. Amazon's Glacier[7] was one of the earliest offerings to specifically target that use case. Other providers have special archive tiers for their storage service; for example, Azure Storage Archive Tier[8] and GCP Coldline Cloud Storage[9].

---

[6]https://en.wikipedia.org/wiki/Equifax#May%E2%80%93July_2017_data_breach
[7]https://aws.amazon.com/glacier/
[8]https://azure.microsoft.com/en-us/services/storage/archive/
[9]https://cloud.google.com/storage/docs/storage-classes

Archiving data in the cloud makes good sense:

- Backing up and restoring data usually occurs separate from regular operations, so it allows you to take advantage of the cloud without having to migrate or re-architect applications.
- For older applications, data storage cost can make up a significant percentage of the overall operational costs, so storing it in the cloud can give you instant cost savings.
- For archiving purposes, having data in a location separate from your usual data center increases the resilience against disaster scenarios such as a fire in your data center.

Alas, this approach also has limitations:

- Data recovery costs can be high, so you'd only want to move data that you rarely need.
- The data you'd want to back up likely contains customer or other proprietary data, so you might need to encrypt or otherwise protect that data, which can interfere with optimizations such as data de-duplication.

Still, using cloud backup is a good way for enterprises to quickly start benefiting from the cloud.

Operational State: Disaster vs. Business-as-Usual

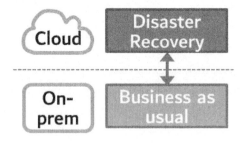

Separating by operational state

Lastly, one can split workloads by the nature of the system's operational state. The most apparent division in operational state is whether things are going well (business-as-usual) or whether the main compute resources are unavailable (disaster). While you or your regulator may have a strong preference for running systems on premises, during a data-center outage you might find a system running in the cloud preferable over none running at all. This reasoning can apply, for example, to critical systems like payment infrastructure.

This approach to slicing workload is slightly different from the others as the same workload would be able to run in both environments, but under different circumstances:

- No workloads run in the cloud under normal operational conditions, meeting potential regulatory requirements.
- Cloud usage is temporary, making good use of the cloud's elastic billing approach. The cost of the cloud environment is low during normal operations.

However, life isn't quite that simple. There are drawbacks, as well:

- To run emergency operations from the cloud, you need to have your data synchronized into a location that's both accessible from the cloud and unaffected by the outage scenario that you are planning for. More likely than not, that location would be the cloud, at which point you should consider running the system from the cloud in any case.
- Using the cloud just for emergency situations deprives you of the benefits of operating in the cloud in the vast majority of the cases.
- You might not be able to spool up the cloud environment on a moment's notice. In that case, you'd need to have the environment on standby, which will rack up charges with little benefit.

So, this approach may be suitable mainly for compute tasks that don't require a lot of data. For example, for an on-premises e-commerce site that faces an outage, you could allow customers to place orders by picking from a (public) catalog and storing orders until the main system comes back up. It will likely beat your customers seeing a nonchalant HTTP 500 page.

Workload Demand: Burst vs. Normal Operations

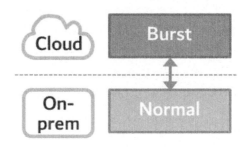

Separating by workload demand

Last, but not least, we may not have to conjure an outright emergency to occasionally shift some workloads into the cloud while keeping it on premises under normal circumstances. An approach that used to be frequently cited is "bursting" into the cloud, meaning you keep a fixed capacity on premises and temporarily extend into the cloud when additional capacity is needed.

Again, you gain some desirable benefits:

- The cloud's elastic billing model is ideal for this case given that short bursts are going to be relatively cheap.
- You retain the comfort of operating on premises for most of the time and are able to utilize your already paid for hardware.

But there are reasons that people don't talk about this option quite as much anymore:

- Again, you need access to data from the cloud instances. This means that you either replicate the data to the cloud, which is likely what you tried to avoid in the first place. Alternatively, your cloud instances need to operate on data that's kept on premises, which likely implies major latency penalties and can incur significant data access cost.
- You need to have an application architecture that can run on premises and in the cloud simultaneously under heavy load. That's not a small feat and means significant engineering effort for a rare case.

Rather than bursting regular workloads into the cloud, this option works best for dedicated compute-intensive tasks, such as simulations, which are regularly run in financial institutions. It's also a great fit for one-time compute tasks where you rig up machinery in the cloud just for one time. For example, this worked well for the *New York Times* digitizing six million photos[10] or for calculating *pi* to 31 trillion digits[11]. To be fair, though, these cases had no on-premises equivalent, so it likely wouldn't qualify as a hybrid setup.

Putting It into Practice

For most enterprises, a hybrid-cloud scenario is inevitable, so you'd better have a good plan for how to make the best use of it. Because there are quite a few options to slice your workloads across the cloud and your on-premises compute environments, cataloging these options helps you make well-thought-out and clearly communicated decisions. It also keeps you from wanting to proclaim that "one size fits all" and will lead you to a more nuanced strategy.

Happy slicing and dicing!

---

[10]https://www.nytimes.com/2018/11/10/reader-center/past-tense-photos-history-morgue.html
[11]https://www.theverge.com/2019/3/14/18265358/pi-calculation-record-31-trillion-google

20. The Cloud—Now on Your Premises

From the buzzword down the rabbit hole into a new universe.

The previous chapter showed many ways to split workloads across cloud and on-premises environments. Equally interesting is how cloud providers make hybrid model possible in the first place; that is, how they enable a cloud operating model on your premises. Because different vendors follow different philosophies and choose different approaches, it's the architects' job to look behind the slogans and understand the assumptions, decisions, and the ramifications that are baked into the respective approaches. "Doors closing. Elevator going down..."

Bringing the Cloud to Your Premises

A cloud operating model brings many great benefits. But since they're mostly available in commercial cloud environments, what to do about the applications that remain on premises due to regulatory constraints, corporate policies, or specific hardware dependencies? Declaring everything that remains on premises as legacy would be foolish. True, there are inherent limitations on premises, such as the rate at which you can scale (physical hardware won't spawn) and the overall scale you can reach (you're not Google). Still, on-premises applications deserve to enjoy modern architectures and automated deployments. "Bringing the cloud to you" was even the slogan of a now revamped hybrid-cloud platform.

Hybrid vs. Cloud On Premises

Similar to *multicloud* (Chapter 18), enterprises have a range of options regarding how much uniformity across their cloud and on-premises environments they want to achieve. Initially, there are three fundamental choices:

- Option 1: Largely leave the on-premises environment as is, which for most enterprises means a virtualized IaaS environment based on VMware or Microsoft Hyper-V.
- Option 2: Achieve cloud-like capabilities on premises, but operate separately from the cloud.
- Option 3: Consider on premises an extension of the cloud and manage both environments uniformly. This management unit is often called "control plane", a term borrowed from network architecture.

Hybrid cloud ambitions

(The astute reader will have noticed that the diagrams are rotated by 90 degrees from the ones in the previous chapter, now showing cloud and on-premises environments side by side. This is the artistic license I took to make showing the layers easier.)

The first option isn't as horrible as it might sound. You could still use modern software approaches like CI/CD, automated testing, and frequent releases. In many cases, option #2 is a significant step forward, assuming that you are clear on *what you expect to gain from moving to the cloud* (Chapter 11). Lastly, if you want to achieve a true hybrid-cloud setup, you don't just enable cloud capabilities on premises, but also want uniform management and deployment across the environments.

Which one is the correct target picture for your enterprise depends largely on *how you will split applications* (Chapter 19). For example, if applications run either in the cloud or on premises, but not half-half, uniform management may not be as relevant for you. Once again, you must keep in mind that not every available feature translates into an actual benefit for your organization.

Why On Premises Is Different

Architecture lives in context. Before thinking about the implementation of hybrid-cloud frameworks, you should therefore consider how on premises is a different ballpark from commercial cloud. Even though it's all made from racks and servers, cables, and network switches, power supplies and air conditioning, you'll also find quite a few significant differences:

Scale
> Most on-premises data centers are two or more orders of magnitude smaller than so-called hyperscaler data centers. The smaller scale impacts economics but also capacity management; that is, how much hardware can be on standby for instant application scaling. For example, running one-off number crunching jobs on hundreds or thousands of VMs likely won't work on premises, and if it did, it would be highly uneconomical.

Custom hardware
> Virtually all cloud providers use custom hardware for their data centers, from custom network switches and custom security modules, to custom data-center designs. They can afford to do so based on their scale. In comparison, on-premises data centers have to make do with commercial off-the-shelf hardware.

Diversity
> On-premises environments have usually grown over time, often decades, and therefore look like they contain everything including the proverbial kitchen sink. Cloud data centers are neatly built and highly homogeneous, making them much easier to manage.

Bandwidth
> Large-scale cloud providers have enormous bandwidth and super-low latency straight from the internet backbone. Corporate data centers often have thin pipes. Network traffic also typically needs to make many hops: 10, 20, or 30 milliseconds isn't uncommon just to *reach* a corporate server. By that time, Google's search engine has already returned the results.

Geographic reach
> Cloud data centers aren't just bigger, they're also spread around the globe and supported by cloud endpoints that give users low-latency access. Corporate data centers are typically confined to one or two locations.

Physical access

In your own data center, you can usually "touch" the hardware and conduct manual configurations or replace faulty hardware. Cloud data centers
are highly restricted and usually do not permit access by customers.

Skills

An on-premises operations team typically has different skill sets than
teams working for a cloud service provider. This is often the case because on-premises teams are more experienced in traditional operational
approaches. Also the operational tasks might be outsourced altogether to
a third party, leaving very little skill in house.

In summary, despite many similarities on the surface, on-premises environments operate in a substantially different context and with different constraints
than commercial cloud environments. Hence, we need to be cautious not to
place an abstraction that's appealing at first but ultimately turns out to be an
illusion. IT isn't a magic show, not even cloud computing.

Hybrid Implementation Strategies

Given the different constraints in the cloud and on premises, it's no surprise
that providers approach the problem of bringing the cloud to your premises
in different ways and sometimes in combinations thereof. That's a good thing
because it lets you choose the approach that best matches your strategy.

The primary approaches I have observed are:

1. Layering a uniform run-time and management layer across both environments
2. Replicating the cloud environment on your premises, with either a hardware or software solution
3. Replicating your existing on-premises virtualization environment in the
   cloud
4. Building an interface layer on existing on-premises virtualization tools to
   make it compatible with the cloud management layer; aka control plane

Each of these approaches deserves a closer look. Naturally, architects are going to
be most interested in the decisions and trade-offs that sit beneath each particular
path.

1. Define a Shared Abstraction Layer

When an architect is going to look for a uniform solution, the first thought that comes to mind is to add an abstraction layer. Following the old saying that "all problems in computer science can be solved with another level of indirection", attributed to David Wheeler[1], this layer absorbs the differences between the underlying implementations (we're glancing over the difference between indirection and abstraction for a moment). Great examples are SQL to abstract database internals, and the Java Virtual Machine (JVM) to abstract processor architectures, which ironically are less diverse nowadays than when that layer was created back in 1994.

So, it's natural to follow the same logic for clouds, as illustrated in the following diagram:

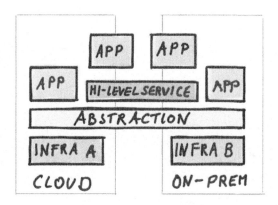

Layering a common abstraction across cloud and on premises

With cloud and on-premises data centers containing quite different hardware infrastructures, the abstraction layer absorbs such differences so that applications "see" the same kind of virtual infrastructure. Once you have such an abstraction in place, a great benefit is that you can layer additional higher-level services on top, which will "inherit" the abstraction and also work across cloud and on-premises environments, giving this approach a definite architectural elegance.

By far the most popular example of this approach is Kubernetes, the open-source project that has grown from being a container orchestrator to look like a universal deployment/management/operations platform for any computing

[1]https://en.wikipedia.org/wiki/David_Wheeler_(computer_scientist)

infrastructure, sort of like the JVM but focused on operational aspects as opposed to a language run time.

Advantages

Naturally, this approach has several advantages:

- The abstraction layer simplifies application deployment across environments because they look identical to the application.
- You might be able to pull the abstraction not only over on-premises but also across multiple cloud providers, yielding a *multi-hybrid* solution.
- You can build new abstractions on top of this base abstraction. For example, this is the approach KNative follows in the Kubernetes ecosystem.
- A common abstraction can enable unique features like failover or resiliency across environments, (mostly) transparent to the application.
- You need to learn only one tool for all environments, reducing the learning curve and improving skills portability.

Considerations

Of course, what looks good in theory will also face real-life limitations:

- A shared abstraction can become a lowest common denominator, meaning that features available in one platform won't be reflected in the abstraction, thus leading to costly *underutilization* (Chapter 21). An abstraction is, for example, unlikely to support cloud services like machine learning that are impractical to implement on premises due to the required hardware scale. The effect is exacerbated if the abstraction spans multiple cloud providers, which may or may not provide certain features. Also, the layer may face a time lag when new features are released in the cloud platform, leaving you without access to the latest features.
- The new abstraction layer adds another moving part, increasing overall system complexity and potentially reducing reliability. It also requires developers to have to learn a new layer in addition to the cloud service they usually already know. Admittedly, once they learn this layer, they can work in any cloud to the extent that the abstraction holds.

- The abstraction runs the risk of conveying a model that doesn't match the underlying reality, resulting in a dangerous illusion. A well-known example is the Remote Procedure Call[2], which pretends that a remote call across the network is just like a local method call. A fantastic abstraction that, unfortunately, doesn't hold[3] because it ignores the inherent properties of remote communication such as latency and new failure modes. Likewise, a cloud abstraction on premises might ignore the limited scalability.
- Different implementations of the abstraction might have subtle differences. Applications that depend on those are no longer portable. For example, despite the SQL abstraction, very few applications can be ported from one relational database to another without changes.
- Implementation details, especially those for which it is difficult to define a common denominator, often leak through the abstraction. For example, many cross-cloud automation tools define a common automation syntax but can't abstract away platform-specific details, such as the options available to configure a VM. Raising the abstraction higher (so you don't need to deal with VMs) can overcome some of these differences but in return increases complexity.
- Most *failure scenarios break the abstraction*[4]. If something goes wrong underneath—let's say your on premises network environment is flooded or faces other issues—the abstraction can't shield you from having to dive into that environment to diagnose and remedy the problem.
- The abstraction likely doesn't cover all your applications' needs. For example, Kubernetes primarily focuses on compute workloads. If you use a managed database service such as DynamoDB, which might be a great convenience for your application, this dependency resides outside the common abstraction layer.
- The abstraction only works for applications that respect it. For example, Kubernetes assumes that your application is designed to operate in a container environment, which may be suboptimal or not possible for traditional applications. If you end up having multiple abstractions for different types of applications, things get a lot more complicated.
- Using such an abstraction layer likely *locks you into a specific product* (Chapter 21). So, while you can perhaps change cloud providers more

[2]https://en.wikipedia.org/wiki/Remote_procedure_call
[3]https://www.enterpriseintegrationpatterns.com/patterns/messaging/EncapsulatedSynchronousIntegration.html
[4]https://architectelevator.com/architecture/failure-doesnt-respect-abstraction/

easily, changing to a different abstraction or removing it altogether will be very difficult. For most enterprise users, VMware comes to mind. An open-source abstraction reduces this concern somewhat, but certainly doesn't eliminate it. You are still tied to the abstraction's APIs and you won't be able to just fork it and operate it on your own.

 A common abstraction resembles Esperanto. Intellectually appealing but unlikely to gain broad traction because it's an additional burden for folks already speaking their native language.

I label this approach the Esperanto[5] ideal. It's surely intellectually appealing—wouldn't it be nice if we all spoke the same language? However, just like Esperanto, broad adoption is unlikely because it requires each person to learn yet another language and they won't be able to express themselves as well as in their native language. And sufficiently many people speak English, anyway.

2. Copy the Cloud to Your Premises

If you feel like your cloud is good as it is and you don't want to place a whole new abstraction layer on top of it, a natural idea is to have the vendor bring the cloud to your corporate data center:

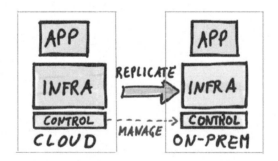

Replicating the cloud on premises

Once you have a carbon copy of your cloud on premises, you can shift applications back and forth or perhaps even split them across cloud and on premises

---

[5]https://en.wikipedia.org/wiki/Esperanto

without much additional complexity. You can then connect the on-premises cloud to the original cloud's control plane and manage it just like any other cloud region. That's pretty handy.

Different flavors of this option vary in how the cloud will be set up on your premises. Some solutions are fully integrated as a hardware/software solution, whereas others are software stacks to be deployed on third-party hardware.

The best-known products following this approach are AWS Outposts[6], which delivers custom hardware to your premises, and Azure Stack[7], a software solution that's bundled with certified third-party vendors' hardware. In both cases, you essentially receive a shipment of a rack to be installed in your data center. Once connected, you have a cloud on premises! At least that's what the brochures claim.

Advantages

Again, this approach has some nice benefits:

- You can get a true-to-the-original experience on premises. For example, if you know AWS or Azure well, you don't need to relearn a whole new environment just to operate on premises.
- Because vendor hardware is deployed on your premises, you benefit from the same custom hardware that's available only to hyperscalers. For example, servers may include custom security modules or the rack might have an optimized power supply that powers all servers, rendering it a rack-size blade[8].
- You can get a fully certified and optimized stack that assures that what runs in the cloud will also run on premises. In contrast, the abstraction layer approach runs the risk of a disconnect between the abstraction and the underlying infrastructure.
- You don't need to do a lot—the cloud comes to you in a fully integrated package that essentially needs only power and networking.

Considerations

Of course, we need to keep a few things in mind, also:

[6]https://aws.amazon.com/outposts/
[7]https://azure.microsoft.com/en-in/overview/azure-stack/
[8]https://en.wikipedia.org/wiki/Blade_server

- Not all cloud services can meaningfully scale down to an on-premises setup that's orders of magnitudes smaller than a commercial cloud data center. On premises, you might have a physical capacity of a handful of racks, which won't work for services like BigTable or RedShift. So, the services offered won't be exactly identical in the respective environments.
- Shipping custom hardware might make it difficult to update on-premises systems, especially given the rapid pace of evolution on cloud services. Also, most enterprises will have stringent validation processes before they allow any hardware, especially a new kind, into their data centers.
- To achieve unified management, the on-premises appliances will connect back ("phone home") to the cloud provider. Hence, this solution doesn't provide a strict isolation between the cloud provider and your on-premises systems. Given that isolation is a key driver for keeping applications and data on premises in the first place, this aspect can be a show stopper for some enterprises. You're relying on the internal segregation between the cloud appliance's control plane and the user plane where your applications and data reside.
- Bringing a vendor's cloud to your premises means that you increase your commitment, and hence the potential lock-in, with that vendor. This might be okay for you if you've already considered the *Return on Lock-in* (Chapter 21), but it's still something to factor in. To counterbalance, you could place a common abstraction layer on top of the environments; for example, by running managed Kubernetes in your on-premises cloud environment. But that'll invite some of the limitations from approach #1 back in.
- Just like the other approaches, bringing a cloud appliance on premises can't overcome some of the inherent limitations of the on-premises environments, such as limited hardware and network capacity.

3. Copy On Premises to the Cloud

If one can bring the cloud to your premises, one can also consider bringing your on-premises systems to the cloud. Although such an approach might seem unusual at first, it does make sense if you consider that many traditional applications won't easily run in the "regular" cloud. Replicating your on-premises environment in the cloud therefore eases "as-is" migration—a welcome option when you need to vacate your existing data center before an upcoming contract renewal.

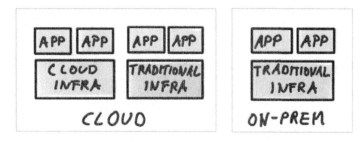

Replicating on premises in the cloud

A popular example of this approach is AWS' VMware Cloud, which allows you to migrate VMs straight from vCenter and, for example, supports operating systems that aren't offered in EC2.

Some might debate whether this approach counts as "hybrid cloud" or whether it's closer to "hybrid virtualization" because you're not operating in a cloud-optimized model but might just copy the old way of working into the cloud data center. Still, as an intermediate step or when you're close to shutting down an on-premises data center, it can be a viable option.

4. Make On Premises Look Like the Cloud

Lastly, rather than bringing a whole new abstraction or even custom hardware into your data center, why not take what you have and give it a cloud-compatible API? Then, you could interact with your on-premises environment the same way you do with the cloud without tossing everything you have on premises.

Naturally, this approach makes most sense if you're heavily invested in an existing on-premises infrastructure that you're not prepared to let go anytime soon. The most common starting point for this approach is VMware's ESX virtualization, which is widely used in enterprises. VMware is planning to support Kubernetes on this platform via *Project Pacific*[9], which embeds Kubernetes into vSphere's control plane to manage VMs and containers alike.

---

[9]https://www.vmware.com/products/vsphere/projectpacific.html

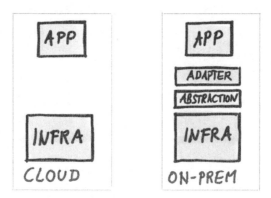

Making on premises look like the cloud

Questions to Ask

The good news is that different vendors have packaged the presented solutions into product offerings. Understanding the relevant decisions behind each approach and the embedded trade-offs allows you to select the right solution for your needs. Based on the prior discussions, here's a list of questions you might want to ask vendors offering products based on the listed approaches:

1. Define a Shared Abstraction Layer

- To what extent does the abstraction address non-compute services such as databases or machine learning?
- How are you expecting to keep up with several major cloud providers' pace of innovation?
- What underlying infrastructure is needed on premises to support the abstraction?
- Why do you believe that a common abstraction works well across two very different environments?
- How would you minimize lock-in into your abstraction layer? Which parts aren't open source?

2. Copy the Cloud to Your Premises

- What service coverage does the on-premises solution provide compared to the cloud?

- What are your environmental requirements, e.g., power and cooling density?
- How can we monitor the traffic back to your control plane to make sure our data doesn't leak out?
- To what extent will the solution run while being detached from the control plane?
- What are the legal and liability implications of bringing your solution to our data center?

3. Copy On Premises to the Cloud

- How well is the solution integrated into your cloud?
- What's the minimum sizing at which this solution is viable?
- What's the best path forward for migration; in other words, how much easier is it to migrate from this solution as opposed to from on premises?

4. Make On Premises Look Like the Cloud

- How does your solution compare to the ones mentioned in approach #1?
- Won't adding yet another layer further increase complexity?
- How are you keeping pace with the rapid evolution of the open-source frameworks you are embedding?

Asking such questions might not make you new friends on the vendor side, but it will surely help you make a more informed decision.

Additional Considerations

Deploying and operating workloads aren't the only elements for a hybrid cloud. At a minimum, the following dimensions come into play, also:

Identity and Access Management

A key element of cloud is to manage, enable, and restrict access to compute resources and their configurations. If you are looking to unify management across on-premises and cloud environments, you'll also want to integrate identity and access management, meaning that developers and administrators use the same user name and authentication methods and receive similar privileges.

Monitoring

If you have applications that spread across on premises and the cloud, you'd want to have consistent monitoring across environments. Otherwise, when you encounter an operational issue, you might have to chase down the source of the problem in different monitoring tools, which may make it difficult to correlate events across the whole environment.

Deployment

Ideally, you'd be able to deploy applications to the cloud and on premises in a uniform way. If you have the same run-time environment available in both environments, harmonized deployment is greatly simplified. Otherwise, a uniform continuous build and integration (CI) pipeline coupled with several deployment options allows you to minimize the diversity.

Data Synchronization

Lastly, being able to manage workloads uniformly isn't sufficient, because all your applications also need access to data. For new applications, you might be able to abstract data access via common APIs, but most commercial or legacy applications won't easily support such an approach. A variety of tools promise to simplify data access across the cloud and on premises. For example, the AWS Storage Gateway[10] allows you to access cloud storage from your premises while solutions like NetApp SnapMirror enable data replication.

Plotting a Path

So, once again, there's a lot more behind a simple buzzword and the associated products. Because each vendor tends to tell the story from its point of view—which is to be expected—it's up to us architects to "zoom out" to see the bigger picture without omitting relevant technical decisions. Making the trade-offs inherent in the different approaches visible to decision makers across the entire organization is the architect's responsibility. Because otherwise there'll be surprises later on, and one thing we have learned in IT is that there are no good surprises.

---

[10]https://aws.amazon.com/storagegateway/features

21. Don't Get Locked Up Into Avoiding Lock-In

Architecture isn't binary.[1]

An architect's main job is often seen as avoiding being locked into a specific technology or solution. That's not a huge surprise: wouldn't it be nice if you could easily migrate from one database to another or from one cloud provider to another in case the product no longer meets your needs or another vendor offers you favorable commercial terms? However, lock-in isn't a true-or-false situation. And while reducing lock-in surely is desirable, it also comes at a cost. Let's develop some decision models that will keep your cloud strategy from getting locked up into trying to avoid lock-in.

Architecture Creates Options

One of an architect's major objectives is to create options[2]. Options allow you to postpone decisions into the future, at known parameters. For example, the option to scale out an application allows you to add compute capacity at any time. Applications built without this option require hardware sizing up front. Options are valuable because they allow you to defer a decision until more information (e.g., the application workload) is available as opposed to having to make a best guess at the very beginning. Options, hence, make a system change tolerant: when needed, you can exercise the option without having to rebuild the system. Lock-in does the opposite: once decided, it makes switching from the selected solution to another difficult or expensive.

Many architects may therefore consider lock-in their archenemy during their noble quest to protect IT's freedom of choice in face of uncertainty. Sadly,

---

[1]This article is an adaptation of my original article posted to Martin Fowler's website: https://martinfowler.com/articles/oss-lockin.html

[2]https://architectelevator.com/architecture/architecture-options/

architecture isn't that simple—it's a business of trade-offs. Thus, experienced architects have a more nuanced view on lock-in:

- First, architects realize that lock-in isn't binary: you're always going to be locked into some things to some degree—and that's OK.
- Second, you can avoid lock-in by creating options, but those options have a cost, not only in money, but also in complexity or, worse yet, new lock-in.
- Lastly, architects need to peek behind common associations; for example, open-source software supposedly making you free of lock-in.

At the same time, there's hardly an IT department that hasn't been held captive by vendors who knew that migrating off their solutions is difficult. Therefore, wanting to minimize lock-in is an understandable desire. No one wants to get fooled twice. Alas, folks trying to avoid any kind of commitment are bound to fall victim to *Gregor's First Law of Architecture*:

 Excessive complexity is nature's punishment for organizations that are unable to make decisions.

So, let's see how to best balance lock-in when defining a cloud strategy.

One Cloud, Please, but with Lock-In on the Side!

Cloud folks talk a lot about lock-in these days: all the conveniences that cloud platforms bring us appear to be coming at the expense of being locked into a specific platform. A cure is said to be readily available in the form of *hybrid-multi-cloud abstractions* (Chapter 18). Such solutions might give us more options, but they also bring additional complexity and constraints.

Deploying applications used to be fairly simple. Nowadays, things seem to be more complicated with a multitude of choices. For modern applications, deploying in *containers* (Chapter 25) is one obvious route, unless you're perhaps aiming straight for *serverless* (Chapter 26). Containers sound good, but should you use AWS' Elastic Container Service (ECS) to run them? It integrates well with the platform but it's a proprietary service, specific to Amazon's cloud. So, you may prefer Kubernetes. It's open source and runs on most environments, including on premises. Problem solved? Not quite: now you are tied to Kubernetes—think of all those precious YAML files you'll be writing! So you traded one lock-in for another, didn't you? And if you use a managed Kubernetes services such as Amazon's Elastic Kubernetes Service (EKS), Azure's Kubernetes Service (AKS), or Google's Kubernetes Engine (GKE), it may also tie you to a specific version of Kubernetes and proprietary extensions.

If you need your software to run on premises, you could also opt for AWS Outposts[3] and run your ECS there, so you do have that option. But that again is based on proprietary hardware, which could be an advantage or a liability. Or over on the Kubernetes route, you could deploy GKE on your premises. That in turn is installed on top of VMware, which is also proprietary and hence locks you in. However, more likely than not, you're already locked into that one and have little motivation to switch, so does it really make a difference? Or you could try to make all of these concerns go away with Google's Anthos, which is largely built from open-source components, including GKE. Nevertheless, it's a proprietary offering: you can move applications to different clouds—as long as you keep using Anthos. Now that's the very definition of lock-in, isn't it?

Taking a whole different angle, if you neatly separate your deployment automation from your application run time, doesn't that make it much easier to switch infrastructures, mitigating the effect of all that lock-in? Hey, there are even cross-platform Infrastructure as Code (IaC) tools. Aren't those supposed to help make some of these concerns go away altogether?

It looks like avoiding cloud lock-in isn't quite so easy and might even get you locked up into trying to escape from it. Therefore, we need an architecture point of view so that our cloud strategy doesn't get derailed by unqualified fear of lock-in.

Shades of Lock-In

As we have seen, lock-in isn't a binary property that has you either locked in or not. Actually, lock-in comes in more flavors than you might have expected:

Vendor lock-in
This is the kind that IT folks generally mean when they mention "lock-in".

---

[3]https://aws.amazon.com/outposts/

It describes the difficulty of switching from one vendor to a competitor. For example, if migrating from Siebel CRM to Salesforce CRM or from an IBM DB2 database to an Oracle one will cost you an arm and a leg, you are "locked in". This type of lock-in is common as vendors generally (more or less visibly) benefit from it. It can also come in the form of commercial arrangements, such as long-term licensing and support agreements that earned you a discount off the license fees back then.

Product lock-in

Related, although different nevertheless is being locked into a product. Open-source products may avoid the vendor lock-in, but they don't remove product lock-in: if you are using Kubernetes or Cassandra, you are certainly locked into a specific product's APIs, configurations, and features. If you work in a professional (and especially enterprise) environment, you will also need commercial support, which will again lock you into a vendor contract—see above. Heavy customization, integration points, and proprietary extensions are forms of product lock-in: they make it difficult to switch to another product, even if it's open source.

Version lock-in

You may even be locked into a specific product version. Version upgrades can be costly if they break existing customizations and extensions you have built. Some version upgrades might even require you to rewrite your application—AngularJS vs. Angular 2 comes to mind. You feel this lock-in particularly badly when a vendor decides to deprecate your version or discontinues the whole product line, forcing you to choose between being out of support or doing a major overhaul.

Architecture lock-in

You can also be locked into a specific kind of architecture. Sticking with the Kubernetes example, you are likely structuring your application into services along domain context boundaries, having them communicate via APIs. If you wanted to migrate to a serverless platform, you'd want your services finer-grained, externalize state management, and have them connected via events, among other changes. These aren't minor adjustments, but a major overhaul of your application architecture. That's going to cost you, so once again you're locked in.

Platform lock-in

A special flavor of product lock-in is being locked into a platform, such as our cloud platforms. Such platforms not only run your applications, but they also hold your user accounts and associated access rights, security policies, network segmentations, and trained machine learning models. Also, these platforms usually hold your data, leading to *data gravity*. All of these make switching platforms harder.

Skills lock-in

Not all lock-in is on the technical side. As your developers are becoming familiar with a certain product or architecture, you'll have skills lock-in: it will take you time to retrain (or hire) developers for a different product or technology. With skills availability being one of the major constraints in today's IT environment, this type of lock-in is very real.

Legal lock-in

You might be locked into a specific solution for legal reasons, such as compliance. For example, you might not be able to migrate your data to another cloud provider's data center if it's located outside your country. Your software provider's license might also not allow you to move your systems to the cloud even though they'd run perfectly fine. As I said, lock-in comes in many flavors.

Mental lock-in

The most subtle and most dangerous type of lock-in is the one that affects your thinking. After working with a certain set of vendors and architectures, you'll unconsciously absorb assumptions into your decision making. These assumptions can lead you to reject viable alternative options. For example, you might reject scale-out architectures as inefficient because they don't scale linearly (you don't get twice the performance when doubling the hardware). Even though it is technically accurate, this way of thinking ignores the fact that in the internet age, scalability trumps local efficiency.

So, the next time someone speaks about lock-in, you can ask them which of these eight dimensions they are referring to. While most of our computers work in a binary system, architecture does not.

Accepted Lock-In

Although we typically aren't looking for more lock-in, we might be inclined, and well advised, to accept some level of lock-in. Adrian Cockcroft of AWS is famous for starting his talks by asking who in the audience is worried about lock-in. While looking at the many raised hands, he follows up by asking who is married. Not many hands go down as the expression on people's faces suddenly turns more contemplative.

Apparently, there are some benefits to being locked in, at least if the lock-in is mutual. And back in technology, many of my friends are fairly happily locked into an Apple iOS ecosystem because they appreciate the seamless integration across services and devices.

 You will likely accept some lock-in in return for the benefits you receive.

Back in corporate IT, some components might lock you into a specific product or vendor, but in return give you a unique feature that provides a tangible benefit for your business. While we generally prefer less lock-in, this trade-off might well be acceptable. For example, you may happily and productively use a product like Google Cloud Spanner or AWS Bare Metal Instances. The same holds for other native cloud services that are better integrated than many cross-cloud alternatives. If a migration is unlikely, you might be happy to make that trade-off.

On the commercial side, being a heavy user of one vendor's products might allow you to negotiate favorable terms. Or as a major customer you might be able to exert influence over the vendor's product roadmap, which in some sense, and somewhat ironically, reduces the severity of your lock-in: being able to steer the products you're using gives you fewer reasons to switch. We often describe such a mutual lock-in as a "partnership", which is generally considered a good thing.

In all these situations, you realize that you are locked in and decided to be so based on a conscious decision that yielded a positive "ROL"—your *Return On Lock-In*. It actually demonstrates a more balanced architecture strategy than just proclaiming that "lock-in is evil". Architecture isn't a Hollywood movie in which good battles evil. Rather, it's an engaging murder mystery with many twists and turns.

The Cost of Reducing Lock-In

Even though lock-in isn't the root of all evil, reducing it is still generally desirable. However, doing so comes as a cost—there are no free lunches in architecture (even those "free" vendor lunches come at a price). Although we often think of cost in terms of dollars, the cost of reducing lock-in also comes in a bigger variety of flavors than we might have thought:

Effort
> This is the additional work to be done in terms of person-hours. If you opt to deploy in containers on top of Kubernetes to reduce cloud provider lock-in, this item would include the effort to learn new concepts, write Docker files, and get the spaces lined up in your YAML files.

Expense
> This is the additional cash expense; for example, for product or support licenses, to hire external providers, or to attend KubeCon. It can also include operational costs if wanting to be portable requires you to operate your own service instead of utilizing a cloud-provider-managed one. I have seen cost differences of several orders of magnitude in the case of secrets management.

Underutilization
> This cost is indirect but can be significant. Reduced lock-in often comes in the form of an *abstraction layer* (Chapter 20) across multiple products or platforms. However, such a layer may not provide feature parity with the underlying platforms, either because it's lagging behind or because it won't fit the abstraction. In a bad case, the layer may be the lowest common denominator across all supported products and may prevent you from using vendor-specific features. This in turn means that you get less utility out of the software you use and pay for. If it's an important platform feature that the abstraction layer doesn't support, the cost can be high.

Complexity
> Complexity is another often underestimated cost in IT, but one of the most severe ones. Adding an abstraction layer increases complexity because there's yet another component with new concepts and new constraints. IT routinely suffers from excessive complexity, which drives up cost and reduces velocity due to new learning curves. It can also hurt system availability because complex systems are harder to diagnose and prone

to systemic failures. While you can absorb monetary cost with bigger budgets, reducing excessive complexity is very hard—it often leads to even more complexity. It's so much easier to keep adding stuff than taking it away.

New lock-ins

Lastly, avoiding one lock-in often comes at the expense of another one. For example, you may opt to avoid AWS CloudFormation[4] and instead use Hashicorp's Terraform[5] or Pulumi[6], both of which are great products and support multiple cloud providers. However, now you are tied to another product from an additional vendor and need to figure out whether that's okay for you. Similarly, most multicloud frameworks promise to let you move workloads across cloud providers but lock you into the framework. You'll need to decide which form of lock-in concerns you more.

The Real Enemies: Complexity and Underutilization

So, the cost of reducing lock-in isn't just very real but comes in many forms. Out of this list, underutilization and complexity should concern architects the most because they are both severe and most often overlooked. Both stem from the fact that a reduction in lock-in is often achieved by adding another layer on top of existing tools and platforms.

 Complexity and underutilization can be the biggest but least obvious price you pay for reducing lock-in.

For example, not being able to take advantage of DynamoDB or Cloud Spanner because you want your solution to be portable across clouds bears a real, concrete cost of reduced features or value delivered. You're paying with underutilization: a feature or product is available, but you're not using it.

The cost of not being able to use a feature is real and incurred right now, whereas the potential return in reduced switching cost is deferred and hypothetical. It's

---

[4]https://aws.amazon.com/cloudformation/
[5]https://www.terraform.io/"
[6]https://www.pulumi.com/

realized only when a full migration is needed. If your product fails in the market because avoiding a specific service led to poor performance or a delayed launch, the option of a later migration will be worthless because your product won't be around. That's why ThoughtWorks' widely respected Technology Radar[7] designated *Generic Cloud Usage* as *Hold* already in late 2018. Reducing lock-in is a delicate decision that's certainly not binary.

 You bear the cost of the option, such as increased complexity or underutilization, today. The payoff in form of flexibility gained comes only in the future and is limited to specific scenarios.

The cost in terms of complexity is incurred due to the addition of yet another layer of abstraction, such as JDBC (Java Database Connectivity) connectors, container orchestration, and common APIs. While all these are useful tools, such layers add more moving parts, increasing the overall system complexity. A quick look at the Cloud Native Computing Foundation's product landscape[8] illustrates this complexity vividly. The complexity increases the learning effort for new team members, makes debugging more difficult, and increases the chance of systemic errors.

Not all abstractions are troublesome, though. Some layers of abstraction can greatly simplify things: most developers are happy to read from byte streams instead of individual disk blocks. Such abstractions can work for narrow interfaces, but rarely across broad platforms, and especially those from competing vendors. The industry standard graveyard is littered with such attempts—remember SCA[9]? And, even though abstraction may shield you from some complexity during happy times, it's well known that *Failure Doesn't Respect Abstraction*[10].

Optimal Lock-in

With both being locked-in and avoiding it carrying a cost, it's the architect's job to balance the two and perhaps find the sweet spot. We might even say that this sums up the essence of the architect's job: dismantle the buzzwords, identify the

---

[7]https://www.thoughtworks.com/radar/techniques/generic-cloud-usage
[8]https://landscape.cncf.io/
[9]https://en.wikipedia.org/wiki/Service_Component_Architecture
[10]https://architectelevator.com/architecture/failure-doesnt-respect-abstraction/

real drivers, translate them into an economic risk model, and then find the best spot for the given business context.

 It's the architect's job to dismantle the buzzwords, identify the real drivers, translate them into an economic/risk model, and then find the best spot for the given business context.

Sometimes you can find ways to reduce lock-in at low (overall) cost; for example, by using an Object-Relational Mapping (ORM) framework like Hibernate[11] that increases developer productivity and reduces database vendor lock-in at the same time. Those opportunities don't require a lot of deliberation and should just be done. However, other decisions might deserve a second, or even third look.

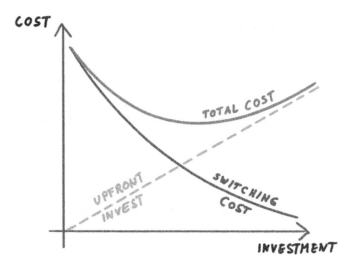

The total cost of lock-in

To find the optimal degree of lock-in, you need to sum up two cost elements (see preceding graph):

1. The expected cost of lock-in, measured by the chance of needing to switch multiplied by the cost in case it happens (blue curve going down)
2. The up-front investment required to reduce lock-in (dashed green line)

---

[11]https://hibernate.org/orm/

In the world of financial options, the first element is considered the option's strike price; that is, the price to pay when you exercise the option you hold. The second will be the price of the option itself; in other words, how much you pay for acquiring the option. The fact that Messrs. Black and Scholes received a Nobel prize in Economics[12] for option pricing tells us that this is not a simple equation to solve. However, you can imagine that the prize of the option increases with a reduced strike price—the easier you want the later switch to be, the more you need to prepare right now.

For us, the relevant curve is the red line (labeled "total"), which tracks the sum of both costs. Without any complex formulas, we can easily see that minimizing switching cost isn't the most economical choice, because it will drive up your up-front investment for diminishing returns.

Let's take a simple example. Many architects favor not being locked into a specific cloud provider. How much would it cost to migrate your application from the current provider to another one? You'd need to re-code automation scripts, change code that accesses proprietary services, and so on. $100,000? That's a reasonable chunk of money for a small-to-medium application. Next, you'll need to consider the likelihood of needing to switch clouds over the application's lifespan. Maybe 5%, or perhaps even lower? Now, how much would it cost you to bring that switching cost down to near zero? Perhaps a lot more than the $5,000 ($100,000 x 5%) you are expected to save, making it a poor economic choice. Could you amortize the up-front investment across many applications? Perhaps, but a significant portion of the costs would also multiply.

 Minimizing switching cost won't be the most economical choice for most enterprises. It's like being over-insured.

A well-greased CI/CD pipeline and automated testing will drastically reduce your switching cost, perhaps by half. Now the expected cost of switching is only $2,500. Note that building the CI/CD pipeline doesn't equate to buying an option—it's a mechanism that helps you right here and now to release higher-quality software at lower cost every time.

Therefore, minimizing the switching cost isn't the goal—it's about minimizing total cost. Architects that focus on switching cost alone will over-invest into re-

---

[12]https://en.wikipedia.org/wiki/Black%E2%80%93Scholes_model

duced lock-in. It's the equivalent of being over-insured: paying a huge premium to bring the deductible down to zero may give you peace of mind, but it's not the most economical, and therefore rational, choice.

Open Source and Lock-In

Lastly, a few thoughts to the common notion that using open-source software eliminates lock-in. From the many forms of lock-in that we looked at, we can see that open-source software primarily addresses a single one: vendor lock-in. Most other forms of lock-in remain. You'll still be facing architecture, product, skills, and mental lock-in, for example. That doesn't mean open source is not worth considering, but it means that it isn't the easy way out of lock-in that it's sometimes portrayed to be.

In the context of cloud, open source is often positioned as a natural path to multicloud because most open-source frameworks can be operated on all commercial clouds as well as on premises. But here we need to be careful whether open source also means that you have to operate the software yourself as opposed to subscribing to a fully managed, but perhaps proprietary, service. After all, the transformational aspect of the cloud isn't to have a database, but being able to provision one at a moment's notice, never having to deal with operations, and paying only per usage. There are efforts to offer fully managed open-source platforms across cloud providers, but those are again proprietary offerings. There are no magic answers.

The argument that open source avoids lock-in rests on the notion that "in the worst case you can pack up your software and leave your cloud provider". While this argument might hold true for the software's functionality (most vendors include proprietary "enterprise" extensions, though), it doesn't cover operational aspects. Architects know best that the non-functional aspects or "ilities" are a critical element of enterprise IT. Therefore, reverting from a managed platform (e.g., GKE/EKS/AKS for Kubernetes) back to operating the upstream open-source version yourself will eliminate virtually all operational advantages that came with the proprietary control planes. In many cases, this can amount to losing a significant portion of the overall benefit, not even considering the enormous effort involved.

Another common point regarding open source is that in principle everyone can contribute to or influence the product, much in contrast to commercial offerings that put you at the mercy of the vendor's product roadmap (which makes it important to understand the vendor's product philosophy—see "The IT World is Flat" in *37 Things*[13]). Although this is a significant benefit for community-driven projects, many "cloud-scale" open-source projects see roughly half of the contributions from a single commercial vendor, who is often also the instigator of the project and a heavy commercial supporter of the affiliated foundation. Having the development heavily influenced by that vendor's strategy might work well for you if it aligns with yours—or not, if it doesn't. So, it's up to you to decide whether you're happily married/locked-in to that project.

Although many open-source products operate across multiple cloud platforms, most can't shield us from the specifics of each cloud platform. This effect is most apparent in automation tools, such as Terraform, that give us common language syntax but can't shield us from the many vendor-specific constructs; that, is what configuration options are available for a VM. Implementation details thus "leak" through the common open-source frame. As a result, such tools reduce the switching cost from one cloud to another, because you don't have to learn a new language syntax. But they certainly don't bring it down to zero. In return, you might pay a price in feature lag between a specific platform and the abstraction layer. Solving that equation is the architect's job.

In summary, open source is a great asset for corporate IT. Without it, we wouldn't have Linux operating systems, the MySQL database, the Apache web server, the Hadoop distributed processing framework, and many other modern software amenities. There are many good reasons to be using open-source software, but it's the architect's job to look behind blanket statements and simplified associations, for example, related to lock-in.

Maneuvering Lock-In

Consciously managing lock-in is a key part of a cloud architect's role. Trying to drive potential switching costs down to zero is just as foolish as completely ignoring the topic. Some simple techniques help us reduce lock-in for little cost, whereas others just lock us into the next product or architectural layer. Open standards, especially interface standards such as open APIs, do reduce lock-in because they limit the blast radius of change.

---

[13]https://architectelevator.com/book

Lock-in has a bad reputation in enterprise, and generally rightly so. Most any enterprise has been held hostage by a product or vendor in the past. Cloud platforms are different in several aspects:

- Most cloud platform vendors aren't your typical enterprise tool vendors (the one that might have been, has transformed substantially).
- An application's dependence on a specific cloud platform isn't trivial, but it's generally less when compared with complete enterprise products like ERP or CRM software.
- A large portion of the software deployed in the cloud will be custom-developed applications that are likely to have a modular structure and automated build and test cycles. This makes a potential platform switch much more digestible than trying to relocate your Salesforce APEX code or your SAP ABAP scripts.
- In the past a switch between vendors was often necessitated by severe feature disparity or price gouging. In the first decade of cloud computing, providers have repeatedly *reduced* prices and released dozens of new features each year, making such a switch less likely.

So, it's worth taking an architectural point of view on lock-in. Rather than getting locked up in it, architects need to develop skills for picking locks.

22. The End of Multitenancy?

The cloud makes us revisit past architecture assumptions.

Most architecture decisions aim to balance conflicting forces and constraints. Often we consider such architecture decisions the "long-lasting" decisions that are difficult to reverse. New technology or a new operating model, such as the cloud, can influence those constraints, though, making it worthwhile to revisit past architecture decisions. Multitenant architectures make for an excellent case study.

Multitenancy

Multitenant systems have been a common pattern in enterprise software for several decades. According to Wikipedia[1]:

> Multitenant systems are designed to provide every tenant a dedicated share of a single system instance.

The key benefit of such a multitenant system is the speed with which a new share or (logical) customer instance can be created. Because all tenants share a single system instance, no new software instances have to be deployed when a new customer arrives. Also, operations are more efficient because common services can be shared across tenants.

That's where this architectural style derives its name—an apartment building accommodates multiple tenants, so you don't need to build a new house for each new tenant. Rather, a single building efficiently houses many tenants, aided by common infrastructure like hallways and shared plumbing.

---

[1]https://en.wikipedia.org/wiki/Multitenancy

No Software!

In recent IT history, the company whose success was most directly based on a multitenant architecture was Salesforce. Salesforce employed a Software as a Service (SaaS) model for its Customer Relationship Management (CRM) software well before this term gained popularity for cloud computing platforms. Salesforce operated the software, including updates, scaling, and so on, freeing customers from having to install software on their premises.

The model, aided by an effective "no software" marketing campaign, was extremely successful. It capitalized on enterprises' experience that software takes a long time to install and *causes all sorts of problems along the way* (Chapter 13). Instead, Salesforce could sign up new customers almost instantaneously. Often the software was sold directly to the business under the (somewhat accurate) claim that it can be done without the IT department. "Somewhat", because integrations with existing systems are a significant aspect of a CRM deployment.

No software (to install)

From an architecture point of view, Salesforce ran a large database segregated by customer. The application logic would make sure all functions are executed on the current customer's data set. When a new customer purchased the CRM suite, Salesforce essentially only set up a new logical "tenant" in its system, identified by a so-called OrgID field in the database. Every so often, more hardware needed to be added to accommodate the additional data and computational demands, but that was independent from the actual customer sign-up and could be done in advance.

Tenant Challenges

Multitenant systems have apparent advantages for customers, but they pose several architectural challenges. To make a single system appear like a set of individual systems, data, configuration, and non-functional characteristics such as performance must be isolated between the tenants—people want thick walls in their apartments. This isolation introduces complexity into the application and the database schema; for example, by having to propagate the tenant's identity through the code base and database structure for each operation. Any mistake in this architecture would run the risk of exposing one tenant's data to another—a highly undesired scenario. Imagine finding your neighbor's groceries in your fridge, or worse.

Also, scaling a single system for a large number of tenants can quickly hit limits. So, despite its great properties, multitenancy, like most other architectural decisions, is a matter of trade-offs. You have to manage a more complex system for the benefit of adding customers quickly and easily. Past systems architects chose the optimum balance between the two and succeeded in the market. Now, cloud computing platforms challenge some of the base assumptions and might lead us to a new optimum. Oddly, the path to insight leads past waterfowl...

Duck Typing

The object-oriented world has a notion of *duck typing*[2], which indicates that instead of classifying an object by a single, global type hierarchy, it's classified by its observable behavior. So, instead of defining a duck as being a waterfowl, which is a bird, which in turn is part of the animal kingdom, you define a duck by its behavior: if it quacks like a duck and walks like a duck, it's considered a duck.

In software design, this means that the internal makeup or the type hierarchy of a class takes a back seat to the object's observable behavior: if an object has a method to get the current time, perhaps it's a *Clock* object, regardless of its parent class. Duck typing is concerned with whether an object can be used for a particular purpose and is less interested in an overarching ontology. Hence, it allows more degrees of freedom in system composition.

---

[2]https://en.wikipedia.org/wiki/Duck_typing

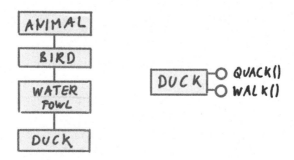

Typing via hierarchy (left) vs. duck typing (right)

Duck Architecture

It's possible to apply the same notion of typing based on behavior to large-scale system architecture, giving us a fresh take on architecture concepts like multitenancy. Traditionally, multitenancy is considered a structural property: it describes how the system was constructed; for example, by segmenting a single database and configuration for each user/tenant.

Following the "duck" logic, though, multitenancy becomes an observable property. Much like quacking like a duck, a multitenant system's key property is its ability to create new and isolated user instances virtually instantaneously. How that capability is achieved is secondary—that's up to the implementer.

 The sole purpose of a system's structure is to exhibit a desirable set of observable behaviors.

The "duck architecture" supports the notion that the sole purpose of a system's structure is to exhibit a desirable set of observable behaviors. Your customer's won't appreciate the beauty of your application architecture when that application is slow, buggy, or mostly unavailable.

Revisiting Constraints

The goal of a system's structure is to provide desirable properties. However, the structure is also influenced by a set of constraints—not everything can be implemented. Therefore, the essence of architecture is to implement the desirable properties within the given set of constraints:

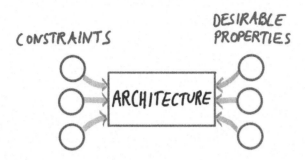

Constraints and desirable properties shape architecture

Now, certain constraints that have shaped architectural decisions in the past may have changed or disappeared. The result is that past architectural decisions can and should be revisited.

For multitenant systems, the key constraint driving the design is that deploying a new system instance is a complex and time-consuming process. Hence, if you want to give independent users near-instant access to their own logical instance, you need to build a system that's based on a single existing instance that's logically segmented into seemingly isolated instances. Such a system doesn't have to deploy a new instance for each new customer and can therefore set up new customers easily.

A secondary constraint is that having many separate system instances, each with its own hardware infrastructure, is rather inefficient. Each instance carries the overhead of an operating system, storage, monitoring, and so on, which would be duplicated many times, wasting compute and storage resources.

The Cloud Removes Constraints

We already learned that *cloud computing isn't just an infrastructure topic* (Chapter 12). It's as much about software delivery and automation as it is about run-time infrastructure. And this very aspect of automation is the one that allows us to reconsider multitenancy as a structural system property.

Thanks to cloud automation, deploying and configuring new system instances and databases has become much easier and quicker than in the past. A system can therefore exhibit the properties of a multitenant system without being architected like one. The system would simply create *actual* new instances for each tenant instead of hosting all tenants in a single system. It can thus avoid the complexity of a multitenant architecture but retain the benefits. So, it behaves like a multitenant system (remember the duck?) without incorporating the structural property.

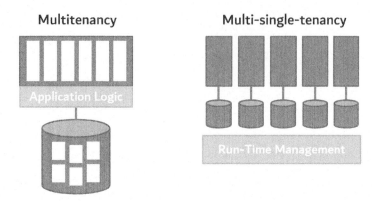

Multitenancy vs. multi-single-tenancy

Additionally, container and lightweight VM technologies significantly reduce the overhead associated with each individual instance because they don't duplicate the complete operating system each time.

But what about the operational complexity of managing all these instances? Container orchestration tools like Kubernetes are designed to help operate and manage large numbers of container instances, including automated restarts, workload management, traffic routing, and so on. It's not uncommon to run several thousand container instances on a large Kubernetes cluster.

In combination, this means that cloud automation and containers allow a traditional system with a multitenant architecture to be replaced with what we can call a *multi-single-tenant system*. This system exhibits comparable properties but follows a much simpler application architecture by relying on a more powerful run-time infrastructure.

 A multi-single-tenant system exhibits the behavior of a multi-tenant system without the complexities of building one. It simplifies the application architecture thanks to a more powerful run-time infrastructure.

Under the covers, a cloud provider ultimately implements a typical multitenant design, for example by isolating clients sharing the same physical server. Luckily that complexity has been absorbed by the cloud provider so there's no reason for us to reinvent it for each application, vastly simplifying our application logic. While in many cases we shift responsibilities *up the stack* (Chapter 12), in this case we're lucky enough to be able to push them down.

Efficient Single Family Homes

To stretch the building metaphor from the beginning of this chapter a bit, cloud computing allows us to move away from apartment buildings into easily replicated and efficient single-family homes: they are easier to build and each tenant gets its own building. Luckily we can do this quite efficiently in cloud computing as compared to the real world, so we don't have to worry about urban sprawl.

23. The New "ility": Disposability

When it comes to servers, we don't recycle.

Tossing servers may cost you—or not

Architects are said to focus on the so-called "ilities", a system's non-functional requirements. Classic examples include availability, scalability, maintainability, and portability. Cloud and automation add a new "ility", *disposability.*

Speeding Up Is More Than Going Faster

As discussed earlier, the cloud isn't just about replacing your existing infrastructure, but more so about speeding up software delivery to successfully compete in *Economies of Speed* (Chapter 2). One of the key mechanisms to achieve speed is automation—things that are automated can be done faster than by hand. Getting things done faster is definitely useful—I haven't heard a business complain that their IT delivers too quickly.

However, if things can be done a lot faster, you can do more than just be quicker. You can start to work in a fundamentally different model, as long as you also change the way you think about things. Handling servers is a great example.

Software development doesn't have a lot of tangible assets, making servers the most visible IT asset: they're big metal boxes with many blinking lights that cost a good chunk of money. So, it's natural that we want to treat them well and use them for as long as possible.

  Servers aren't assets; they're a liability.

Following our insight that the cloud is a fundamental *lifestyle change* (Chapter 1), we can rethink that assumption and come to realize that servers aren't assets—they're a liability. In fact, *no one wants one* (Chapter 12) because they're expensive, consume a lot of energy, and depreciate quickly. If a server is a liability, we should minimize the number we have. For example, if we don't need a server anymore, or need a different configuration, we should just throw it away.

Longevity Considered Harmful

Generally, we consider recycling to be a good thing because it preserves resources. I am personally a big fan of repairing old things, being particularly fond of having been able to repair my venerable Bang & Olufsen Beolab 4000 speakers (a shorted FET muted the speaker) and my 1992 Thurlby lab power supply (a potentiometer went out and cut the current limiter to zero).

So, it's no surprise that we apply the same thought to servers: we use them over and over again, thanks to a little patching and new software being installed. Such behavior leads to the well-known notion of a "pet server", which is pampered like a favorite pet, possibly even has a cute name, and is expected to live a long and happy life.

Actually, in my opinion the "pet" metaphor doesn't quite hold. I have seen many servers that had a bit of space left being (ab-)used as a mail or DHCP server, development machine, experimentation ground, or whatever else came to developers' minds. So, some of those servers, while enjoying a long life, might resemble a pack mule more than a cute bunny. And, in case there's any doubt, Urban Dictionary confirms[1] that mule skinners and bosses alike take good care of their pack mules.

Automation allows us to reconsider this tendency to prolong a server's life. If setting up a new server is fast and pain-free, and tearing one down means we don't have to pay for it anymore, we might not have to hold on to our favorite server until death do us part. Instead, we are happy to throw (virtual) servers away and provision new ones as we see the need.

 Disposing of servers is sometimes also referred to as the "cattle" model, suggesting that sick animals be shot instead of being pampered like a pet. As a devout vegetarian, I am not so fond of metaphors that involve killing, so I prefer to stick with servers and suggest the term *disposability*.

Automation and related practices such as software-defined infrastructure allow us to trade longevity in favor of *disposability*—a measure of how easily we can throw something away and re-create it, in our case servers.

Throwing Away Servers for Good

Changing our attitude to favor disposability gives us several benefits, most important among them being consistency, transparency, and less stress.

Consistency

If servers are long-lived elements that are individually and manually maintained, they're bound to be unique. Each server will have slightly different software and versions thereof installed, which is a great way of building a test laboratory. It's not that great for production environments, where security and

---

[1]https://www.urbandictionary.com/define.php?term=pack%20mule

rapid troubleshooting are important. Unique servers are sometimes referred to as *snowflakes*, playing off the fact that each one of them is unique.

Disposing and re-creating servers vastly increases the chances that servers are in a consistent state based on common automation scripts or so-called *golden images*. It works best if developers and operations staff refrain from manually updating servers, except perhaps in emergency situations. In IT jargon, not updating servers makes them *immutable* and avoids *configuration drift*.

Disposing and re-creating your systems from scripts has another massive advantage: it assures that you are always in a well-defined, clean state. Whereas a developer who "just needed to make that small fix" is annoying, a malware infection is far more serious. So, disposability makes your environment not only more consistent, but also consistently clean and, therefore, safe.

Transparency

One of the main hindrances in traditional IT is the astonishing lack of transparency. Answering simple questions like how many servers are provisioned, who owns them, what applications run on them, or what patch level they are on typically requires a mini-project that's guaranteed to yield a somewhat inaccurate or at least out-of-date answer.

Of course, enterprise software vendors stand by to happily address any of IT's ailments big or small, including this one. So, we are sure to find tools like a Configuration Management Database (CMDB) or other system management tools in most enterprises. These tools track the inventory of servers including their vital attributes, often by scanning the estate of deployed systems. The base assumption behind these tools is that server provisioning occurs somehow through a convoluted and nontransparent process. Therefore, transparency has to be created in retrospect through additional, and expensive, tooling. It's a little bit like selling you a magic hoverboard that allows you to levitate back out of the corner you just painted yourself into. Cool, for sure, but not really necessary had you just planned ahead a little.

 Many IT tools are built under the assumption that servers are provisioned somehow and transparency therefore has to be created in retrospect.

The principle of disposability allows us to turn this approach around. If all servers are easily disposed of and re-created from scripts and configuration files, which are checked into a source control system, then as long as you minimize manual configuration drift, you'll inherently know how each server is configured simply by looking at the scripts that created them. That's a different and much simpler way to gain transparency *a priori* as opposed to trying to reverse engineer reality in retrospect.

Transparency via detection (left) vs. inherent transparency (right)

Isn't creating such scripts labor intensive? Surely, the first ones will have an additional learning curve, but the more you minimize diversity, the more you can reuse the same scripts and thus win twice. Once you factor in the cost of procuring, installing, and operating a CMDB or similar tools, you're bound to have the budget to develop many more scripts than the tool vendors would want you to believe.

Less Stress

Lastly, if you want to know whether a team embraced disposability as one of its guiding principles, there's a simple test. Ask team members what happens if one of their servers dies (not assuming any data loss, but a loss of all software and configuration installed on it). The fewer tissue packs are needed (or expletives yelled) in response to such a scenario, the closer the team is to accepting disposability as a new -ility.

If their systems are disposable, one of them keeling over isn't anything unexpected or dramatic—it becomes routine. Therefore, disposability is also a stress reducer for the teams. And with all the demands on software delivery, any reduction in stress is highly welcome.

Better Life with Less Recycling (in IT Only!)

As a result, life with disposable resources is not only less stressful, but also makes for a better operational model. And if we're worried about environmental impact, disposing servers in IT is 100% environmentally acceptable—it's all just bits and bytes[2]! So, go on and toss some servers!

---

[2]In reality, each IT operation also has an environmental cost due to energy consumption and associated cooling cost. In the big scheme of IT operations, server provisioning is likely a negligible fraction.

Part V: Building (for) the Cloud

The cloud is a platform on which you deploy applications. Unlike traditional setups in which application and infrastructure were fairly isolated and often *managed by different teams* (Chapter 7), cloud applications and the associated tooling interact closely with their environment. For example, platforms that offer resilient operations usually require applications to be automatically deployable. Similarly, serverless platforms expect applications to externalize their state and be short lived. So, when we talk about cloud platforms, we should also talk about building applications.

Application Complexity Increases

Although cloud gives applications amazing capabilities like resilience, autoscaling, auto-healing, and updates without downtime, it has also made application delivery more complex. Listening to modern application developers speak about green/blue deploys, NoOps, NewOps, post-DevOps, FinOps, DevSecOps, YAML indentation, Kubernetes operators, service meshes, HATEOAS, microservices, microkernels, split brains, or declarative vs. procedural IaC might make you feel like application delivery was invaded by aliens speaking a new intergalactic language.

Many of these mechanisms have a viable purpose and represent major progress in the way we build and deliver software. Still, the tools that bring us such great capabilities have also caused a jargon proliferation like we haven't seen since the days when database column names were limited to six characters. Explaining these many tools and techniques with intuitive models instead of jargon will help us understand cloud's implications on application design and delivery.

Removing Constraints Impacts Architecture

The *environment's constraints* (Chapter 22) shapes the structure of applications. For example, if deploying software is difficult, you'd lean toward deploying a large piece of software once. Likewise, if communications are very slow and nontransparent, you might prefer to keep all parts together to avoid remote communication. Cloud platforms, in conjunction with modern software stacks, have reduced or eliminated many such constraints and hence enabled new kinds of software application architecture to emerge. Microservices, likely the most well-known example, became popular because lower run-time overhead and advances in software deployment made dividing applications into smaller components practical. Understanding such architectural shifts helps lay out a path for application evolution on the cloud.

Platforms Expand and Contract

Platforms to improve application delivery have existed for quite a while. For example, PaaS (Platform as a Service) products simplified application deployment with prefabricated build packs that included common dependencies. However, most of these platforms were designed as "black boxes" that didn't easily support replacing individual components. After plateauing for a while, the pace of innovation picked up again, this time favoring loose collections of tools, such as the Kubernetes ecosystem. Shifting toward sets of tools allows components to evolve independently but usually leaves the end user with the complexity of assembling all the bits and pieces into a working whole.

 I have seen projects where the build and deployment system became more complex than the application itself.

Over time, as approaches stabilize, we can expect platforms to again become more prescriptive, or "opinionated" in modern IT vernacular, and hence better integrated. Anticipating such platform cycles can help us make better IT investment decisions.

Applications for the Cloud

Many existing resources describe how applications should be built for the cloud. This part in the book isn't intended to be an application development guide but rather looks at those aspects of application development and delivery that directly relate to cloud platforms:

- An *application-centric cloud* (Chapter 24) looks very different from an infrastructure-centric one. We could say it's more flowery.
- You can't be in the cloud without containers, it seems. But what's really packed up *inside that container metaphor* (Chapter 25)?
- Serverless isn't really server-less, but perhaps it's *worry-less* (Chapter 26)?
- Many frameworks and buzzwords want to tell us what makes an application suitable to the cloud. But it can also be simple and punchy like *FROSST* (Chapter 27).
- Things break, even in the cloud. Let's *stay calm and operate on* (Chapter 28).

24. The Application-Centric Cloud

Sketching out the modern application ecosystem.

Because *no one wants a server* (Chapter 12), the cloud should make it easier to build useful applications. Applications are the part of IT that's closest to the customer and thus the essence of a so-called digital transformation. Application delivery allows organizations to innovate and differentiate. That's why rapid feature releases, application security, and reliability should be key elements of any cloud journey. However, application ecosystems have also become more complex. Models have helped us make better decisions when architecting the cloud, so let's look at a model for an application-centric view of the cloud.

Applications Differentiate

Once you realize that *running software you didn't build is a bad deal* (Chapter 13), you should make it a better deal to build software. Custom software is what gives organizations a competitive edge, delights their customers, and is the anchor of innovation. That's what's behind the shift from IT as service provider to IT as competitive differentiator. So, it behooves everyone in an IT organization to better understand the software delivery life cycle and its implications. Discussing software applications typically starts by separating software delivery (when software is being made) from operations (when software is being executed and available to end users).

The Four-Leaf Clover

Developing a strategy for an application-centric cloud needs more than just building and running software. And once again, the connection between the pieces is at least as interesting as the pieces themselves. To make building an application-centric cloud meaningful but also intuitive, we can follow a model which I dubbed the "four-leaf clover":

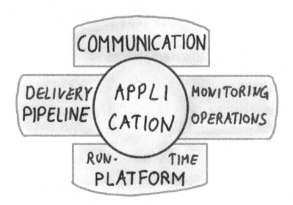

A four leaf clover represents the application ecosystem

The clover leaf appropriately places the application in the center and represents the essential ecosystem of supporting mechanisms as the four leaves. Going counterclockwise, the model contains the following leaves:

Delivery pipeline

The build, deployment, and configuration mechanisms compile and package code into deployable units and distribute them to the run-time platform. A well-oiled delivery pipeline speeds up software delivery because it constitutes a software system's *first derivative* (Chapter 2). The oil comes in the form of automation, which enables approaches like Continuous Integration (CI) and Continuous Delivery (CD).

Run-time platform

Running software needs an underlying environment that manages aspects like distributing workloads across available compute resources, triggering restarts on failure, and routing network traffic to the appropriate places. This is the land of virtualization, VMs, containers, and serverless run times.

Monitoring/operations

Once you have applications running, especially those consisting of many individual components, you're going to need a good idea of what your application is doing. For example, is it operating as expected, are there unexpected load spikes, is the infrastructure out of memory, or is CPU consumption significantly increased from the last release? Ideally, monitoring can detect symptoms before they become major problems and cause customer-visible downtime. This is the realm of log processing, time series databases, and dashboard visualizations.

Communication

Last but certainly not least, applications and services don't live in isolation. They'll need to communicate with related services, with other applications, and often with the outside world via public APIs. Such communication should take place securely (protecting both messages and participants), dynamically (e.g., to test a new version of a service), and transparently (so that you have an idea which component depends on which others). Communication is handled via API gateways, proxies, and service meshes.

Application

Of course, the center of the clover leaf holds the application (or the service). There's a good bit to say about applications' structure and behavior that makes them best suited for the cloud. That's why this book includes an entire chapter on making applications good citizens for the cloud: "*Keep Your FROSST* (Chapter 27)".

The simple model shows that there's more to a software ecosystem than just a build pipeline and run-time infrastructure. An application-centric cloud would want to include all four elements of the clover-leaf model.

Good Models Reveal Themselves

The clover leaf shares one property with most good models: it is intuitive at first sight but reveals itself upon closer inspection, much like a Rothko painting (I wish it would also fetch similar prices). Upon closer inspection, you'll find that the leaves aren't positioned arbitrarily. Rather, the elements on the leaves run along two defined axes. The horizontal axis represents the application life cycle from left to right. Hence, we find the build pipeline on the left because that's how software is "born". The run time sits in the middle, and monitoring on the right because it takes place after the software is up and running.

Good models are intuitive at first sight but reveal themselves upon closer inspection, like a Rothko painting.

The vertical axis represents the software "stack" where the lower layers indicate the run time "underneath" the application. The communications channels that connect multiple applications sit on top. So, we find that the positioning of the leaves has meaning. However, the model still makes sense without paying attention to this finer detail.

Models like this one that can be viewed at different levels of abstractions are the ones architects should strive for because they are suited to communicating with a broad audience across levels of abstraction—the essence of the *Architect Elevator*.

Diversity vs. Harmonization

Infrastructure architecture is typically driven by the quest for standardization as IT looks to limit the number of different types of servers, storage, middleware, an so on. Much of it is motivated by the pursuit of Economies of Scale—less diversity means larger purchases and bigger discounts in a traditional IT setting. The cloud's linear pricing makes this approach largely obsolete: 10 servers cost you exactly 10 times as much as one server (modest enterprise discounts aside). Harmonization also means complexity reduction, which is a worthwhile goal in any IT environment, pre- or post-cloud.

So, it's no surprise that when building an environment that places applications into the center of attention, the topic of standardization also creeps up. What to standardize and what to leave up to developers' preferences can be a hotly debated issue. After all, applications are meant to be diverse and allow for experimentation and innovation. But do you really need to use a different programming language and database for each service?

 Some Silicon Valley companies known for giving developers substantial leeway in many regards, including their outfit, are surprisingly strict when it comes to source code. For example, they strictly enforce an 80-character limit per line of code (after many months of debate, Java code was granted an exception to stretch to a dizzying 120 characters).

Many companies are looking to narrow the number of development editors, operating systems, or hardware to be used. The motivation comes again from aiming to reduce management complexity (if something breaks, it's easier to diagnose if all is the same), utilizing economies of scale (carried over from the old IT days), or security (diversity widens the attack surface).

However, equally loud are the screams from software developers feeling crippled by needless standards that *deprive them from their favorite tool* (Chapter 10). I have seen developers set up completely separate networks so that they can use their favorite online drawing tool. The unfortunate side effect was no one else being able to see the documentation containing said drawings. As is so often the case, the right approach probably lies somewhere in the middle of the two extremes. However, what's a fair or reasonable split?

Standards Have Value and Cost

Just like providing *options* (Chapter 21) has a value and a cost, the same holds true for standards. Standards can help reduce complexity, which is often an inhibitor of delivery velocity. Standards can also limit choice, meaning the best tool for the job might not be available—that's a cost. Limiting choice doesn't necessarily mean limiting creativity, though (see "A4 Paper Doesn't Stifle Creativity" in *The Software Architect Elevator*).

Architects understand that standards are not a black-or-white decision and look to balance cost and benefit. Standardizing those elements where harmonization provides a measurable value and has a justifiable cost should be highest on the list. In the context of application delivery, a common source-code repository boosts reuse and thus reduces development effort and cost. Hence, standardizing on one repository has measurable value and speeds up software delivery. Likewise, common systems monitoring can help diagnose issues more easily than having to consult many different systems and manually trying to correlate data across them.

 Standardize those elements that resemble a connecting element; that is, where harmonization improves reuse or interoperability.

As a result, I tend to favor standardizing those elements that resemble a connecting element. For example, developers should have a free choice of code editor or IDE as that's an individual decision. Diversity in these items may annoy standards committees but carries little real cost. Programming languages are somewhat of a hybrid. They are usually a team's choice, so some coordination is helpful. Services written in different languages can interact well through standard APIs, reducing the cost of diversity. However, using many different languages might impair skills reuse across teams, increasing the cost. Lastly, elements like monitoring or version control connect many different parts of the organization and thus are more valuable to standardize.

A section on standards wouldn't be complete without highlighting that standardization spans many levels of abstractions. Whereas much of traditional IT concerns itself with standardizing products, additional levels of standards can have a bigger impact on the organization. For example, relational databases can be standardized at the product level, the data model or schema level, consistent field naming conventions, and more. The following illustration compares a standardized database product with diverse schema (left) with diverse products but harmonized schema (right).

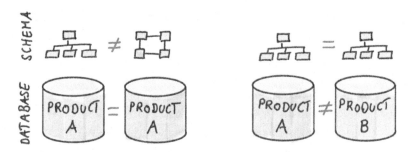

Standardizing products (left) or schemata (right)

The left side applies traditional IT thinking to reduce operational complexity; the right side is more relevant for the integration of different data sources. The left side focuses on bottom line, whereas the right side looks at top line—integration across systems is often a driver of business value plus a better user experience. Once again, we find that seemingly simple decisions have more nuances than might be initially apparent. Teasing out these subtleties is one of an architect's key value contributions.

Growing Leaves

Building an application platform for the cloud—for example, by means of an *engineering productivity team* (Chapter 7)—takes time. A common question, therefore, is in which order to grow the leaves on the clover. Although there is no universal answer, a common guideline I give is that you need to grow them somewhat evenly. That's the way nature does it—you won't find a clover that first grows one leaf to full size, then two, then three. Instead each leaf grows little by little. The same holds true for application delivery platforms. Having a stellar run-time platform but absolutely no monitoring likely isn't a great setup.

Growing the application ecosystem little by little

If I were pressed for more specific advice, building the platform in counter-clockwise circles around the clover leaf is most natural. First, you'd want to have software delivery (left) worked out. If you can't deploy software, everything else becomes unimportant. If you initially deploy on basic VMs, that's perhaps satisfactory, but soon you'd want to enhance your run time to become automated, resilient, and easily scalable (bottom). For that, you'll need better monitoring (right). Communications (top) is also important, but can probably wait until you established solid operational capabilities for the other parts (Martin Fowler's famous article reminds us that you must be this tall to use microservices[1]). From there, keep iterating to continue growing the four petals.

Pushing the Model

Once you have a good model, you can try to stretch it to reveal yet more detail without negatively impacting the initial simplicity. It won't always work but because it's hard to know without trying, it's always worth a try. Looking back at the clover after some time, I was wondering whether it can be augmented

---

[1]https://martinfowler.com/bliki/MicroservicePrerequisites.html

to also explain and position some of the common buzzwords that float around modern software delivery.

I felt that Infrastructure as Code (IaC), which is equally useful and over-hyped, can be summed up as using the build pipeline to not only deploy software artifacts,but to also instantiate the necessary infrastructure components. In the clover model, it could therefore be depicted as a new petal on the bottom left, between *delivery pipeline* and *run-time platform*.

When you think about it, you could also place *GitOps* here, another frequent buzzword (you know to be cautious when the top search result describes something as a "paradigm"). GitOps roughly describes the useful practice of checking your infrastructure deployment and configuration scripts (used in a broad sense here, including declarative specifications) into your source code repository. Infrastructure changes can then be tracked via Git logs and approved via pull requests. So, GitOps also sits at the intersection of delivery pipeline and run time and hence could occupy the same petal.

Stretching the model further, one could position Site Reliability Engineering (SRE) as a new petal at the bottom right between *monitoring* and *run-time platform*. SRE brings a software engineering mindset to infrastructure and operations, suggesting practices like automation and balancing delivery velocity and reliability via so-called *error budgets*.

If we feel lucky with our model, we should try to find matching elements for the top half also. The term that's been buzzing around communications quite a bit is *service mesh*. Again, it's not easy to find a precise definition— the Wikipedia page is flagged as having issues. Erring on the site of simplicity, a service mesh aims to provide better control (such as dynamic traffic routing) and better transparency (such as latencies and dependencies) of service-to-service communications. Following this logic we could place it on the top right.

This leaves us one petal short, the one on the top left. Since I have been working in integration for decades, the closest technique that comes to my mind is IDL— an *Interface Description Language*[2]. Although for some this term would trigger flashbacks of CORBA (Common Object Request Broker Architecture), Google's Protocol Buffers and tools like Swagger have made IDL cool again.

---

[2]https://en.wikipedia.org/wiki/Interface_description_language

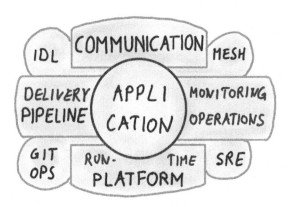

Adding buzzword petals to the four leaf clover

Is this model better than the original? You be the judge—it's certainly richer and conveys more in a single picture. But showing more isn't always better—our model has become more noisy. You could perhaps show the two versions to different audiences. Developers might appreciate the small petals, whereas executives might not.

Defusing buzzwords and positioning them in a logical context is always helpful. Finding simple models is a great way to accomplish that. Once they're done, such models might seem obvious. However, that's one of their critical quality attributes: you want your good ideas to look obvious in hindsight.

25. What Do Containers Contain?

Metaphors help us reason about complex systems.

Container technology has become an indispensable staple of cloud architecture. Much like it's hard to imagine shipping and logistics without the shipping container, Docker containers have become virtually synonymous with being *cloud native* (and perhaps some smuggled in *cloud immigrants...*). Now that containers are being increasingly associated with *multicloud* (Chapter 18) approaches, it's worth having a closer look behind the scenes of their runaway success. And we'll unpack the container metaphor along the way.

Containers Package and Run

When IT folks mention the word "container", they are likely referring to Docker containers, or, more recently, container images compliant with the *Open Container Initiative*[1] (OCI). Despite all the buzz around containers and associated tools, there's still occasional confusion about the exact role containers play in the software life cycle. The debate isn't helped by most "architecture diagrams" of Docker showing run-time components, such as the Docker host and the client API, as opposed to capabilities. Let's try to do better.

In my view, containers combine three important mechanisms that redefine how we deploy and operate applications:

---

[1]https://www.opencontainers.org/

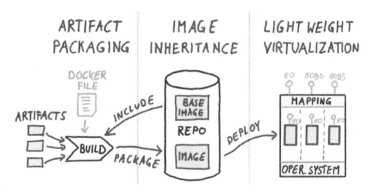

A functional architecture of Docker containers

Artifact packaging

Containers package application artifacts based on a *Dockerfile*, a specification of the installation steps needed to run the application. The Dockerfile would, for example, include the installation of libraries that the application depends on. From this specification, Docker builds an image file that contains all required dependencies.

Image inheritance

A particularly clever feature that Docker included in the generation of the container image files is the notion of a *base image*. Let's say that you want to package a simple Node.js application into a Docker image. You'd likely need the run time, libraries, npm, and a few other items installed for your application to run. Instead of having to figure out exactly which files are needed, you can simply reference a Node.js base image that already contains all of the necessary files. All you need to do is add a single line to your Dockerfile, like so: `FROM node:boron`.

Lightweight virtualization

Folks talking about containers will often refer to two Linux kernel mechanisms: cgroups[2] and namespaces[3]. cgroups support lightweight virtualization by limiting resource usage (disk, main memory, or CPU). Namespaces allow a container to "see" its own set of resources, such as file-system paths or network ports. For example, running multiple containerized web servers on a single VM allows each web server to listen to "their" virtual port 80, which is mapped to a distinct global host port.

---

[2]https://en.wikipedia.org/wiki/Cgroups
[3]https://en.wikipedia.org/wiki/Linux_namespaces

Much confusion arises when folks refer to different aspects when mention the word "container". It also becomes clear why containers revolutionized the way modern applications are deployed and executed: the concept of modern containers spans all the way from building to deploying and running software.

Container Benefits

My *Architect Elevator Workshops*[4] include an exercise that asks participants to develop a narrative to explain the benefits of using containers to senior executives. Each group pretends to be talking to a different stakeholder, including the CIO, the CFO, the CMO (Chief Marketing Officer), and the CEO. They each get two minutes to deliver their pitch.

The exercise highlights the importance of avoiding jargon and *building a ramp*[5] for the audience. It also highlights the power of metaphors. Relating to something known, such as a shipping container, can make it much easier for the audience to understand and remember the benefits of Docker containers.

Having run this exercise many times, we distilled a few nice analogies that utilize the shipping container metaphor to explain the great things about Docker containers. Let's have a look:

Containers Are Enclosed

If you load your goods into a container and seal the doors, nothing goes missing while en route (as long as the container doesn't go overboard, which does occasionally happen).

The same is true for Docker containers. Instead of the usual semi-manual deployment that is bound to be missing a library or configuration file, deploying a container is predictable and repeatable. Once the Dockerfile is well defined, everything is inside the container and nothing falls out.

Containers Are Uniform

While you could package goods in large boxes or crates to avoid stuff getting lost, shipping containers are unique in that their dimensions and exterior features,

---

[4]https://architectelevator.com/workshops
[5]https://architectelevator.com/book

such as the hook-up points, are highly standardized. Containers are likely one of most successful examples of standardization, perhaps outside of A4 paper[6]. I tend to highlight this important property by reminding people that:

 Containers look the same from the outside, whether there's bags of sand inside or diamonds.

Thanks to this uniformity, tooling and "platforms" can be highly standardized: you only need one type of crane, one kind of truck, and one type of ship as the "platform" for the containers. This brings both flexibility and efficiency. The fact that an incoming container can be loaded onto any truck or another vessel makes operations more efficient than waiting for specialized transport. But the uniformity also brings critical Economies of Scale for investment into specialized tools, such as highly optimized cranes.

Uniformity in Docker containers brings the same advantages: you need only one set of tools to deal with a wide variety of workloads. This allows you better Economies of Scale to develop sophisticated tooling, such as container orchestration, that would be hard to justify as a one-off.

Containers Stack Tightly

Shipping containers are designed to stack neatly so that more freight can be loaded onto a single ship. Large container ships hold upward of 20,000 Twenty-foot Equivalent Units (TEU), which means 20,000 of the "smaller" 20-foot containers or proportionally fewer of the "larger" 40-foot containers. Those ships stack containers 16 units high, which equates to about a 13-story building. The regular, rectangular shape of shipping containers means that very little cargo space is wasted on these ships. The resulting packing density makes container shipping one of the most efficient modes of transport in the world.

Docker containers also stack more tightly because, unlike VMs, multiple containers can share a single operating system instance. The reduced overhead makes deployment of small services, like we often use in microservices architectures, significantly more efficient. So, packing density is a benefit for both physical and logical containers.

---

[6]Hohpe, *The Software Architect Elevator*, 2020, O'Reilly

Containers Load Fast

On my business trips to Singapore, the Asia Square Westin hotel often afforded me a clear view of Singapore's container port. Seeing a giant container ship being unloaded and reloaded within just a few hours is truly impressive. Highly specialized and efficient tooling, made possible through the standardized container format, minimizes expensive wait times for vessels. Container loading is also sped up because the packaging process (i.e., placing goods into the container) is handled separately from the loading/deployment process of the container. It thus minimizes the potential bottleneck of ship loading—there are only so many cranes that can service a vessel at the same time.

Docker containers also have shorter deployment times because they don't require a whole new VM and operating system instance to be deployed. As a result, most IT containers spin up in less than a minute as opposed to roughly 5 to 10 minutes for a complete VM. Part of that speed gain is attributable to the smaller size, but also to the same strategy as with physical containers: all little application details and dependencies are loaded into the container image first, making deployment more efficient.

Rapid deployment isn't just a matter of speed, but also *increases resilience* (Chapter 28) at lower cost than traditional standby servers.

So, it turns out that the shipping container analogy holds pretty well and helps us explain why containers are such a big deal for cloud computing. The following table summarizes the analogies:

Property	Benefit	Shipping Containers	Docker Containers
Enclosed	Self-containment	Nothing gets lost	No missing files
Uniform	Consistent tooling	Cranes and trucks	Container registries, orchestration
Stacking	Higher density	25000 TEU Vessels	Dozens per VM
Packing vs. Loading	Fast loading	Short vessel downtime	Rapid deployment, resilience

Not Everything Ships in Containers

Now that we have done quite well with relating the benefits of IT containers to shipping containers, let's stretch the metaphor a little bit. Despite the undisputed advantages of container ships, not all goods are transported in containers. Liquids, gas, and bulk material are notable examples that are transported via oil tankers, LPG vessels, or bulk vessels, which actually outnumber container vessels[7]. Other materials, especially perishable ones, are also better transported by aircraft, which do use specialized palettes and containers but generally of much smaller size and weight.

If our analogy holds, perhaps not all applications are best off running in containers. For large applications, so-called *monoliths*, the efficiency advantage is smaller because the application size is bigger in comparison to the operating system image overhead. And, deployment can be automated with a variety of tools, such as Ansible, Chef, or Puppet. Now, of course we're told that such applications are *bad* and should all be replaced with numerous microservices. Architects, however, know that one size doesn't necessarily fit all, and your IT won't come to a standstill if not every last application runs in containers.

Also, although containers, and even container orchestration with *k3s*, can run on a Raspberry Pi, embedded systems may not need to pack many applications onto a single device[8]. Similarly, performance-critical applications, especially those heavy on input/output, might not want to pay the overhead that containers introduce, for example, to virtualize network connections. And some of them, especially databases, have their own multitenant mechanisms, again reducing the operating system overhead and the need for rapid deployment. You can pack quite a few logical databases onto a single database server that runs on a pair of heavy-duty VMs or even physical servers.

Thin Walls

Shipping containers provide pretty good isolation from one another—you don't care much what else is shipping along with your container. However, the isolation isn't quite as strong as placing goods on separate vessels. For example,

---

[7]https://www.statista.com/statistics/264024/number-of-merchant-ships-worldwide-by-type/
[8]Late-model Raspberry Pi's have compute power similar to Linux computers from just a decade ago, so they might not be a perfect example for embedded systems that operate under power and memory constraints.

pictures circulating on the internet show a toppling container pulling the whole stack with it overboard. The same is true for compute containers: a hypervisor provides stronger isolation than containers.

Some applications might not be happy with this lower level of isolation. It might help to remember that one of the largest container use cases plus the most popular container orchestrator originated from an environment in which all applications were built from a single source-code repository and highly standardized libraries, vastly reducing the need for isolation from "bad" tenants. This might not be the environment in which you're operating, so once again you shouldn't copy and paste others' approaches, but first seek to understand the trade-offs behind them.

It's alright if not everything runs in a container—it doesn't mean they're useless. Likewise, although many things can be *made to run* in a container, that doesn't mean that it's the best approach for all use cases.

Shipping Containers Don't Re-Spawn

Alas, physical analogies don't necessarily translate to the ephemeral world of bits and bytes. For example, analogies between a physical building and IT architecture are generally to be taken with a grain of salt. Also, as we learned in an earlier chapter, *disposability* (Chapter 23) is a great feature in the IT world, but not in the physical one. Bits just recycle better than plastic.

 Docker containers have a few tricks up their sleeves that shipping containers can't do.

In my workshops, we stumbled upon a specific break in the analogy when one team tried to stretch the metaphor to explain the concept of *disposability* (Chapter 23). Because Docker containers can be easily deployed, multiple running instances of one container image are straightforward to create. After trying to weave a storyline that if your shipping container goes overboard, a new instance can be spawned, the team had to admit that it had likely overstretched the metaphor. This wasn't just fun but also educational because you don't know the limits of a metaphor until you test them.

Border Control

If containers are opaque, meaning that you can't easily look inside, the question arises whether containers are the perfect vehicle for smuggling prohibited goods in and out of a country[9]. Customs offices deal with this problem in multiple ways:

- Each container must have a signed-off manifest. I'd expect that the freight's origin and the shipper's reputation are a consideration for import clearance.
- Customs may randomly select your container for inspection to detect any discrepancies between the manifest and its actual contents.
- Most ports have powerful X-ray machines that can have a good look inside a container.

We also should not blindly trust IT containers, especially base containers that you inherit from. If your Dockerfile references a compromised base image, chances are that your container image will also be compromised. Modern container tool chains therefore include scans for containers before deploying them. *Container Security Scanning* has a firm place on ThoughtWorks' Technology Radar[10]. Companies will also maintain private container registries that will (or at least should) hold only containers with a proven provenance.

Containers Are for Developers

Hopefully, examining analogies between shipping containers and Docker containers has helped shed some light on the benefits of using containers. One additional aspect played an important role, though, in Docker's surge as a container format, despite the underlying run-time technology having been available for several years and VMware having deployed powerful virtualization tools to virtually (pun intended) every enterprise.

And that difference is as important as it is subtle: Docker is a tool for developers, not for operations. Docker was designed, developed, and marketed to developers.

---

[9]Recent world news taught us that a musical instrument case might be a suitable vehicle to smuggle yourself out of a country.

[10]https://www.thoughtworks.com/radar/techniques/container-security-scanning

It features text-based definition files, which are easy to manage with version control, instead of the shiny but cumbersome GUI tools perennially peddled by enterprise operations vendors.

 Docker was designed and built for developers, not operations staff. It liberated developers by supporting a DevOps way of working detached from traditional IT operations.

Also, Docker was open—open source actually—something that can't be said of many traditional operations tools. Lastly, it provided a clean interface to, or rather separation from, operations. As long as a developer could obtain a VM from the operations team, it could install Docker and be able to spawn new containers at will without ever having to submit another service request.

Beware of Résumé–Driven Architecture!

As much as Docker deserved to become a staple of modern delivery, the popularity of tools isn't always a function of merit. Even open-source tools can enjoy seven-figure marketing budgets and effectively eliminate the competition before setting up their own trademarks, certifications, conferences, and paid vendor memberships. Tying the notion of a modern enterprise with deploying a particular tool is a great marketing story but shouldn't impress architects.

Popular tools drive the demand for developers possessing relevant experience. In a dynamic market, that demand quickly translates into higher salaries and job security. Therefore, some developers might favor a specific tool because it's good for their resume—and their pay grade. It's been asserted that adding "Kubernetes" to your resume can earn you a 20% pay hike.

This tendency leads you to an unusual and undesired type of architecture: *résumé-driven architecture*. It's probably not the one you're after! So, "everyone else does it" shouldn't be a sufficient argument for technology adoption, even if the technology looks useful and has wide adoption. Architects look beyond the buzz and aim for concrete value for their organization. Being able to do that is also the most attractive item you can have on your resume.

26. Serverless = Worry Less?

If no one wants a server, let's go serverless!

As an industry, we generally earn mediocre marks for naming things. Whether microservices are really "micro" as opposed to "mini" or "nano" has caused some amount of debate. Meanwhile, is it really useful to define something by what it isn't, like NOSQL has done? Lastly, you have probably noticed by now that I'm not a fan of calling things *native*. But the winning prize for awkward naming likely goes to the term *serverless*, which describes a run-time environment that surely relies on servers. It's time to put the buzzword aside and have a look.

Architects Look for Defining Qualities

Dissecting buzzwords is one of enterprise architects' most important tasks. Buzzwords are a slippery slope toward a strategy that's *guided by wishful thinking* (Chapter 3). As an architect, the question I like to ask any vendor touting a popular buzzword is: "Could you please enumerate the defining qualities for that label?" Based on these qualities I should be able to determine whether a thing I am looking at is worthy of the label or not. The vendor's initial response is invariably "That's a good question." Surely we can do better than that.

Server-Less = Less Servers?

Tracking down the origin of the term leads us to an article by Ken Fromm from 2012[1]. Here we learn that:

> *Their worldview is increasingly around tasks and process flows, not applications and servers—and their units of measure for compute cycles are in seconds and minutes, not hours. In short, their thinking is becoming serverless.*

---

[1]https://readwrite.com/2012/10/15/why-the-future-of-software-and-apps-is-serverless

AWS, whose Lambda service placed serverless architectures into the main-stream, makes the explanation[2] quite simple, giving support to the moniker server-worry-less:

> *Serverless computing allows you to build and run applications and services without thinking about servers.*

Looking for a bit more depth, Mike Robert's authoritative article on serverless architectures[3] from 2018 is a great starting point. He distinguishes serverless third-party services from FaaS (Function as a Service), which allows you to deploy your own "serverless" applications. Focusing on the latter, those are applications...

> *...where server-side logic is run in stateless compute containers that are event-triggered, ephemeral, and fully managed by a third party.*

That's a lot of important stuff in one sentence, so let's unpack this a bit:

Stateless
> I split the first property into two parts. In a curious analogy to being "server-less", stateless-ness is also a matter of perspective. As I mused some 15 years ago[4], most every modern compute architecture outside of an analog computer holds state (and the analog capacitors could even be considered holding state). So, one needs to consider context. In this case, being stateless refers to application-level persistent state, such as an operational data store. Serverless applications externalize such state instead of relying on the local file system or long-lived in-memory state.

Compute containers
> Another loaded term—when used in this context, the term "containers" appears to imply a self-contained deployment and run-time unit, not necessarily a *Docker container* (Chapter 25). Having self-contained units is important because ephemeral applications (addressed in a moment) need to be automatically re-incarnated. Having all code and dependencies in some sort of container makes that easier.

---

[2]https://aws.amazon.com/lambda/faqs/
[3]https://martinfowler.com/articles/serverless.html
[4]https://www.enterpriseintegrationpatterns.com/ramblings/20_statelessness.html

Event-triggered

If serverless applications are deployed as stateless container units, how are they invoked? The answer is: per event. Such an event can be triggered explicitly from a front end, or implicitly from a message queue, a data-store change, or similar sources. Serverless application modules also communicate with one another by publishing and consuming events, which makes them loosely coupled and easily recomposable.

Ephemeral

One of those fancy IT words, ephemeral means that things live for only a short period of time. Another, more blunt way of describing this property is that things are easily *disposable* (Chapter 23). So, serverless applications are expected to do one thing and finish up because they might be disposed of right after. Placing this constraint is a classic example of an application programmers accepting higher complexity (or more responsibility) to enable a more powerful run-time infrastructure.

Managed by third party

This aspect is likely the main contributor to serverless' much-debated name. Although "managed" is a rather "soft" term (I manage to get out of bed in the morning...), in this context it likely implies that all infrastructure-related aspects are handled by the platform and not the developer. This would presumably include provisioning, scaling, patching, dealing with hardware failure, and so on.

But There's More

Although Mike's carefully worded sentence is astonishingly comprehensive, its focus is on applications running on a serverless (or FaaS) platform. The platform itself also needs to possess a number of defining qualities to deserve the coveted label. In fact, Mike wrote another article just on this topic, titled Defining Serverless[5]. So let's see what else is commonly assumed when a platform provider labels a service as serverless:

Auto-scales

A serverless platform is expected to scale based on demand, giving substance to the term server-worry-less, meaning you don't have to

---

[5]https://blog.symphonia.io/posts/2017-06-22_defining-serverless-part-1

worry about servers; the platform does that. This property sets serverless platforms aside, for example, from container orchestration where the application operations team typically has to provision nodes (VMs) managed by the orchestration.

Scales to zero

Although we are most interested in scaling up, scaling down can be equally important and sometimes more difficult to achieve. If we follow the cloud's promise of elastic pricing, we shouldn't have to pay anything if we don't incur any processing, perhaps because our site isn't seeing any traffic. The reality, though, is that traditional applications keep occupying memory and usually demand at least one VM under any circumstance, so zero traffic doesn't become zero cost. Truly paying zero dollars is unlikely to ever be true—all but the most trivial services will store operational data that keeps incurring charges. Nevertheless, idling serverless applications will cost you significantly less than with traditional deployment on VMs.

Packaged deployment

This one is a bit more fuzzy. It appears that serverless platforms make it easy to deploy code, at least for simple cases. Best examples are likely Node.js applications deployed to AWS Lambda or Google Cloud Functions with just a simple command line.

Precise billing

Cost based on precise usage[6] is also one of Mike's properties. AWS Lambda bills in 100-ms increments of usage, making sporadically used applications incredibly cheap to run.

Is It a Game Changer?

So now that we have a better idea of what types of systems deserve to be called "serverless", it's time to have a look at why it's such a big deal. On one hand, serverless is the natural evolution of handing over larger portions of the *non-differentiating toil* to the cloud providers. Whereas on a VM you have to deal with hardening images, installing packages, and deploying applications, containers and container orchestration simplified things a lot by allowing you to deploy prepackaged units to a pool of nodes (VMs). However, you still manage cluster sizes, scaling units and all sorts of other machinery that, unless

---

[6]https://blog.symphonia.io/posts/2017-06-26_defining-serverless-part-3

you believe YAML is the nirvana for DevOps disciples, ends up being rather cumbersome.

Serverless makes all this go away by handling deployment (and recycling) of instances, node pool sizes, and everything under the covers, *really* allowing you to focus on application functionality as opposed to infrastructure.

Additionally, just like cloud computing, serverless shifts the business model in a subtle but important way. As Ben Wilson, my former colleague and now group product manager at Google Cloud, and myself laid out in a blog post titled Rethinking commercial software delivery with serverless[7], serverless incurs cost per execution of a single fine-grained application function. You can therefore compare the value (and profit) generated by that function to the cost of executing that function at a level of granularity never before thought possible. Ben aptly called this capability "transparent, transaction-level economics". Now that's a game changer.

Building Serverless Platforms

Architects tend to be those folks who routinely took their childhood toys apart to see how they worked. So, as architects we are naturally curious how the magic of serverless is implemented under the hood. As I revealed in *37 Things*, for me architecture is rooted in the non-trivial decisions that were made. So, when our favorite cloud providers built their serverless platforms, what critical decisions would they make? Let's play serverless platform architect for a minute.

Layering vs. Black Box

A serverless platform could be a "black box" ("opaque" would be a nicer term) or built by layering additional capabilities on top of another base platform. Interestingly, we find examples of both approaches, even within a single cloud provider.

Both Google App Engine, a serverless platform that existed well before the term was coined, and AWS Lambda, AWS' category-defining service, follow the opaque model. You deploy your code to the platform from the command

---

[7]https://cloud.google.com/blog/topics/perspectives/rethinking-commercial-software-delivery-with-cloud-spanner-and-serverless

line or via a ZIP file (for Lambda) without having to know what the underlying packaging and deployment mechanism is.

Google Cloud Run follows the opposite approach by layering serverless capabilities on top of a container platform. One critical capability being added is scale-to-zero, which is emulated using Knative[8] (talk about another not-so-stellar-name...) to route traffic to a special Activator[9] that can scale up container pods when traffic comes in.

From an architectural point of view, both approaches have merit but reflect a different point of view. When considering the architecture as a product line, layering is an elegant approach because it allows you to develop a common base platform both for serverless and traditional (serverful? servermore?) container platforms. However, when considering the user's point of view, an opaque platform provides a cleaner overall abstraction and gives you more freedom to evolve the lower layers without exposing this complexity to the user.

Language Constraints

A second key decision is what languages and libraries to support. Closely related is the decision as to whether to constrain the developer to better assure the platform's capabilities. For example, most platforms will limit the ability to run native code or the spawning of additional threads. One of the earliest serverless platforms, Google App Engine, placed numerous restrictions on the application, allowing only Java and limiting library use. Together with the lack of ancillary services like managed SQL databases, these limitations likely contributed to the slow uptake when compared with AWS Lambda.

Many of the modern FaaS platforms began with a limited selection of languages, usually starting from Node.js, but now support a wide range. For example, in 2020 AWS Lambda supported Java, Golang, PowerShell, Node.js, C#, Python, and Ruby. Container-based serverless platforms aren't really limited in the choice of language as long as it's practical to include the run time in a container.

Salesforce's Apex language is another important but sometimes omitted serverless platform (as in FaaS). Salesforce decided to impose constraints in favor of better platform management, going as far as defining its own programming language. I am generally skeptical about business applications defining custom

---

[8]https://knative.dev/docs/serving/configuring-autoscaling/
[9]https://github.com/knative/serving/tree/26b0e59b7c1238abf6284d17f8606b82f3cd25f1/pkg/activator

languages because not only is language design really hard, but most of them also lack in tooling and community support. In Salesforce's case creating a new language might have been a plausible avenue because its platform provides many higher-level services and wasn't intended to be running generic applications.

Platform Integration

An additional decision is how much a serverless platform should be integrated with the cloud platform; for example, monitoring, identity and access management, or automation. A tighter integration benefits developers but might make the platform less portable. In the current market, we see AWS Lambda being fairly well integrated with platform services such as CloudWatch, IAM, or CloudFormation. Google Cloud Run largely relies on the Kubernetes ecosystem and associated products bundled into Anthos, which is starting to look a bit like a "cloud on a cloud".

Is Serverless the New Normal?

Enterprise cloud strategies often lay out a path from virtual machines to containers and ultimately serverless. I take issue with such an association for multiple reasons. First, your strategy should be a lot more than following an industry trend—it needs to define critical decisions and trade-offs you are making. Second, just like containers, not all applications are best off running in a serverless model. So, it's much more about choosing the most suitable platform for each kind of application than blindly following along the platform evolution. Else you don't need an architect.

27. Keep Your FROSST

The cloud doesn't love all applications equally much.

Cloud platforms are amazing, but they don't love all applications equally much. I've seen old-school monoliths, which require special storage hardware because trivial business actions trigger 200 database queries, and snapshotting the database is the only cure for a batch process that regularly corrupts customer data. Such applications can be made to run in the cloud but honestly won't benefit a whole lot. On the other end of the spectrum we have 12-factor, cloud-native, stateless, ephemeral, post-DevOps, microservices applications that were awaiting the cloud before it was even conceived.

After seeing someone claim their application was 66% cloud ready because it met 8 of the 12 factors[1] commonly cited for modern applications, my team set out to craft a better definition of what makes applications well suited for the cloud. My colleague Jean-François Landreau authored this nice description that he labeled "FROSST". I consider it a perfect piece of pragmatic, vendor-neutral architecture advice and am happy to include it in this book.

By Jean-François Landreau

Our architecture team regularly authored compact papers that shared the essence of our IT strategy with a broad internal audience of architects, CIOs and IT managers. Each paper, or *Tech Brief*, tackled a specific technology trend, elaborated the impact for our specific environment, and concluded with actionable guidance. I was assigned to write such a Tech Brief to give development teams and managers directions for moving applications to our new cloud platform. The paper was intended as useful guidance but also as a form of guard rail for us to avoid someone deploying the mother of all brittle, latency-sensitive monoliths

---

[1] https://12factor.net/

on our platform just to highlight that the platform didn't produce an instant miracle.

Titled *Five Characteristics of Cloud-Ready Applications*, the Tech Brief was widely read by colleagues across the globe and referenced in several senior management slides decks. Encouraged by this positive feedback, I evolved the five characteristics into the moniker "FROSST"—vaguely inspired by the chilly Munich winters.

Cloud Applications Should Be FROSST

I wasn't looking for an all-encompassing but difficult-to-remember set of attributes (tell me those 12 factors again...), but a description that's meaningful, intuitive, and easy to remember. I therefore chose simple words and intentionally avoided buzzwords or jargon. Lastly, I wanted the characteristics to support one another so that they can make a cohesive whole as opposed to a "laundry list".

I ended up with *FROSST*—an acronym that helps me remember the key characteristics of applications that look to be good friends with the cloud. Those applications should be:

- Frugal
- Relocatable
- Observable
- Seamlessly updatable
- internally Secured
- failure Tolerant

Let's look at each one, discuss why it's relevant and how it relates to the other characteristics.

Frugal

Frugality means that an application should be conservative in the amount of CPU and memory it uses. A small deployment footprint, such as a Docker image, is also a sign of frugality. Being frugal doesn't mean being cheap—it doesn't imply premature optimization via incomprehensible code that ekes out every last bit of memory and every CPU cycle (we leave that to microcontrollers). It mainly means to not be unnecessarily wasteful; for example, by using an n^2 algorithm when a simple n or $n\ log(n)$ version is available.

Being prudent with memory or CPU consumption will help you stay in budget when your application meets substantial success and you have to scale horizontally. Whether your application or service consumes 128 or 512 MB of RAM might not matter for a handful of instances, but if you're running hundreds or thousands, it makes a difference. Frugality in application start-up time supports the application's *relocatability* and *seamless updatability* thanks to quick distribution and launch times.

Frugality can be achieved in many ways, such as by using efficient library implementations for common problems instead of clunky one-offs. It can also mean not lugging around huge libraries when only a tiny fraction is required. Lastly, it could mean storing large in-memory data sets in an efficient format like Protocol Buffers if it's infrequently enough accessed to justify the extra CPU cycles for decoding (letting the bit-twiddling happen under the covers).

Relocatable

Relocatable applications expect to be moved from one data center to another or from one server to the next without requiring a full-on migration that has a project manager executing countless tasks to make sure that everything still works. The cloud moves applications frequently and expects applications to be prepared for such events.

Cloud applications need to relocate for different reasons. First, to scale an application horizontally, new instances need to be deployed. It's not strictly being re-located, but the relocatability characteristic allows additional instances to run on different servers. The second occasion is when either the application or the underlying infrastructure fail, necessitating a quick redeployment. AWS' auto-scaling groups and Kubernetes' replication controllers are typical examples. To make these relocation mechanisms work, *observability* is needed. Additionally, relocatability also comes in handy during the update of the application when a new version is deployed, perhaps in parallel to the existing version. Lastly, relocatability can pay off when deploying applications on so-called *spot* (or *preemptible*) instances, discounted cloud instances that can be reclaimed at any point in time.

Externalizing state, implementing an `init` function to collect environment details, or not relying on single instances (singletons) help make an application relocatable. The application may still need singletons; however, a singleton will now be a role, assigned via an election protocol rather than a single physical instance.

Observable

Observability means that there is no need to plug a debugger into an application to analyze a problem. While it's never been a good solution, horizontally scaling and relocating cloud applications make debugging highly impractical.

The observability characteristic supports several scenarios. It enables *relocatability* by helping frameworks detect or, better yet, predict failure. It also increases *failure tolerance* when used as part of a circuit breaker[2]. Finally, it's an essential part of platform or application operations that need to meet specific Service-Level Agreements (SLAs). For example, observability allows you to build dashboards measuring compliance with these SLAs.

The simplest implementation of observability is by exposing endpoints that report the application's readiness and liveness; for example, to be used by a load balancer or orchestrator. Start-up parameters, connected dependencies, the error rate of incoming requests, and so on can be instrumental for distributed tracing and troubleshooting. Logs are also a useful form of observability particularly when trying to debug on a widely distributed system. A classic and immensely useful implementation of observability is Google's varz[3] coupled with Borgmon, replicated in the open-source world via Prometheus[4].

Seamlessly Updatable

On the internet there are no nights, no weekends, and no low-usage windows for scheduled downtime. To be honest, performing upgrades at night or over the weekend wasn't much fun, anyway. To make matters worse, often the development teams were not present, leaving the operations team to trigger a deployment they couldn't fully qualify. It's a lot better to deploy during business hours with the stakeholders directly available thanks to seamlessly updatable applications.

[2]https://en.wikipedia.org/wiki/Circuit_breaker_design_pattern
[3]https://landing.google.com/sre/sre-book/chapters/practical-alerting
[4]https://prometheus.io/

As outlined in the previous sections, *frugality*, *relocatability*, and *observability* contribute to this characteristic. Automation and tooling, for example to perform green/blue deploys, complete the implementation. This characteristic is therefore not fully intrinsic to the application, but relies on additional external tooling. A developer who has access to an environment that supports seamless updates (like Kubernetes or auto-scaling groups) has no excuse for needing downtime or requiring simultaneous updates of dependent components.

Making application service APIs backward compatible makes updates seamless. New features should be activated via feature toggles to separate component deployment from feature release. Also, applications should be able to exist simultaneously in different versions to support canary releases.

Internally Secured

Traditionally, security was managed at the perimeter of the data center. The associated belief that everything running inside the perimeter was in a trusted environment meant that applications were often poorly secured. Companies realized that it was not enough and started to implement *security in depth*, which extends security considerations into the application. This approach is mandatory in the cloud, particularly for regulated companies.

All other characteristics presented so far contribute to application security. For example, redeploying the application every day from a verified source can enhance security because it could overcome a Trojan horse or another attack that compromised the application's integrity. Close observation of the application can enable the early detection of intrusions or attacks. However, on top of this the application must be *internally* secured: it cannot count on the runtime platform being a fully secured environment, be it on premises or on the public cloud. For example, do not expect an API gateway to always protect your web service. Although it can clearly do a major part of the job, a web service application has to authenticate both the API Gateway and the end user at the origin of the call to prevent unauthorized access. "Trust no one" is a good guideline for applications that can be deployed into a variety of environments.

Developers should test applications at a minimum against OWASP Top Ten Web Applications Security Risks[5]. If there is no embedded authorization or authentication mechanism, there is probably something missing. Testing that

---

[5]https://owasp.org/www-project-top-ten/

the values of the parameters are within the expected range at the beginning of a function is a good practice that shouldn't be reserved only to software running mission-critical systems on airplanes or rockets.

Failure Tolerant

Things will break. But the show must go on. Some of the largest e-commerce providers are said to rarely be in a "100% functioning state", but their site is very rarely down. Users may not be able to see the reviews for a product, but they are still able to order it. The secret: a composable website with each component accepting failure from dependent services without propagating them to the customer.

Failure tolerance is supported by the application's *frugality, relocatability,* and *observability* characteristics, but also has to be a conscious design decision for its internal workings. Failure tolerance supports *seamless updates* because during start-up, dependent components might not be available. If your application doesn't tolerate such a state and refuses to start up, an explicit start-up sequence has to be defined, which not only makes the complete start-up brittle, but also slower.

On the cloud, it's a bad practice to believe that the network always works or that dependent services are always responding. The application should have a degraded mode to cope with such situations and a mechanism to recover automatically when the dependencies are available again. For example, an e-commerce site could simply show popular items when personalized recommendations are temporarily unavailable.

When to Use FROSST

I hinted that FROSST is a necessary set of characteristics and highlighted how they sustain one another. I'm not yet able to demonstrate that they are sufficient and complete. However, I used them on numerous occasions in my work:

- Let's say that you have to establish a set of architecture principles to guide the development of a platform, perhaps running on a public cloud. Based on your specific context, your principles can be guided by the FROSST catalog.

- Next, you'll need to establish a list of non-functional requirements (NFRs) for this platform. You can now use FROSST as a checklist to ensure that the NFRs support these characteristics.
- Likely, development teams will ask you for guidelines for their applications. Instead of building a list of NFRs and architecture principles for them to follow, you can point them directly to FROSST.
- Lastly, working for a big company, you will likely evaluate third-party software solutions. You may use FROSST as a prism through which you evaluate their solutions regarding compatibility with your cloud strategy. Using a consistent framework assures that your evaluation is consistent and unencumbered by sales pitches.

FROSST can be used on many kinds of run-time platforms, be it VMs or containers, on premises or on public clouds. These characteristics are still valid even when you move to a higher level of abstraction, such as *Functions as a Service* (Chapter 26), where a good portion of the FROSST implementation is done by the infrastructure framework. Most important, you likely already remember the six characteristics.

28. Keep Calm And Operate On

What kills us makes us stronger.

No one likes to pay for systems that aren't running. Hence, it's not surprising that system uptime is a popular item on a CIO's set of goals. That doesn't mean it's particularly popular with IT staff, though. The team generally being tasked with ensuring uptime (and blamed in case of failure) is IT operations. That team's main objective is to assure that systems are up and running, and functioning properly and securely. So, it's no surprise that this team isn't especially fond of outages. Oddly enough, the cloud also challenges this way of working in several ways.

Robustness: Prevent Failure

The natural and obvious way to assure uptime is to build systems that don't break. Such systems are built by buying high-quality hardware, meticulous testing of applications (sometimes using formal methods) and providing ample hardware resources in case applications do leak (or need) memory. Essentially, these approaches are based on up-front planning, verification, and prediction to avoid later failure.

IT likes systems that don't break, because they don't need constant attention and no one is woken up in the middle of the night to deal with outages. The reliability of such systems is generally measured by the number of outages encountered in a given time period. The time that such a system can operate without incident is described by the system's Mean Time Between Failure (MTBF), usually measured in hours.

High-end critical hardware, such as network switches, sport an MTBF of 50,000 hours or more, which translates into a whopping six years of continuous operation. Of course, there's always a nuance. For one, it's a mean figure assuming some (perhaps normal) distribution. So, if your switch goes out in a year, you can't get your money back—you were simply on the near end of the probability distribution. Someone else might get 100,000 hours in your place. Second, many MTBF hours, especially astronomical ones like 200,000 hours, are theoretical values calculated based on component MTBF and placement. Those are design MTBF and don't account for oddball real-life failure scenarios. Real life always has a surprise or two in store for us, such as someone stumbling over a cable or a bug shorting a circuit[1]. Lastly, in many cases, a high MTBF doesn't actually imply that nothing breaks but rather that the device will keep working even if a component fails. More on that later.

Systems that don't break are called *robust*. They resist disturbance, like a castle with very thick walls. If someone decides to disturb your dwelling by throwing rocks, those rocks will simply bounce off. Such systems are convenient because you can largely ignore the disturbance—unless, of course, someone shows up with a trebuchet and a very large stone. Also, living in a castle with very thick walls may be all cool and retro, but not the most comfortable option.

Recovering from Failure

While maximizing MTBF is a worthwhile endeavor, ultimately the time of "F"—as in failure—comes (a picture of *Sesame Street* pops up in my head). That's when another metric comes into play—Mean Time To Repair (MTTR); that is, how long does it take for the system to be back up and running?

A system's availability, the most indicative measure of a system's operational quality, derives from both metrics. If you do actually get the 50,000 hours out of your switch (remember, it's just a statistical measure) and it puts you out of business for a day, so 24 hours, you still got 99.95% (1 − 24/50000) availability—not bad. If you want to achieve 99.99%, you'd need to reduce the relative downtime by a factor of five, either by increasing the MTBF or by decreasing the MTTR. It's easy to see that stretching MTBF has limits. How do you build something with an MTBF of 250,000 hours (28.5 years) and actually test for that? Somewhere, some time, something will break. Because there's a point of diminishing returns for increasing MTBF, you should also reduce MTTR.

 Increasing MTBF is useful, but to reach high uptime guarantees, minimizing MTTR is equally important.

---

[1]https://www.computerhistory.org/tdih/september/9/

This example also shows that simply counting the number of outages is a poor *proxy metric* (see *37 Things*): an outage that causes 30 seconds of downtime should not be counted the same as one that lasts 24 hours. The redeeming property of traditional IT is that it might not be able to detect the 30-second outage and doesn't even count it. However, poor detection shouldn't be the defining element!

An essential characteristic of robust systems is that they don't break very often. This means that repairs are rare, and therefore often not well practiced. You know you have robust systems when you have IT all up in arms during an outage, running around like carrots with their heads cut off (I am a vegetarian, you remember). People who drive a German luxury car will know an analog experience: the car rarely breaks, but when it does, oh my, will it cost you! The ideal state, of course, is that if a failure occurs nothing really bad happens. Such systems are resilient.

Resilience: Absorb Failure

Resilient systems absorb disturbance. They focus on fast recovery because it's known that robustness can only go so far. Rather than rely on up-front planning, such systems bet on redundancy and automation to quickly detect and remedy failures. Rather than a castle with thick walls, such systems are more like an expansive estate—if the big rock launched by the trebuchet annihilates one building, you move to another one. Or, you build from wood and put a new roof up in a day. In any case, you have also limited the *blast radius* of the failure—a smashed or burnt down building won't destroy the entire estate.

In IT, robustness is usually implemented at the infrastructure level, whereas resilience generally spans both infrastructure and applications. For example, applications that are deployed in small units, perhaps in containers, can exhibit resilience by using orchestration that automatically spawns new instances in case the underlying hardware fails.

Infrastructure often has some amount of redundancy, and hence some resilience, built in. For example, redundant power supplies and network interfaces are standard on most modern hardware. However, these mechanisms cannot protect against application or systemic failure. Hence, true resilience requires collaboration from the application layer.

Antifragile Systems

Resilient systems absorb failure, so we should be able to test their resilience by simulating or even actually triggering a failure without causing user-visible outages. That way we can make sure that the resilience actually works.

 A major financial services provider once lost a major piece of converged infrastructure—almost 10,000 users were unable to access the core business application. The cause was identified as a power supply failure that wasn't absorbed by the redundant power supply, as it was designed to do. Had they tested this scenario during planned downtime, they would have found the problem and likely avoided this expensive and embarrassing outage.

So, when dealing with resilient systems, causing disturbance can actually make the system stronger. That's what Nassim Taleb calls *antifragile systems*[2]—these aren't systems that are not fragile (that'd be robust), but systems that actually benefit from disturbance.

Although at first thought it might be difficult to imagine a system that welcomes disturbance, it turns out that many highly resilient systems fall into this category. The most amazing system, and one close to home, deserves the label "antifragile": our human body (apologies to all animal readers). For example, immunizations work by injecting a small disturbance into our system to make it stronger.

 What do firemen do when there's no fire and all the trucks have been polished to a mirror perfect shine? They train! And they train by setting an actual fire so that the first time they feel the heat isn't when they arrive at your house.

Antifragile systems require an additional level to be part of the scheme: the systemic level.

---

[2]Nassim Taleb: *Antifragile: Things That Gain From Disorder*, Random House, 2012

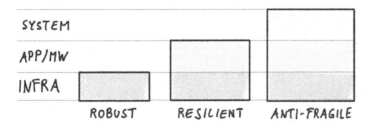

Different models require a different scope

The system level includes ancillary systems, such as monitoring, but also processes and staff behavior. In fact, most critical professions for which accidents are rare but costly rely on proverbial "fire drills" in which teams actively inject failure into a system to test its resilience but also to hone their response. They are antifragile.

Systems Controlling Systems

Thinking about the application you are managing as a complex system (see "Every Systems Is Perfect" in *The Software Architect Elevator*[3]) highlights the difference between the three approaches:

A robust application is a very simple system. It has a *system state* that is impacted by *disturbance.* If your server fails, the system will be unavailable. Resilient applications form a more powerful system that consists of a self-correcting (sometimes called goal-seeking) feedback loop. If there is a *discrepancy* between a desired and actual system state (e.g., a failing server), a *correcting action* is invoked, which returns the system to the desired state. The correction—for example, failing over to another server or scaling out to additional instances—is usually neither instant nor perfect, but it does a good job at absorbing minor disturbances.

---

[3]Hohpe, *The Software Architect Elevator,* 2020, O'Reilly

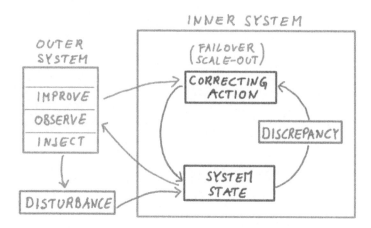

An outer system improves the inner system

Antifragile systems add a second, *outer system* to this setup. The outer system injects disturbances, observes the system behavior, and improves the *correcting action* mechanism.

 Antifragile organizations are those that embrace a systems-thinking attitude toward their operations.

Such compensating mechanisms are similar to many control circuits in real life. For example, most ovens have a thermostat that controls the heating element, thus compensating for heat loss due to limited insulation or someone opening the door (the disturbance). That's the inner system. During development of the oven, the engineers will calibrate the heater and the thermostat to ensure a smooth operation; for example, enabling the oven to reach the desired temperature quickly without causing heat spikes. That's the outer loop.

Chaos Engineering

When the fire brigade trains, it usually does so in what I refer to as the "preproduction" environment. The brigade has special training grounds with charred up buses and aircraft fuselage mock-ups that is set on fire to inject disturbance and make the overall system, which heavily depends on the preparedness of the brigade, more resilient.

In software, we deal with bits and bytes that we can *dispose of at will* (Chapter 23). And because we don't actually set things on fire, it's feasible for us to test in production. That way we know that the resilient behavior in preproduction actually translates into production, where it matters most.

Naturally, you might wonder how smart it is to inject disturbance into a production system. It turns out that in a resilient system, routinely injecting small disturbances builds confidence and utilizes the antifragile properties of the overall system (including people and processes). That insight is the basis for *Chaos Engineering*[4], described as *discipline of experimenting on a system in order to build confidence in the system's capability to withstand turbulent conditions in production.*

The Chaos Monkey Governs Like No Other

One of the better known tools associated with chaos engineering is the *Chaos Monkey*[5], a process that randomly terminates virtual machine instances and containers. While traditional organizations would feel that this is the last thing they want to run in their data center, it is actually a governance mechanism that has an effectiveness that other governance bodies can only dream of. The Chaos Monkey assures that all software that is released is resilient against a single-VM outage. Non-compliant applications fall victim to the monkey test and are shut down. Now that's governance!

 The Chaos Monkey is the ultimate governance tool, shutting down non-compliant applications.

A gentler version of governance through deliberate failure are systems that periodically return errors even when they are operating fine. Doing so forces their clients to perform error checking, which they might otherwise neglect when interacting with a highly available system. A well-known example is Google's Chubby Service[6], which sported an amazing 99.99958% availability. Due to this "excess" availability, the service's site reliability engineers started forcing periodic outages.

---

[4]http://principlesofchaos.org/
[5]https://github.com/Netflix/chaosmonkey
[6]https://static.googleusercontent.com/media/research.google.com/en//pubs/archive/45855.pdf

Diversity Breeds Resilience

Much of IT concerns itself with reducing diversity. Diversity drives up operational complexity (multiple ways of essentially doing the same thing), reduces negotiation power (enterprise sales still largely functions by economies of scale), and can compromise security (the more stuff you have, the more likely one of them is vulnerable).

There is one area, though, for which diversity is desired: highly resilient systems. That's so because diversity limits the blast radius of software failure. If one piece of software suffers from a defect, if all components rely on the same software, this defect can propagate to redundant components and thus compromise the anticipated resilience. The extreme cases are space probes and such, which are sometimes built with fully redundant systems that perform the same function but share no implementation details. In such scenarios, even the teams aren't allowed to speak to each other to maintain complete diversity of ideas.

From Fragile to Antifragile

Even though everyone would dream of running only antifragile systems, systems that don't die from disturbance but only grow stronger, it's a long path for most organizations. The following table summarizes the individual stages and implications.

	Robust	Resilient	Antifragile
Model	Prevent failure	Recover from failure	Inviting failure
Motto	"Hope for the best"	"Prepare for the worst"	"Bring it on!"
Attitude	Fear	Preparedness	Confidence
Mechanism	Planning & verification	Redundancy & automation	Chaos engineering
Scope	Infrastructure	Middleware/Application	Whole System

It's easy to see that although antifragility is an amazing thing and a worthwhile goal, it's a full-on *lifestyle change* (Chapter 1). Also, it can be achieved only by working across infrastructure, middleware, application layer, and established processes, something that often runs counter to existing organizational barriers. It's therefore best attempted on specific projects for which one team is in charge of end-to-end application management.

 Don't try to be antifragile before you are sure that you are highly resilient!

Likewise, you must be careful to not be lured into wanting to be antifragile before all your systems are highly resilient. Injecting disturbance into a fragile system doesn't make it stronger, it simply wreaks havoc.

Resilience Do's and Don'ts

DON'T...

- Make availability the sole responsibility of infra/ops teams
- Just count outages, considering them "bad luck"
- Rely on failover mechanisms that weren't explicitly tested
- Inject disturbance unless you have resilient systems

DO...

- Progress from robustness (MTBF) to also consider resilience (MTTR)
- Use monitoring and automation to help achieve resilience
- Link organizational layers to achieve antifragility
- Conduct regular "fire drills" to make sure you know how to handle an outage

Part VI: Embracing the Cloud

By now you have migrated existing applications and built new ones so that they take advantage of the cloud computing platform. But you're not quite done yet. A cloud journey isn't a one-time shot, but an ongoing series of learning and optimization.

The Journey Continues

Your initial migration has likely yielded promising benefits, but there's surely some optimization work left to do. Also, as your cloud consumption increases, your financial management might take notice and have a different view on the savings you achieved. Lastly, with new powers come new responsibilities, so the cloud might bring you a few surprises.

Embracing the cloud permeates all parts of the organization, whether it's IT, business, finance, or HR, because it influences core business processes, financial management, and hiring/re-skilling.

To round off this book, this last part discusses aspects to consider as your organization fully embraces the cloud as a new lifestyle:

- Cloud savings don't arrive magically; they *have to be earned* (Chapter 29).
- You may find that migrating to the cloud *increased your run budget* (Chapter 30). That's likely a good thing!
- Traditionally, we think of *automation as being about efficiency* (Chapter 31). That's not so in software and in the cloud.

- Small items do add up, also in the cloud. *Beware the Supermarket effect* (Chapter 32)!

29. Cloud Savings Have to Be Earned

There ain't no such thing as a free lunch. Not even in the cloud.

The cloud savings challenge, Stage One

Many cloud initiatives are motivated, and justified, by cost savings. Cost is always a good argument, particularly in traditional organizations, which still view IT as a cost center. And although lower cost is always welcome, once again things aren't that simple. It's time to take a closer look at reducing your infrastructure bill.

278   Cloud Savings Have to Be Earned

How Much Cheaper Is the Cloud?

When migrating traditional, monolithic, non-elastic applications to the cloud, many organizations are surprised to find that the hardware cost isn't that much lower than on premises. Well, the cloud providers still have to pay for the hardware and electricity just like you do. They also invest in significant infrastructure around it.

Admittedly, they have better Economies of Scale, but hardware mark-ups aren't that rich and, depending what operating system you run, licenses also have to be paid. As of early 2020, running an AWS EC2 *m5.xlarge* instance with 4 vCPU and 16 GB of RAM (comparable to a decent laptop) with Windows will cost you about 40 cents per hour, or $288 per month. To that, you need to add the cost for storage, networking, egress traffic, and so on, so watch for the *Supermarket Effect* (Chapter 32)! Including a second server as standby or development server, data backup, and a few bells and whistles, $10,000 a year isn't a stretch by any means, no matter which provider you choose. Larger instances, as they are typical in classic IT, can easily hit a multiple of that. But wasn't the cloud meant to be cheap?

Server Sizing

I am somewhat amused that when discussing cloud migrations, IT departments talk so much about cost and saving money. The amusement stems from the fact that most on-premises servers are massively oversized and thus waste huge amounts of money. So, if you want to talk about saving money, perhaps look at your server sizing first!

I estimate that existing IT hardware is typically two to five times larger than actually needed. The reasons are easy to understand. Because provisioning a server takes a long time, teams would rather play it safe and order a bigger one, just in case. Also, you can't order capacity at will, so you need to size for peak load, which may take place a few days a year. And, let's be honest, in most organizations spending a few extra dollars on a server gets you in less trouble than a poorly performing application.

 In most IT organizations overspending on a server gets you into less trouble than a poorly performing application.

Server sizing tends to be particularly generous when it's done by a software vendor. After all, they're spending your money, not theirs. I have seen relatively simple systems proposing a run-time footprint of many dozen VMs, because the vendor recommended so. Many vendors calculate license fees based on hardware size, so the vendor actually earns by oversizing your servers. And the teams have little incentive to trim hardware cost once the budget is approved. To the contrary, how much hardware your application "needs" has become an odd sort of bragging right in corporate IT.

 I tend to joke that when big IT needs a car, they buy a Rolls Royce. You know, just in case, and because it scored better on the feature comparison. When they forget to fill the tank and the car breaks down, their solution is to buy a second Rolls-Royce. Redundancy, you know!

Even though "hardware is cheap" it isn't so cheap that having a second look at your sizing isn't worth it. In many cases, you can easily shave off $100,000 or more from your hardware bill per year. I'd be inclined to add that to my list of accomplishments for the next performance review.

Earn Your Savings

Migrating your bloated servers to the cloud may reduce your run cost a little bit thanks to better Economies of Scale and lower operational overhead. Still, migration itself isn't free either, and many organizations are somewhat disappointed that migrating to the cloud didn't magically knock 30, 40, or even 50% off their operations budget.

The reality is that savings don't just appear, but must be earned, as illustrated in the following diagram:

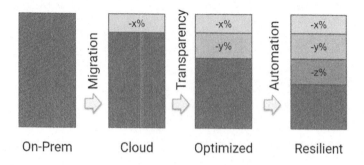

Cloud savings have to be earned

If savings is your goal, you must complete at least two more important steps after the actual cloud migration:

Optimization Through Transparency

Simply lifting and shifting existing systems to the cloud might provide some savings, but to significantly reduce your cloud bill, you need to optimize your infrastructure. Now, you might think that no one has money to give away, so your infrastructure must have been optimized at some point or another. As we so frequently find, cloud computing changes the way we can do things in subtle but important ways: it gives us more *transparency*.

Transparency is the key ingredient into being able to optimize and turns out to be one of the most underappreciated benefits of moving to the cloud. Typical IT organizations have relatively little insight into what's happening in their infrastructure, such as which applications run on which servers, how heavily the servers are utilized, and what run cost to attribute to each application. The cloud gives you significantly more transparency into your workloads and your spend. Most clouds even give you automated cost-savings reports if your hardware is heavily underutilized.

 Transparency is the most underappreciated benefit of moving to the cloud. It's the critical enabler for cost reduction.

The nice thing about the cloud is that, unlike your on-premises server that was purchased already, you have many ways to correct oversized or unneeded hardware. Thanks to being *designed for the first derivative* (Chapter 2) the formula for cloud spend is quite simple: you are charged by the size of hardware or storage multiplied by the unit cost and by the length of time you use it. You can imagine your total cost as the volume of a cube:

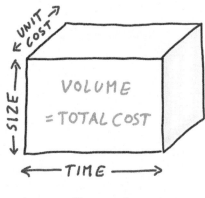

The cost cube

For the more mathematically inclined, the formula reads like this:

$$Cost[\$] = size\ [units]\ x\ time\ [hours]\ x\ unit\ cost\ [\$/unit/hour]$$

Because the unit cost is largely fixed by the provider (more on that later), you have two main levers for saving: resource size and lifetime. Let's take a quick look at each.

Optimizing Size

Optimizing size is a natural first step when looking to reduce cost. Servers that are mostly idling around are good candidates. Also, cloud providers offer many combinations of CPU and RAM so that applications that are particularly compute or memory intensive can be deployed on VMs that more closely match their needs. Some cloud providers offer custom machine sizes so that you can pick your favorite combination of memory and CPU.

Optimizing Time

Reducing the amount of time a server is running also presents ample opportunity for cost savings. A typical development and test environment is utilized about

40 to 50 hours per week, which is roughly one quarter of the week's 168 hours. Stopping or downscaling these environments when they're not needed can cut your cost dramatically. Winding down and reprovisioning servers also assures that your systems are *disposable* (Chapter 23).

When aiming to reduce a server's size or running time, you need to consider load peaks or intermittent loads. What if the seemingly idling server is heavily utilized once per week or once each month? In those cases, the savings potential is limited by the time and complexity of resizing the system or bringing it back online. This consideration leads us to the second major cost savings vector: automation.

Resilience Through Automation

When organizations look to optimize spend, I usually ask them which server is the most expensive one. After a lot of speculation, I let them in on a little secret:

 The most expensive server is the one that's not doing anything. Even at a 30% discount.

The sad part is that if you negotiate a 30% discount from your vendor, that server is still your most expensive one. Now if I want to really get the executives' attention, particularly CFOs, I tell them to imagine that half the servers in their data center aren't doing anything. Most of them won't be amused because they'd consider it a giant waste of money and dearly hope that my exercise is a hypothetical one, until I let them in on the fact that this is true for most data centers.

Why are half the servers in a data center not doing anything? They're there in case another server, which is doing something, breaks. "Warm standby" they're called. Warm standby servers take over in a failure scenario to minimize system downtime. The poor economics of warm standby servers are easily explained:

 A single server can conservatively achieve around 98% of uptime. Adding a redundant server can increase that to 99 or 99.5%, but at double the hardware cost! So you bought yourself 1 percent of uptime for 100% increase in hardware cost.

The way out of this conundrum is *automation* (Chapter 31). If your software provisioning is fully automated, meaning that you can spool up a new instance in mere minutes or even seconds as opposed to days or hours, then you may not need that redundant hardware—you simply deploy a new instance when the primary instance fails. Let's say you have a 99.5% Service-Level Objective (SLO), which allows you 30 days x 24 hours x 0.5% = 3.6 hours of downtime a month. If it takes you 3 minutes to deploy and start a new server to take over from the old one, you could do that 72 times each month without missing your SLO. Try doing that by hand.

The big shift here is from a *robust* architecture, one that's designed not to break, to a *resilient* architecture, one that can absorb failure and remain available—see *Stay Calm and Operate On* (Chapter 28). Shifting from robustness and redundancy to resilience and automation is one of several ways how the cloud can defy existing contradictions, such as providing better uptime at lower cost (see my Google Cloud blog post on Connecting the Dots[1]).

Changing Cloud Providers

You might be surprised that changing providers wasn't on the list of major savings vehicles. After all, we do see numerous press releases of dramatic cost savings from migrations in one direction or another. When looking at these reports, more often than not there are two critical factors at play:

Architecture changes
The case study often involves a drastic shift in architecture that allowed optimizing usage. Classic examples are data warehouse analytics that are used sporadically but require lots of compute power. Running a constant estate of servers for such usage can indeed cost you 10 or 100 times more than a managed pay-per-use data analytics service. Many on-premises Hadoop environments have gone this route as long as the data can be reasonably transferred to and stored in the cloud. Interestingly, the choice of cloud provider is a distant second factor to the change in model.
Pricing model differences
Different cloud providers have different pricing models for some of their services. Again, these are most noticeable in fully managed services like

---

[1] https://blog.google/products/google-cloud/how-the-cloud-operating-model-meets-enterprise-cio-needs/

data warehouses. Some providers charge for such a service per query (by compute power used and amount of data processed), others for the compute infrastructure (by size and time). Most charge you for storage on top of the compute charges. To make things more interesting, in some cases compute power and storage size are interlinked, so as your data set grows, you'll need more compute nodes.

Which model will be cheaper? The answer is a resounding "it depends!" If you run a lot of queries in a short time interval (e.g., for your month-end analysis), being charged for compute/storage likely comes out better because you pay for the nodes only for a limited time and can utilize them heavily before tearing them down (shown on the left side of the following diagram). However, if you run queries intermittently over time, paying per query likely comes out cheaper (shown on the right) because you would otherwise have to keep the infrastructure in place the entire time—setting it up for a single query would be highly impractical.

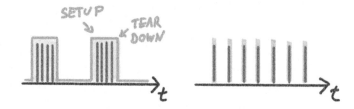

Batched usage (left) vs. sporadic usage (right) favor different pricing models

Additionally, if your data is largely static, you can save a lot in the pay-per-query model by creating interim results tables that hold aggregated results. Once again, it shows that knowing your needs is the most important ingredient into reducing cost.

Sounds complicated? Yes, it can be. But such is the double-edged sword of cost control (and transparency): you have much more control over pricing but need to work to realize those savings. As usual, there is no magic bullet. The good news is that in our example, both models likely will result in a bill that's much lower than setting up a traditional data warehouse that's idle 99% of the time.

 Knowing your needs and usage patterns is the most important ingredient into reducing cost.

When comparing prices, don't expect huge differences in pricing between providers—open market competition is doing its job just fine. You'll gain if a particular model fits your situation and usage pattern particularly well. Always take a critical look at the case studies that claim "moving from provider X to Y reduced our cost by 90%." Most of the time there's an architecture change involved or the use case was a particularly poor fit for the pricing model. It's a bit like "I traded my Mercedes for a BMW and also decided to ride my bike to work. Now I use 80% less gas." That's why architects look for causality[2].

When reviewing case studies related to cost savings, make sure to look for causality. Often it's not just the product change that led to the savings.

Many teams will start to compare prices by comparing unit prices for basic services such as compute nodes. This is likely a sign that you're stuck in a traditional data-center-oriented frame of mind. In the cloud, your biggest levers are sizing and resource lifetime. Data often has the longest lifespan, so there it makes sense to look at cost per unit.

Comparing unit cost charts for compute nodes can be a sign that you're looking at cloud cost from an outdated data-center mindset.

Luckily, history has shown that the competition between the "big three" generally works in your favor: most cloud providers have reduced prices many times.

Doing Nothing

Cynics might note that some cloud providers being rumored to be incurring significant losses means that you're in fact getting more than you pay for, at least for as long as the investors keep bankrolling the operation. There's another, slightly less cynical cost-savings strategy that most are too shy to mention: doing *nothing* (after migrating to the cloud, that is). Not only does compute power become cheaper all the time, the cloud providers also deal with

---

[2]https://architectelevator.com/architecture/architects-causality

depreciation and hardware refresh cycles for you, letting you enjoy a continuous negative price inflation. So, you'll save by doing nothing—perhaps some things in the cloud are a kind of magic.

Premature Optimization

Premature optimization is widely considered the root of much evil in computer science. So, when is the time mature to optimize cost? In the end, it's a simple economic equation: how much savings can you realize per engineer hour invested? If your overall cloud run rate is $1,000 per month, it's unlikely that you'll be getting a huge return on investing many engineer hours into optimization. If it's $100,000 per month, the situation is likely different. In any case, it's good to establish a culture that makes *cost a first-class citizen* (Chapter 32).

Optimizing Globally

Modern frameworks can unexpectedly consume compute power and drive up cost; for example, by requiring five nodes for leader election, a few more as control-plane nodes, another two as logging aggregators, an inbound and an outbound proxy, and so on. Suddenly, your trivial demo app consumes 10 VMs and your monthly bill is in the hundreds of dollars per month.

Such frameworks give you productivity gains in return, though, and servers are cheaper than developers. Higher productivity might also give you an edge in the market, which will outweigh most potential savings. So, once again it's about optimizing globally, not locally. Transparency is your best friend in this exercise.

Cost Is More Than Dollars and Cents

So, once again, there are many factors to be considered, even when it comes to cost. It also means that the cloud is a good time to spend more time with your CFO. More on that in the next chapter.

Savings Do's and Don'ts

DON'T...

- Justify your cloud migration based on cost alone
- Expect miracle cost reductions just by lifting and shifting to the cloud
- Just compare unit prices for VMs
- Attribute cost savings to a change in product or vendor alone
- Over-obsess with cost; place your resources where the return is highest

DO...

- Understand pricing models and how they fit your usage patterns
- Use automation to reduce cost
- Use transparency to understand and manage cost
- Spend time understanding your own usage patterns
- Read price reduction case studies carefully to see what impacted the price and whether that applies to you

30. It's Time to Increase Your "Run" Budget

The cloud challenges budgeting misconceptions.

"We double-checked all the numbers."

An IT organization's health is often measured by what percentage of the available budget is spent on operations ("run") vs. projects ("change"). Most CIOs look to minimize spending on "keeping the lights on" because that would mean more money is available to deliver projects (and value) to the business. Also, the change budget is closely tied to financial models that allow deferring some of the cost that's been incurred. As you might have guessed, a cloud operating model that blurs the line between application delivery and operations can put a wrinkle into that strategy.

Run Isn't Change

Much of internal IT is managed as a cost center. It's no surprise, then, that money spent is a key performance indicator for CIOs. While a reduction in overall spend is generally welcome, a second major metric is comparing the money spent on operations, or "run" (as in running the business), with the money spent on project implementations, usually referred to as "change" or "build" budget.

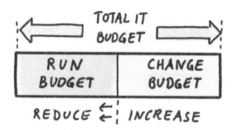

Classic IT looks to minimize the run budget

A CIO who burns too much money just "keeping the lights on" will have a difficult time meeting the demand from the business, which needs projects to be completed. Therefore, almost every CIO's agenda includes reducing the run budget in favor of the project budget. This pressure only builds in times when the business has to compete with "digital disruptors", which places additional demands on IT to deliver more value to the business. Some analysts have therefore started to rephrase "Run vs. Change" as Run-Grow-Transform[1] to highlight that change also incurs expense.

There are many ways to reduce operational costs, including optimizing server sizing, decommissioning data centers, and, of course, moving to the cloud. Somewhat ironically, though, the move to the cloud shifts capital investment toward consumption-based billing, which is traditionally associated with run costs. It can also highlight operational costs that were buried in project budgets.

A real story about building an internal cloud platform and cost recovering for it illustrates some of these challenges.

Billing for Shared Platforms

Around 2014, my team and I started to build a private cloud platform for our employer, a major global financial-services company. As chief architect, I had set out to solve what I considered the biggest problem in our IT organization

---

[1]https://www.gartner.com/smarterwithgartner/align-it-functions-with-business-strategy-using-the-run-grow-transform-model/

at the time: it took us far too long to deploy software. Being convinced that if you can't deploy software, most other problems become secondary, we set out to correct this state of affairs. We thus deployed a private cloud platform that included a fully automated software delivery tool chain, an application run time, and application monitoring.

Being enormously proud of what we built and finding strong demand inside the organization, we were surprised to hit a snag with our charging model. As is common in enterprise IT, we intended to recover the money we spent on hardware, licenses, and project cost by charging our internal customers in the business units. We therefore had to define a charging model to determine how much each of our customers would have to pay. Having built an elastic platform that allows customers to increase and decrease their usage at will, billing based on consumed capacity seemed natural. As main memory was the limiting element in our infrastructure (we had 3 TB of RAM, but had to serve many memory-hungry applications), we decided to charge by memory allocated per month. So, if you'd allocate 1 GB for your application, you'd pay twice as much as if you could make do with 512 MB. We also charged for the containerized build tool chain by the capacity it used and the usage of our on-premises GitHub repository by seat.

Although usage-based billing has become the "new normal" these days, charging for a tool chain and other application development services by usage was fairly novel back then. But, despite our Economies of Scale allowing us to provide such services at a significantly lower cost than each project developing a one-off implementation, our pricing model turned out to be a hurdle for many projects.

False Assumptions About Cost

As I discussed in *37 Things*, organizations operate based on existing assumptions that are rarely documented anywhere. When you develop a new solution that breaks these assumptions, you may find unexpected resistance. That's what had happened to us. Specifically, we stumbled upon two assumptions regarding cost:

Invisible Cost = No Cost

Cost accounting generally breaks down spend by line item. A project budget is split into many line items, including personnel cost, software licenses, hardware, team dinners, consulting services, and many more. The dangerous assumption built into this model is that any cost that doesn't explicitly show up as a line item is assumed to be zero.

So, where would the money a project spent on building operational tools such as a one-off CI/CD pipeline show up? Generally, it would be rolled up into the same line items as the software development cost; in other words, personnel cost, hardware, and so on. However, that line item is assumed to be delivering functionality that provides value to the business. Hence, the time and money spent on setting up project tooling isn't really visible—once a project was approved based on a positive business case, no one would look too deeply inside to see how many developer hours were spent on building delivery infrastructure as opposed to delivering business functionality.

Because a project cost breakdown by features vs. building and maintaining tooling is uncommon, projects were rarely asked about the cost of the latter. In contrast, our shared platform, which provided tooling as a service, billed projects explicitly for this expense every month. Usage of the CI/CD pipeline, source repository, and so forth now showed up quite visibly as "internal IT services" on the project budget. Some of the project managers were surprised to see that their project spent $500 a month on delivery infrastructure, notwithstanding the fact that the 10 or 20 person days they would have spent building and maintaining it would have cost them a multiple. So, these project managers had never worried about the cost of software delivery tooling because it had never shown up anywhere.

 Lowering costs but making them visible in the process can be perceived as "costing more" by your internal customers.

Another version of this fallacy were developers claiming that running their own source-code repository would cost them nothing. They used the open-source version, so they had no license cost. When asked who maintains the installation, they pointed out that "an engineer does it in her spare time." At that point, you should become slightly suspicious. Probing further, we found that the software ran on a "spare" server that obviously cost nothing. Backups weren't really done, so storage cost was also "pretty much zero". The real answer is that of course all these items have associated costs; they are just assumed to not exist because they don't show up anywhere. When your software engineer spends half a day with a Jenkins version upgrade or an operational issue, you're simply missing half a person-day from delivering value to the business.

Recurring Cost = Operations

The second assumption that we uncovered was that traditional organizations associate any recurring cost with operations. So, if they'd pay a monthly fee for version control and the build tool chain, they would lump that into their operational cost as opposed to software development cost, where it would wind up if they had built it themselves.

When these items are rolled up, to the CIO it would appear that the project spend on operations increased, a trend that's not desired. Because there was no distinction between recurring costs that are needed to operate the software and recurring costs for software development, project managers preferred to build their own tooling as opposed to using a shared service despite the clearly better economics of the latter, especially if you account for the developer's opportunity cost.

Cloud Cost Blurs the Line

Enterprises moving to the cloud can encounter similar challenges as the scope of cloud platforms is rapidly expanding to not just include infrastructure services, such as VMs, but also software development tooling, such as AWS CodeBuild and CodeDeploy, Google Cloud Build and Cloud Repository, and many others. Just like our shared software delivery platform, they can also appear to increase total "run" cost because you now see a line item for cost that might have been buried in project budgets up to now. Rolling up, the consumption-based billing model might portray an increase in the portion of the IT budget that is spent on operations.

 Spending a larger portion of your IT budget on items that would traditionally be considered "operational" is to be expected with the transition to a cloud operating model and is a good thing.

A "serverless" model, which makes software deployment seamless, totally blurs the line between deployment tools and application run time, showing that the strict separation between build and run might no longer make much sense in modern IT organizations. The same is true for a DevOps mindset that favors "you build it, you run it", meaning project teams are also responsible for operations. However, as we saw, such a way of working can run up against existing accounting practices.

A Mini Tour of Accounting

Most software developers and architects don't bother looking into the details of project budgeting and financials. However, when you are building a shared platform or are supporting a major cloud transformation, having a basic understanding of financial management can be instructive. The key constructs that might help you better understand budgeting decisions are *depreciation* and *capitalization*.

Depreciation allocates capital expenses spread over a period of time. A classic example is a manufacturing tool, which might cost a significant amount of money but lasts a decade. Although the tool investment is a business expense, and hence tax deductible, most tax authorities won't allow the business to claim the full price of the machine in the year it was purchased. Rather, the business can claim a fraction of the cost each year over the lifespan of the tool to better associate the expense with the ongoing profit generated from the up-front investment. This admittedly simplified example also explains why a business's profit is distinct from its cash flow. You might have spent more than you earned to buy the machine, meaning your cash flow is negative, but you're posting a profit because the machine cost is deducted in fractions over many years.

IT also makes investments that provide value to the business for an extended period of time, much like buying a manufacturing tool: it builds business applications. Because many of these applications carry a large initial investment but can be in operation for decades, it appears logical that the cost of developing them should be allocated proportionally over the asset's useful life. Such expenses are called *capitalized expenses*[2].

This capitalization mechanism helps explain a project manager's love for project costs. Despite spending the cash for developers right now, only a fraction of that cost is allocated to the current fiscal year. The rest is spread over future years,

---

[2]https://www.investopedia.com/terms/c/capitalization.asp

making the cost appear much smaller than the actual spend. Anything that can be bundled into the project cost benefits from this effect. So, the half day that the software developer spent fixing the CI/CD pipeline might show up as only $100 in the current fiscal year because the remaining $400 is pushed to the subsequent years. A shared service will have a difficult time competing with that accounting magic!

The astute reader might have noticed that pushing expenses into the future makes you look better in the current year, but burdens future years with cost from prior investments. That's absolutely correct—I have seen IT organizations for which past capitalization ate most of the current year's budget. It's the corporate equivalent of having lived off your credit card for too long. However, project managers often have short planning and reward horizons, so this isn't as disconcerting to them as it might be for you.

Cloud Accounting

The apparent conflict between a novel way of utilizing IT resources and existing account methods has not escaped the attention from bodies like the IFRS Foundation[3], which publishes the International Financial Reporting Standards, similar to GAAP in the United States. While the IFRS doesn't yet publish rules specific to cloud computing, it does include language on intangible assets that a customer controls, which can apply to cloud resources. The guidance, for example, is that implementation costs related to such intangible assets can be capitalized. The global consulting firm EY published an in-depth paper on the topic[4] in July 2020. If you think reading financial guidance is a stretch for a cloud architect, consider all the executives who have to listen to IT pitching Kubernetes to them.

Spending as Success Metric

The cost accounting for service consumption hints at an interesting phenomenon. If you apply a new operational model to the traditional way of thinking, it might actually appear worse than the old model. As a result,

---

[3] https://www.ifrs.org/about-us/who-we-are/

[4] https://assets.ey.com/content/dam/ey-sites/ey-com/en_gl/topics/ifrs/ey-applying-ifrs-cloud-computing-costs-july-2020.pdf

people stuck in the old way of thinking will often fail to see the new model's huge advantages.

However, a new model can also completely change the business's view on IT spending. Traditionally, hardly any business would be able to determine how much operating a specific software feature costs them. Hence, they'd be unable to assess whether the feature is profitable; that is, whether the IT spending stands in any relation to the business value generated.

Cloud services, especially *fine-grained serverless run times* (Chapter 26), change all this. Serverless platforms allow you to track the operational cost associated with each IT element down to individual functions, giving you fine-grained transparency and control over the Return-on-Investment (ROI) of your IT assets. For example, you can see how much it costs you to sign up a customer, to hold a potentially abandoned shopping cart, to send a reminder email, or to process a payment. Mapping these unit costs against the business value they generate allows you to determine the profitability of individual functions. Let's say you concluded that customer signups are profitable per unit. This should cause you to be excited to see IT spend on sign-ups increase!

 With fine-grained cost transparency you might be excited to see IT spending on profitable functions go up.

Fine-grained financial transparency is another example of the great benefits that await those organizations that are able to adjust their operating model to match the cloud's capabilities. It can even turn your view of IT spending upside down.

Changing the Model

The shared platform example illustrates how IT organizations that are stuck in an old way of thinking will be less likely to reap the benefits from cloud platforms. Not only do their existing structures, beliefs, and vocabulary stand in the way of adoption, they will also miss the major benefits of moving to a cloud operating model.

In the case of "change" vs "run", once IT realizes that they *shouldn't run software that they didn't build* (Chapter 13) in the first place, the obsession with reducing run cost might just go away some day.

Budget Do's and Don'ts

DON'T...

- Assume a cost that doesn't show up explicitly in a line item is zero
- Blame a shared services team or the cloud provider for making these costs visible
- Hide tooling and project setup costs in the project budget
- Measure a new operational model in an old cost model

DO...

- Break out the project cost incurred for building tooling
- Utilize shared platforms to avoid duplicating tooling infrastructure
- Anticipate push-back from projects against a usage-based pricing model
- Use the consumption-based pricing model of the cloud to compare marginal value against marginal cost

31. Automation Isn't About Efficiency

Speeding up is more than going faster.

Highly automated IT operations

Most corporate IT has been born and raised from *automating the business* (Chapter 2): IT took something that was done by pen and paper and automated it. What started mostly with mainframes and spreadsheets (VisiCalc[1] turned 40 in 2019) soon became the backbone of the modern enterprise. IT automation paid for itself largely by saving manual labor, much like automation of a car assembly line. So when we speak about automation these days, it's only natural to assume that we're looking to further increase efficiency. However, the cloud also challenges this assumption.

---

[1]https://en.wikipedia.org/wiki/VisiCalc

Industrializing Software Delivery

Within IT, software development is a relatively costly and largely manual process. It's no surprise then that IT management's quest for efficiency through automation also came across the idea of streamlining its own software development processes. Much of that effort originally focused on the specification and coding parts of software delivery—the translation from ideas into code. Many frameworks and methodologies looking to industrialize this aspect of software development, such as CASE tools, 4GL[2], and executable UML, arrived and disappeared again over the course of the 1990s and 2000s.

 I delivered significant business systems in PowerBuilder during the mid-1990s, a system that was considered a fourth-generation language (4GL) that combined UI design and coding in a single environment. I occasionally still get spam mail recruiting PowerBuilder developers.

Somehow, though, trying to automate the specification and coding steps of software delivery never quite yielded the results that the tools' creators were after. Collectively, we could have saved a lot of effort if we had taken Jack Reeves' article, What is Software Design[3], to heart. Published in 1992, Jack elaborated that coding is actually the *design* of software, whereas compiling and deploying software is the *manufacturing* aspect. So, if you're looking to industrialize software manufacturing, you should automate testing, compiling, and deployment, as opposed to trying to industrialize coding. About a quarter century later, that's finally being done. Some things take time, even in software.

DevOps: The Shoemaker's Children Get New Shoes

Ironically, while IT grew big automating the business, it didn't pay much attention to automating itself for about 50 years. As a result, software builds and deployments, the "manufacturing" of software, ended up being more art

---

[2]https://en.wikipedia.org/wiki/Fourth-generation_programming_language
[3]https://wiki.c2.com/?WhatIsSoftwareDesign

than science: pulling a patch in at the last minute, copying countless files, and changing magic configurations.

The results were predictably unpredictable: every software deployment became a high-wire act, and those who were so inclined said a little prayer each time they would embark on it. A forgotten file, a missed configuration, the wrong version of something—that was the daily life of deployment "engineering" for a long time. What was indeed missing was an engineering approach to this set of tasks. If any more proof was needed, email circulations congratulating the team on a successful software release might be well intended, but they serve only as proof of the awfully low success rate.

 Corporate IT celebrating each major product release of its core system to much applause by upper management is a clear sign of missing build and deployment automation.

A slew of recent software innovations has set out to change this: Continuous Integration (CI) automates software test and build, Continuous Delivery (CD) automates deployment, and DevOps automates the whole thing including operational aspects such as infrastructure configuration, scaling, and resilience. In combination, these tools and techniques take the friction out of software delivery. It also allows teams to embrace a whole new way of working.

The New Value of Automation

With all this automation in place, some IT members, especially in operations, fear that this means it's now their turn to be made redundant through technology. This fear is further stoked by terms like "NoOps", seemingly implying that in a fully automated cloud operating model Ops isn't required anymore.

Even though there may be a tad bit of Schadenfreude coming up from the business side who has lived with being made redundant through technology for decades, reducing manual labor isn't actually the main driver behind this automation. Automation in software delivery has a different set of goals:

Speed
   Speed is the currency of the digital economy because it enables rapid and

inexpensive innovation. Automation makes you faster and thus helps the business compete against disruptors, which can often roll out a feature not 10% faster, but 10 times or even 100 times faster.

Repeatability

Going fast is great, but not if it comes at the expense of quality. Automation not only speeds things up, it also eliminates the main error source in software deployment: humans. That's why you should *Never Send a Human to Do a Machine's Job* (see *37 Things*[4]). Automation takes the error margin out of a process and makes it repeatable.

Confidence

Repeatability breeds confidence. If your development team is afraid of the next software release, it won't be fast: fear causes hesitation, and hesitation slows you down. If deployment followed the same automated process the last 100 times, the team's confidence in the next release is high.

Resilience

It's easily forgotten that a new feature release isn't the only time you deploy software. In case of a hardware failure, you need to deploy software quickly to a new set of machines. With highly automated software delivery, this becomes a matter of seconds or minutes—often before the first incident call can be set up. Deployment automation increases uptime and *resilience* (Chapter 28).

Transparency

Automated processes (in IT deployment or otherwise) give you better insight into what happened when, for what reasons, and how long it took to complete. This level of transparency, for example, allows you to find bottlenecks or common failure points.

Reduced machine cost

When using Infrastructure as a Service (IaaS)—deploying software on virtual machines—higher levels of automation allow you to better take advantage of *preemptible* or *spot* instances, those instances that are available at discounted prices but that can be reclaimed by the provider on short notice. In case such a reclaim happens, automation allows you to redeploy your workloads on new instances or to snapshot the state of the current work and resume it later. Such instances are often available at discounts from 60 to 80% below the on-demand price.

---

[4]https://leanpub.com/37things

Continuous improvement/refinement
Having a repeatable and transparent process is the base condition for continuous improvement: you can see what works well and what doesn't. Often you can improve automated processes without having to retrain people performing manual tasks, which could cause additional quality issues due to relearning.

Compliance
Traditional governance is based on defining manual processes and periodic checks. It goes without saying that the gap between what governance prescribes and the actual compliance tends to differ a good bit. Automation enables guaranteed compliance—once the automation script is defined in accordance with the governance, you're guaranteed to have compliance every time.

Cloud Ops

Because moving to the cloud places a significant part of system operations in the hands of the cloud provider, especially with fully managed Software as a Service (SaaS) offerings, there's often a connotation that the cloud requires little to no operational effort, occasionally reflected in the moniker "NoOps". Although cloud computing brings a new operational model that's based on higher levels of automation and *outsourcing IT operations* (Chapter 6), today's drive to automate IT infrastructure isn't driven by the desire to eliminate jobs and increase efficiency. Operations teams therefore should embrace, not fear automation of software delivery.

 Cloud ops isn't "NoOps"—cloud-scale applications have enormous operational demands.

I am not particularly fond of the "NoOps" label—I regularly remind people that cloud-scale applications have higher operational demands than many traditional applications. For example, modern applications operate around the globe, scale instantly, receive frequent updates without visible downtime, and can self-heal if something goes wrong. These are all operational concerns! The cloud also brings other new types of operational concerns, such as *cost management*

(Chapter 32). So, I have no worry that Ops might run out of valuable things to do. If anything, the value proposition of well-run IT operations goes up in an environment that demands high rates of change and instant global scalability.

Speed = Resilience

After you speed up your software delivery and operations through automation, it does more than just make you go faster: it allows you to work in an entirely different fashion. For example, many enterprises are stuck in the apparent conflict between cost and system availability: the traditional way to make systems more available was to add more hardware to better distribute load and to allow failover to a standby system in case of a critical failure.

Once you have a high degree of automation and can deploy new applications within minutes on an elastic cloud infrastructure, you often don't need that extra hardware sitting around—after all, *the most expensive server is the one that's not doing anything* (Chapter 29). Instead, you quickly provision new hardware and deploy software when the need arises. This way you achieve increased resilience and system availability at a lower cost, thanks to automation!

Automation Do's and Don'ts

DON'T...

- Celebrate every release; releases should be normal
- Equate automation with efficiency
- See moving faster as the only benefit of speeding things up
- Fear that cloud means not needing operations

DO...

- Apply software to solve the problem of delivering software, not the design of software
- Automate to improve availability, compliance, and quality
- Understand that automation boosts confidence and reduces stress

32. Beware the Supermarket Effect!

Small stuff adds up, too.

I just went to pick up some milk...

Have you ever been to the supermarket when you really needed only milk but then picked up a few small items along the way just to find out that your bill at checkout was $50? To make matters worse, because you really didn't buy anything for more than $1.99, you're not sure what to take out of the basket because it won't make a big difference anyway. If you've done this, then you're emotionally prepared for what could happen to you on your journey to the cloud.

Computing for Mere Pennies

When enterprises look at vendors' pricing sheets, they are used to counting zeros—enterprise software and hardware isn't cheap. When the same enterprises look at cloud vendors' pricing sheets, they also count zeros. But this time it's not the ones to the left of the decimal point, but the ones to the right! An API request costs something like $0.00002, whereas an hour of compute capacity on a small server can be had for a dime or less. So, cloud computing should just be a matter of pennies, right? Not quite... A month has 720 hours and many systems make millions or sometimes billions of API calls. And although we routinely talk about hyperscalers and their massive fleet of hardware, the average enterprise still uses a lot more compute capacity than many folks might imagine. With IT budgets in the billions of dollars, we shouldn't be surprised to see cloud usage in the tens of millions for large enterprises.

The Supermarket Effect

Enterprise IT is used to spending money in large chunks, similar to going to have dinner at a restaurant: meals are $20 or, if you're at a fancy place, $40. Even though it isn't cheap, the pricing model makes it relatively easy to guess how much the total bill will be (depending on your locale you might get tricked with a mandatory gratuity, state and local tax, health-care cost recovery charges, resort charge, credit card fee, and all kinds of other creations that share the sole goal of extracting more money from your wallet.)

Cloud computing is more like going to the grocery store: you'll have many more line items, each at a relatively low price. So, if you exercise good discipline it can be significantly cheaper. However, it's also more difficult to predict total costs.

 I routinely play the game of "guess the bill" at the supermarket register and although I am getting better, I am routinely below the actual amount. Ah, yes, I did grab that $4.99 cheese and a second bottle of beer...

So, when enterprises first embark on the cloud journey, they need to get used to a new pricing model that includes more dimensions of charges, such as compute, storage, reserved capacity, network, and API calls. They also need to get used to seemingly minuscule amounts adding up into non-trivial cost. Or, as the Germans say, *"Kleinvieh macht auch Mist"*—even small animals produce manure.

Cost Control

The cloud operating model gives developers previously unheard-of levels of control over IT spend. Developers incur cost both via their applications (for example, a chatty application makes more API calls) as well as with machine sizing and provisioning. Cloud providers generally charge identical amounts for production and development machine instances, causing test and build farms plus individual developer machines to quickly add up despite them likely being much smaller instances.

Although most enterprises place billing alerts and limits, with that power over spending also comes additional responsibility. Being a responsible developer starts with shutting down unused instances, selecting conservative machine sizes, purging old data, or considering more cost-efficient alternatives. Done well, developers' control over cost leads to a tighter and therefore better feed-back cycle. Done poorly, it can lead to runaway spending.

Cost Out of Control

Despite proper planning and careful execution, most enterprises seriously moving to the cloud are nevertheless likely to experience unpleasant surprises on their billing statements. Such surprises can range from minor annoyances to tens of thousands of dollars of extra charges. The reasons might be considered obvious in 20/20 hindsight, but I have seen them happen to many organizations, including those well versed in cloud computing.

In my experience, a handful of different scenarios trigger the majority of the unwelcome spike in charges:

Self-Inflicted Load Spikes

Many managed cloud services feature auto-scaling options. Generally, it's a great feature that enables your online system to handle sudden load spikes without manual intervention. However, they're not quite as great if you accidentally cause a massive load spike that will hit your cloud bill fairly hard. Although the natural question is why anyone would do that, it's a relatively common occurrence. Whereas load tests are a classic, albeit planned, scenario, there's another common culprit of unintentional spikes: batch data loads.

 A fairly sophisticated organization that I worked with employed a very nice message-oriented architecture (my soft spot) to propagate, transform, and augment data between a data source and a cloud-managed data store. One day, though, a complete re-sync was required and conducted via a batch load, which pumped the whole dataset into the serverless pipeline and the data store. Both scaled so flawlessly that the job was done before long. The serverless cost per transaction was moderate, but the substantial load spike in records per second triggered additional capacity units to be instantiated by the managed database service. It had racked up a five-figure bill by the time it was detected.

So, when performing actions that differ from the regular load patterns, it's important to understand the impact it might have on the various dimensions of the pricing model. It might be helpful to either throttle down bulk loads or to observe and quickly undo any auto-scaling after the load is finished.

Infinite Loops

Another classic cost-antipattern are serverless or other auto-scaling solutions that have accidental feedback loops, meaning one request triggers another request, which in turn triggers the original request again. Such a loop will cause the system to quickly escalate up—on your dime. Ironically, fast-scaling systems, such as serverless compute, are more susceptible to such occurrences. It's the cloud equivalent of a *stack overflow.*

The problem of uncontrolled feedback loops itself isn't new. Loosely coupled and event-driven systems like serverless applications are highly configurable but also prone to unforeseen system effects, such as escalations. Additional composition-level monitoring and alerting is therefore important. In a blog post from 2007[1], I describe building simple validators that warn you of unintended system structures like circles in the component dependency graph.

---

[1]https://www.enterpriseintegrationpatterns.com/ramblings/48_validation.html

Orphans

The next category is less dramatic, but also sneaks up on you. Developers tend to try out many things. In the process they create new instances or load datasets into one of the many data stores. Occasionally, these instances are subsequently forgotten unless they reach a volume where a billing alert hints that something is awry.

 I have heard many stories of developers spinning up sizable test infrastructure just before they head on vacation. Returning to work having to explain to your boss why your infrastructure kept working so hard while you were away might unnecessarily add to the usual post-vacation *Case of the Mondays*[2].

With infrastructure being software-defined these days, it looks like some of the hard-learned lessons from CI can also apply to cloud infrastructure. For example, you might institute a "no major provisionings on Friday" rule—a Google image search for "don't deploy on Friday" yields many humorous memes for the source of this advice. Also, when rigging up "temporary" infrastructure, think about the deletion right when you (hopefully) script the creation. Or better yet, already schedule the deletion.

Shutting Down May Cost You

One additional line item is unlikely to hit your bill hard, but will nevertheless surprise you. Some cloud pricing schemes include a dependent service for free when deploying a certain type of service. For example, some cloud providers include an elastic IP address with a VM instance. However, if you stop that instance, you will need to pay for the elastic IP. Some folks who provisioned many very small instances are surprised to find that after stopping them, the cost remains almost the same due to the elastic IP charges.

In another example, many cloud providers will charge you egress bandwidth cost if you connect from one server to another via its external IP address, even if both servers are located in the same region. So, accidentally looking up a server's public IP address instead of the internal one will cost you.

---

[2]https://www.moviequotedb.com/movies/office-space.html

It pays to have a closer look at the pricing fine print, but it would be hard to believe that you can predict all situations. Running a cost optimizer is likely a good idea for any sizable deployment.

Being Prepared

While sudden line items in your bill aren't pleasant, it might bear some relief knowing that you're not the only one facing this problem. And, in this case, it's more than just "misery loves company". A whole slew of tools and techniques have been developed to help address this common problem. Just blaming the cloud providers isn't quite fair given that your unintentional usage actually did incur infrastructure cost for them.

Monitoring cost should be a standard element of any cloud operation, just like monitoring for traffic and memory usage.

As so often, the list of treatments isn't a huge surprise. Having the discipline to actually conduct them is likely the most important message:

Set billing alerts
All cloud providers offer different levels of spending alerts and limits. You would not want to set them too low—the main purpose of the cloud is to be able to scale up when needed. But as development teams gain a major impact over the cost aspect of their deployments, cost should become a standard element of monitoring. Unfortunately, many enterprise cloud deployments detach developers from billing and payments, or don't provide the necessary detail, highlighting the dangers of building an *Enterprise Non-Cloud* (Chapter 14).

Run regular scans
Many cloud providers and third parties also offer regular scans of your infrastructure to detect underutilized or abandoned resources. Using them won't do miracles but is good hygiene for your new IT lifestyle. The cloud gives you much *more transparency* (Chapter 1), so you should use it.

Monitor higher-level system structures
For each automated feedback loop that you employ—for example, auto-scaling—you're going to want another (automated or manual) control

mechanism that monitors the functioning of the automated loop. That way you can detect infinite loops and other anomalies caused by automation.

Manage a new form of error budget

An additional approach is to budget for these kinds of mishaps up front—a special kind of "error budget" as practiced by Site Reliability Engineering (SRE). You want to encourage developers to build dynamic solutions that auto-scale, so the chances that you're going to see some surprises on your bill are high enough that it's wise to just allocate that money up front. That way, you'll have less stress when it actually occurs. Think of it as a special version of Etsy's *Three-armed Sweater Award*[3]. If you think setting money aside for learning from mistakes is odd, be advised that there's a name for it: *tuition*.

Know Your Biggest Problem

Even though spend monitoring should be an integral part of cloud operations, it's likely not going to be your number one problem for a while. Hence, overreacting also isn't a good idea. After all, the cloud is there to give developers more freedom and more control, so trying to lock down spending is the quickest way to arrive at an *Enterprise Non-Cloud* (Chapter 14).

Monitoring spending also ties up resources, so how much you might want to invest in spend control largely depends on how much you're spending in the first place. While it's wise to establish a responsible spending culture from day one (or dollar one), making a concerted effort likely only pays off once you have a six-figure run-rate.

Checking Out

You might have observed how supermarkets place (usually overpriced) items appealing to kids near the cashier's desk so that the kids can toss something into the shopping cart without the parents noticing. Some IT managers might feel they have had a similar experience. Cloud providers routinely dangle shiny objects in front of developers, who are always eager to try something new. And, look, they are free of charge for the initial trial!

---

[3]https://bits.blogs.nytimes.com/2012/07/18/one-on-one-chad-dickerson-ceo-of-etsy

I have before likened developers to screaming children who chant "Mommy, Mommy, I want my Kubernetes operators—all my friends have them!" So, you might have to manage some expectations. On the upshot, I give the cloud providers a lot of credit for devising transparent and elastic pricing models. Naturally, elasticity goes both ways, but if you manage your spend wisely, you *can achieve significant savings* (Chapter 29) even if you find the occasional chocolate bar on your receipt.

Cost Management Do's and Don'ts

DON'T...

- Get fooled by unit prices of $0.0001
- Invest too much time into cost optimization until the amount justifies it
- Rig up compute resources just before heading for vacation
- Get sucked in by free trials; use them to actually try things instead of overcommitting

DO...

- Consider cost management a routine operational task
- Expect to be hit by unexpected cost due to mishaps
- Consider setting aside a "tuition fund" that pays for the expensive learning experiences
- Check the system state, especially scale, after any unusual load pattern
- Consider deploying a cost management and optimization system

Author Biography

Gregor Hohpe is an enterprise strategist with AWS. He advises CTOs and technology leaders in the transformation of both their organization and technology platform. Riding the Architect Elevator from the engine room to the penthouse, he connects the corporate strategy with the technical implementation, and vice versa.

Gregor served as Smart Nation Fellow to the Singapore government, as technical director at Google Cloud, and as chief architect at Allianz SE, where he deployed the first private cloud software delivery platform. He has experienced most every angle of the technology business, ranging from start-up to professional services and corporate IT to internet-scale engineering.

Other Titles by This Author

The Software Architect Elevator, O'Reilly, 2020
Enterprise Integration Patterns, Addison-Wesley, 2003 (with Bobby Woolf)

Michele Danieli is the head of architecture practice at Allianz Technology Global Lines, leading globally distributed architecture teams building platforms. He started his career in the engine room and sees architecture and engineers as best friends. A good diagram and a mind map are his essential tools, and code is not a foe.

Tahir Hashmi has developed large-scale distributed applications at internet businesses serving more than 100 million users, like Flipkart, Zynga, Yahoo, and most recently, Tokopedia, where he now leads the technology strategy as vice president and technical fellow. His mission is to make distributed cloud computing as simple as writing a program on the laptop.

Jean-François Landreau leads the infrastructure team at Allianz Direct. When SRE and DevOps shifted the collective excitement from software development toward operations, he decided to follow along. He is a strong believer that you can't take enlightened enterprise decisions if you are too far away from the engine room.

Printed in Great Britain
by Amazon